THE LIVES OF
DANIEL BINCHY

I and Pangur Bán my cat,
'Tis a like task we are at;
Hunting mice is his delight,
Hunting words I sit all night.

Better far than praise of men
'Tis to sit with book and pen;
Pangur bears me no ill will
He too plies his simple skill.

Anonymous, ninth century

Aoibhinn beatha an scoláire
Bhíos ag déanamh a léighinn;
Is follas díbh, a dhaoine,
Gurab dó is aoibhne in Eirinn.
[Good is the life of the scholar
As he does his reading;
Everyone knows this, that
He has the best lot in Ireland.]

Anonymous, seventeenth century

The legends represent the imagination of the country; they are that kind of history which a nation desires to possess. They betray the ambitions and ideals of the people, and, in this respect, have a value far beyond the tale of actual events and duly recorded deeds, which are no more history than a skeleton is a man.

Standish O'Grady, nineteenth century

We now have a literary movement, it is not very important; it will be followed by a political movement, that will not be very important; then must come a military movement, that will be very important indeed.

Standish O'Grady, nineteenth century

The inevitable tendency of the higher intelligence in all countries has been to separate itself from the practical concerns of men.

John Eglinton (W. K. Magee), twentieth century

If the dismissal of Jewish scientists means the annihilation of German science, then we shall do without science for a few years.

Adolf Hitler, twentieth century

If the various doctrines we have been examining had only been put forward by their respective authors as tentative speculations, there would be no reason to object; after all, in history as in other sciences, opinion is free. But when opinions and speculations – whether plausible, unlikely or impossible – are paraded as historical facts, it is time to enter a protest.

Daniel Binchy, twentieth century

However, golden ages, whether the Athens of Pericles, Augustan Rome, Spain's *siglio de oro* or indeed Ireland's middle ages, are the accomplishment of a small artistic and intellectual cadre, supported and patronised by a much larger and powerful extractive elite that lords it over a wretched mass of toilers, some free, many slaves, all exploited, the sweated and bloodied underbelly of a profoundly unequal society. The privileges and the freedoms these elites arrogated to themselves were denied their inferiors, a denial that may have extended not only to the goods of this life, but to the rewards of the next.

Donnchadh O Corráin, twentieth century

What Maitland said of the Anglo-Saxon sources is even more relevant to those of native Irish law; 'Many an investigator will leave his bones to bleach in that desert before it is accurately mapped.' I had hoped to provide subsequent explorers with a very rough sketch-map. But as things are, I can only offer them a ticket of admission to the desert.

Daniel Binchy, twentieth century

THE LIVES OF DANIEL BINCHY

Irish Scholar, Diplomat, Public Intellectual

TOM GARVIN

IRISH ACADEMIC PRESS

First published in 2016 by

Irish Academic Press
8 Chapel Lane
Sallins
Co. Kildare
Ireland

© 2016 Tom Garvin

British Library Cataloguing in Publication Data
An entry can be found on request

978-1-911024-22-4 (Paper)
978-1-911024-05-7 (Cloth)
978-1-911024-06-4 (PDF)
978-1-911024-07-1 (Epub)
978-1-911024-08-8 (Kindle)

Library of Congress Cataloging in Publication Data
An entry can be found on request

CONTENTS

PREFACE

Many an event or remark only reveals its importance long after it has happened. Many of the older people in this story of Irish intellectual life were known by name to me, by reputation and gossip, when I was a child in Dartry in south Dublin in the fifties. I had heard of Thomas O'Rahilly, Richard Best, Kuno Meyer, Eoin MacNeill, Osborn Bergin and James Carney, while having no notion as to who they were or what they had done. Daniel Binchy, in particular, was a name to be conjured with as an older person, an academic of great knowledge and ability. He was spoken of by the older generation in tones of great respect. However, I never inquired about him or his colleagues, and my interest in the entire area of Celtic Studies remained that of a part-time dilettante or friendly onlooker for decades afterwards. All I really knew about him was that he had been the Irish Minister to Germany during the rise to power of the Nazis, that he had encountered Adolf Hitler and that he had warned the Irish government about him. He had also written interesting essays on German leaders of the time. I was also vaguely aware that he had written a study of Italian Fascism, a study which I now realise was a generally unrecognised (and still unrecognised) classic of political science. My more recent interest in him was kindled by conversations with scholars in linguistics and ancient civilisation. In particular, I was gradually attracted to the topic by conversations over the decades with my old friend Liam Breatnach of the Dublin Institute for Advanced Studies (DIAS). Liam has been an indispensable source of information and encouragement throughout the production of this work.

When I retired from the School of Politics and International Relations in University College Dublin (UCD) in 2008 I had several projects that were incomplete, and over the next few years these kept me busy, eventually materialising in the form of several books (*Judging Lemass*; *News from a New Republic* and, with Bryan Fanning, *The Books that Defined Ireland*). I also turned out a few journal articles about contemporary Irish history and politics. However, the idea of finding out something about this extraordinary man, Daniel Binchy, slowly grew, particularly as I eventually realised, that although he had spent his life in the study of a fairly esoteric academic area, Celtic Studies, with particular reference to medieval Irish Brehon law, he had made quite a noticeable mark on modern Irish political life, particularly in that crucial decade, the thirties. This was when he warned the Irish government and his own colleagues in the Fine Gael party against any flirtations with fascism in any guise, at a time when such ideas enjoyed a certain cachet in parts of the Irish civil service, the teaching profession and in both Fine Gael and the party in government, de Valera's Fianna Fáil.

A few years ago, I started reading Binchy's published work systematically for the first time, and was startled to find how variegated it was; he was a man of many interests and one who had been a privileged observer of European affairs during the crucial inter-war period between 1918 and 1939, a period when he was based mainly in UCD. During those years he had travelled extensively in western Europe and was to become an observer of the rise of Nazism and a student of Italian fascism. He encountered Hitler giving a speech in a beerhall in Munich when he was a student in Germany in 1921, and was struck by his strange mixture of intellectual inferiority, slatternly appearance and rhetorical genius. Binchy admired Kevin O'Higgins and was a good friend of William T. Cosgrave, first prime minister of the Irish Free State.

As the Irish ambassador to Germany between 1929 and 1932 he came to know von Hindenburg, Brüning and other leaders of Weimar Germany. He despised Mussolini, but saw him as an improvement of sorts on Hitler; the Italian dictator was a ruffian, but was at least some kind of human being. Binchy studied the Italian dictator's political system closely for the British Foreign Office during the years leading up to the Second World War. This resulted in a major book-length report on church-state relationships in Italy.

De Valera's opposition to the Treaty of 1922 infuriated him, and reconciliation with the eventual leader of the country took decades. He was good friends with many distinguished Irish people, including Frank O'Connor, Sean O'Faolain, Osborn Bergin, Richard Best and Eoin MacNeill. He hobnobbed with distinguished scholars of many nationalities, including the renowned Celticists Rudolf Thurneysen, Carl Marstrander, Myles

Dillon, Robin Flower and George Thompson. He knew the Blasket islanders in their extraordinary last generation of island and Gaelic-speaking life. His affection for the islanders was deep and eloquently expressed.

In contrast to this public life, at times he led an almost monastic private life as a formidable scholar in the years after the Second World War in Oxford and the DIAS. He was a medieval scholar, a diplomat, an Irish public intellectual, a Catholic liberal democrat, a polyglot, a historian, a political scientist *avant la lettre*, an anti-Communist and, possibly most importantly for nationalist Ireland, a fervent anti-Nazi, a stance rooted, in part, in his very personal contempt for Adolf Hitler. I became fascinated by him. He had a forensic mind derived from early legal training, was always demanding evidence when faced with truth claims of any kind, and he was possessed of a deep dislike of mythological or magical thinking, and the grip such thinking had on the political mentalities of certain kinds of people. Some might have accused him of a certain intellectual destructiveness, but in a culture much given to mythical thinking, he often acted as a stiff dose of sceptical salts in human form. Sometimes his intellectual relentlessness hurt his colleagues' feelings, but he remained a man all his long life whose criticism was sharp, penetrating and much feared.

My intellectual debts are many. Over many years I have benefited from many conversations with, in no particular order, Liam Breatnach, as mentioned already, Bruce Bradley, Donnchadh O Corráin, Helen Burke (née Binchy), Fergus Kelly, Bryan Fanning, Andreas Hess, Francis John Byrne, Michael Kennedy, Martin Egan, Tom Mathews, John Coakley, Maurice Manning, John Whyte, Brian Farrell, Charles Doherty, Muiris Mac Conghail, Conn O Cléirigh, Robin Dudley Edwards, Dáithí O hOgáin, Dermot Foley, Patricia Kelly, Diarmuid O Sé, Bairbre ní Fhloinn, Séamas Breatnach, Michael Laffan, Art Cosgrove, Séamas O Catháin, Proinsias mac Cana, Diarmuid O Muirithe and many others. I owe thanks to the library and archival staffs of UCD, the Royal Irish Academy, the staff of the DIAS for their sterling help, the Archives Department at UCD and the National Library of Ireland. The Dublin library and archival systems, both public and learned, are a magnificent resource and an internationally recognised and important cultural asset of the city; these institutions deserve far more recognition and respect than the Irish government, or certain elements within its civil service, seem willing to concede.

The oldest and longest held debt I have is to the people who taught me modern Irish, in particular Séamus O hEocha (An Fear Mór) of Coláiste na Rinne, Helvick, Co. Waterford, over half a century ago, and Tadhg O Murchada of Belvedere College Dublin, a red-haired, befreckled and tweedy man, an old activist of the folklore administration of the thirties who dinned his lovely Kerry Irish into our adolescent skulls so many years ago. Belvedere gave us a magnificent classical education of a kind that is now denigrated in Ireland by philistines as being essentially useless. Actually, it made you literate, particularly in the English language. In that school, I was also taught French and German to pretty good levels. UCD was something else; back in the early sixties, we were dropped into a kind of intellectual world that captivated some of us. We were introduced to real history, something not taught in schools in any real way at that time or for very many years after, and had our eyes opened by the subject economics. Professor Robert Dudley Edwards, as a teacher in the Department of History, did one vital thing: he imparted a passion for his subject that I, for one, found infectious. He found students and turned some of them into nascent, or at least aspirant, scholars.

My father, John Garvin, similarly imparted to me something of his own preoccupation with the Gaelic past of Ireland and with the history of the classical world, partly through my own use of his library of historical materials and also battered translations from Irish, Welsh, Latin and Greek; many of these works are now in my possession. However, this book is my own responsibility.

T. G.
August 2015

THE DISCOVERY OF THE PAST, 1850–1960

The Cult of the Past

In the wake of the French Revolution, a growing popular fascination with the past of nations accompanied the growth of nationalist awareness across the European continent. This near-obsession with the recent and remote past allied itself commonly not only with local nationalisms but also with an historicist romanticism. It commonly expressed itself in retellings of ancient sagas and hero-tales, often bowdlerised and cleaned up for modern consumption. Commonly, medieval bawdiness was excised from the modern retellings, and some of the savagery of the early stories was muted. Frequently, militarist ideologies were decked out in symbolism derived from old traditions: traditions that were, on the face of it, commonly wildly inappropriate to modern conditions and practices. A major theme was the attempt, in the German states in particular, to substitute an imagined or real heroic native age of 'Germanic' early literature and art for the classical world of Greece and Rome which had been the normal stock-in-trade of European literature and pictorial art for many centuries. All across Europe, Achilles, Odysseus and Aeneas were to be replaced by Siegfried, Arminius/Hermann, Vercingetorix, Arthur and Cú Chulain. Both imperial nations and nations trying to liberate themselves from empires made use of similar mythical and often pseudo-historical systems of ideas. Only Greece and Italy remained loyal to the classical tradition, ready-made as it was for nationalist purposes. Austin Clarke noted of the Irish poets and scholars:

> In turning … to these ancient sources, they broke from the main
> tradition of English poetry, which had for centuries borrowed its

1

mythology from Greece and Rome. Imaginative interest in legend and country lore is due, no doubt, to the Romantic Movement, which started at the end of the eighteenth century and gradually spread throughout Europe. In order to deal, however, with all this mass of tradition, these Irish writers had to turn away deliberately from the modern age of realism. Seen, therefore, from a broader point of view, the movement might be described as one of the last waves of European romanticism. ... If I may quote a sentence which I have used elsewhere: 'When Keats turned to Greek mythology he went to Lempriere's *Classical Dictionary*; our poets went out of doors.'[1]

Ireland was, therefore, no exception to this well-known pattern. In the eighteenth century, because of resentment of British general high-handedness, the wholesale theft of land on a sectarian basis (often resented by local Protestants as well as by Catholics), and outrageous anti-trade discriminatory legislation, tentative claims to continuity with a real or invented heroic past were made by the putative Irish Nation. This 'nation' commonly excluded the vast majority of the inhabitants of the island from its imagined membership on the grounds that they were Catholics. In the early seventeenth century Geoffrey Keating had famously wished to exclude all Protestants from membership of the Irish nation. The republishing in a bowdlerised translation of Keating's *Foras feasa ar Éirinn* (General History of Ireland), O'Flaherty's seventeenth-century pseudo-historical *Ogygia* (essentially an echo of Keating) and the appearance of Major Vallancey's preposterous *Grammar of the Irish Language* in 1773 were symptoms of this nascent historicist nationalism of the Irish Ascendancy, itself seen secretly by the Catholic lower orders as descended from landgrabbers of the previous century.[2] John Hutchinson has put it well: science ('research') was to confirm the pre-existing nationalist doctrine of a glorious and heroic past. Science was to be the handmaiden of myth.

The nationalist historians – Palacky of the Czechs, Michelet of the French, Iorga of the Rumanians, Hrushevsky of the Ukrainians – are no mere scholars but rather 'myth-making' intellectuals who combine a 'romantic' search for meaning with a scientific zeal to establish this on authoritative foundations. For only by recovering the history of the nation through all its tribulations and disasters can its members rediscover their authentic purpose. Their histories typically form a set of repetitive mythic patterns, containing a migration story, a founding myth, a golden age of cultural splendour, a period of inner decay and a promise of regeneration.[3]

Hutchinson suggests three waves of cultural activity occurred in Ireland. The first of these in the mid-eighteenth century was a wave of cultural and academic activity centred round the founding of the Royal Irish Academy. This wave was associated also with the romantic, nostalgic and wildly pseudo-historical writings of Ireland's most famous ballad-maker, Thomas Moore:

> Let Erin remember the days of old
> Ere her faithless sons betrayed her
> When Malachy wore the collar of gold
> That he won from the proud invader.
>
> When kings with banners of green unfurl'd
> Led the Red Branch knights to danger
> Ere the emerald gem of the western world
> Was set in the crown of a stranger.

As far as is known, 'collars of gold' in Ireland were usually Irish, were clearly pre-Viking, were already ancient in the middle ages, and were certainly not particularly of Scandinavian origin. Green or 'emerald' as the Irish national colour is a late-eighteenth century Ulster invention.

A late devotee of creative pseudo-history as a form of tourism was the novelist George Moore, who was one of those Irish people who delights in talking beautifully about things he knows nothing about. In 1900 he wrote to a friend:

> I have had a delightful bicycle tour. I visited all the sacred places – places made sacred by memories and many passings from the mortal to the immortal. The elder civilisations were nearer the immortals than we are, I am sure of that; and round these places they saw the

immortals ascending in circles of fire. So they built their altars there and guarded the mysteries. The Druid crypt at Newgrange is one of the most striking things the world has to show. The passages are so narrow that one has to creep on one's hands and knees, and they open into a small chamber in which there is a vast sacrificial cup. The enormous rocks which these great people piled together are carved with the symbol of the sun. The centre is the earth, the First circle is the circle of the waters, the Second the circle of Tir-na-nogue, the Third is the circle of the infinite Lir.[4]

Moore made Yeats look like a scientist.

The second wave, associated with the birth of Irish archaeology and led by George Petrie, the *Dublin University Magazine* and the *Irish Penny Journal* (1840), witnessed the beginning of a real intellectual movement, particularly in the form of the learned work of John O'Donovan and Eugene O'Curry from 1850 on. The latter's *Manners and Customs of the Ancient Irish* (1873) put forward a scientific thesis concerning the nature of Irish early medieval society derived from philological evidence derived from place-names, ranking systems and archaeological evidence.[5] Much of the writing about this semi-legendary past came in two general forms: firstly, romantic retellings of the tales intended to form young minds around ideas of patriotism, courage and self-sacrifice, and secondly by way of contrast, scientific and academic attempts to divine the realities of Celtic society as distinct from glamorising it. That particular division still exists, echoing rather curiously the division in modern Irish historiography between nationalist narratives and the so-called 'revisionism' of nationalist ideologues, known to the rest of us as real history.

The third wave is dated by Hutchinson, following many others, at 1878 with the publication of Standish O'Grady's romantic *History of Ireland*. This was followed by the founding of the Gaelic Athletic Association in Thurles, Co. Tipperary in 1884, the *Dublin University Review* in 1885, the Irish Literary Society of London (1891), the National Literary Society in Dublin (1892) and, crucially, the founding of the Gaelic League in 1893 by that very odd couple, Douglas Hyde and Eoin MacNeill. The Irish Literary Theatre followed in 1899. Each of these projects was connected with similar projects elsewhere, particularly intellectual coteries concerned with the reconstruction of the Celtic past. Celtic studies was well developed at university level in France, Britain and Germany. In all three cases the academic project received sympathetic support from nationalist political forces; what might otherwise have been seen as a rather ethereal and unrealistic intellectual project was encouraged by very non-academic patriotic alliances. Ireland was seen with some optimistic inaccuracy as 'an island refuge of a unique Celtic cosmology derived from one of the founding civilizations of Europe'.[6]

This 'three waves' system is helpful, but I would add a caveat: Geoffrey Keating's *Foras feasa ar Éirinn*, Charles O'Kelly's *Destruction of Cyprus* and other seventeenth-century polemics against British Protestant rule in Ireland express a nascent Catholic-based angry self-assertion that resembles modern nationalism and is obviously a harbinger of later ideological developments. I would term these works as forming a first 'Jacobite' wave, to be followed by three others. In other words, Irish nationalism has had a very long intellectual past. In any event, as O Luing has put it pithily, the last 'wave' from 1880 onwards can itself be seen to have three 'streams', to risk mixing metaphors:

> At the beginning of the twentieth century in Ireland there was in progress a language and literary movement in which three streams flowed side by side. One was the Gaelic League, the popular nationwide movement for the revival of the Irish language; along with it, and deriving from it, was the literary movement, expressing itself in English, of which William Butler Yeats and Lady Augusta Gregory were representative; the third stream was the Celtic-Irish scholarly movement which was, in effect, also a product of the Gaelic League.[7]

It could be argued that, yet again, there was a fourth stream: militant Irish republican nationalism, admittedly going back to the Fenians or Irish Republican Brotherhood (IRB) of the 1860s with its strong American backing and militarised by the American Civil War, but also heavily influenced by neo-Gaelic thinking after about 1890. James Stephens, the Fenian leader, had walked Ireland in the 1850s under the sobriquet *An Seabhac Siubhalach* (The Wandering Hawk), a title rendered happily by a now English-speaking peasantry as 'Mr. Shooks'. Stephens was trying, with some success, to turn local whiteboy and ribbon lodges, usually agrarian and anti-rent organisations, into local branches of the Fenian or IRB separatist secret society, using American money. This Fenian tradition was to go on to fuel both constitutional Parnellism and the insurrectionist tradition in late-nineteenth-century Ireland.

In 1903, Kuno Meyer, a well-known German academic Celticist, argued for the founding of a 'School of Irish Literature, Philology and History' (SIL). Meyer described the Gaelic revival as:

> one of those almost mysterious phenomena, the suddenness and force of which seemed to carry everything before it, astonishing nobody more, perhaps, than those who started it. Even the most sceptical onlooker could not remain indifferent, because it seemed that the cause being pleaded was the existence of the Irish nation itself which was to be rescued from extinction at the 'eleventh hour'.[8]

The movement had already fired the imagination and enthusiasm of thousands and 'a new zest and spirit' had infused itself into a people who had long had a terrible despondency that was 'the saddest feature in its character'. An important feature of this intellectual movement was its determinedly non-sectarian nature; Catholic and Protestant scholars cooperated willingly; in fact, in the early years Protestant scholars and foreigners commonly tended to predominate intellectually, for fairly obvious sociological reasons; Catholics had no reasonably funded university until 1908.

Over the next few years after Meyer's 1903 oration, the proposed School of Irish Learning was set up gradually, as a summer school with an enthusiastic if somewhat amateur staff, badly paid and poorly equipped. However, it had some very distinguished scholars. Carl Marstrander, a young Norwegian philologist and Olympian athlete lectured on comparative linguistics, drawing comparisons between Irish and Latin, Greek, Norse, Welsh and Gaulish words.[9] An accomplished English scholar, John Strachan, lectured on Celtic philology up to his untimely death in 1909. Much of his learned work remained unpublished.[10] One contemporary linguistic patriot (J. G. O'Keeffe) recalled in 1924 that Strachan's death, in particular, was a blow from which the School never recovered.[11] One abiding theme throughout this time was how tiny the numbers of qualified enthusiasts were and, therefore, the presence or otherwise of a few particular individuals could mean failure or success, something which has always been a characteristic problem for Irish academia.

From the very beginning, Celtic scholars looked upon the new National University of Ireland with some ambivalence. Richard Best, Assistant Director of the National Library of Ireland during the time when the SIL was being established, referred to it casually as a *'Narrenschiff'*.[12] Best, a great scholar with international recognition, had never been to a university. Kuno Meyer apparently had a similar attitude, writing in 1909 to J. G. O'Keefe, treasurer of the SIL, concerning the proposed institutionalisation of Celtic Studies at University College Dublin (UCD), that he feared an intellectual takeover by revivalist ideologues. Of particular concern to him at the time were Douglas Hyde and Eoin MacNeill, with their extremely passionate linguistic agenda.

> As for myself, I would only consent to such a post as director, or to any participation in the University work, if I am given a free hand, and that is not very likely. With Hyde and Mac Neill you cannot found a real school. They are both amateurs, as Hyde will and Mac Neill ought to admit.[13]

Many people were privately sceptical as to the inherent staying power of the entire movement. Meyer recalled in 1911 that twenty years previously, at the very beginning of the movement, Fr. Eugene O'Growney had argued that the prospects of reviving the language depended on a cultural and intellectual revolution.

> They had been talking over the prospects of the revival of interest in the language, and they always came back to this – that if it was not a literary revival as well as a linguistic revival it would not be lasting. He had a sort of feeling that the Gaelic League setting up, as it were, perhaps unintentionally, a contrast between the native speaker and the scholar had done harm to the movement.[14]

Thus, from the very beginning, there was an underlying emotional ambivalence among the scholars themselves about the long-term viability of their project. As we shall see, this ambivalence was to surface again and again throughout the half-century of the movement's lifetime. Desmond FitzGerald, who had been an IRB activist in the south of Ireland at the beginning of the century, perceived the language even then as dying. It was becoming impoverished in vocabulary and syntax, and younger people spoke a more Anglicised version of it, lacking the richness and variety of expression available to older speakers; the language was gradually declining into being a contact vernacular or pidgin. 'We were subconsciously aware that the continued decay of the Irish language was bringing ominously near a further great break with the past.'[15]

Ironically the cultural revival that did take place at exactly the same time was overwhelmingly couched in the English language and produced the works of Yeats, Joyce, Shaw, Synge, Wilde and many others. Arguably, it continues still, in the form of the work of Flann O'Brien (Myles na Gopaleen), Frank O'Connor, Mary Lavin, Sean O'Faolain, Brian Friel, John Banville, Edna O'Brien, Seamus Heaney and their heirs and successors extending into the twenty-first century. Many of these writers, although they did not normally write in the language, have used Irish as a kind of cultural touchstone for dramatic, aesthetic or even comic effect.

Philip O'Leary has commented that Irish linguistic revivalists have always been on the defensive.

> As a result we have the vitriolic internal debates about font, dialect, orthography, terminology, legitimate subject matter and forms of expression, as well as all the other issues that many insisted were relevant if not central to the ultimate goal of an Ireland rooted in an almost mystical nexus of beliefs and practices known as *Gaelachas*.[16]

This insecurity was there at the very beginning, and the hijacking of the Gaelic League by the revolutionary tradition was made easier by this uncertainty. Between 1911 and 1915, the Gaelic League was penetrated by the IRB as part of preparation for some kind of national upsurge. This was eventually to result in the Easter Rising of 1916. Hyde was ousted, and many of the scholars walked away from the League either because they did not share the IRB's politics or because they saw the League as being taken over by a witches' brew of politically motivated revivalists, fanatics or political careerists who had little real interest in the language itself and saw it rather as a political resource for winning the hearts and minds of the young. This quiet secession included many of the real scholars in the original movement.[17] Hyde remarked ruefully afterwards that the Gaelic League had been a very charming organisation until it became large and popular.

The Death of the Past?

The generation of Celticists, born in the late nineteenth century and around the beginning of the twentieth century, sheltered by the Gaelic League and later by both the William T. Cosgrave and the Eamon de Valera Irish governments, were a significant part of what passed for governmentally approved intellectualism in independent Ireland. Rather belatedly, they were also backed by the neo-Gaelic ideology of de Valera's Fianna Fáil and a generally sympathetic educational establishment at all levels of the system, a system bent on the restoration of the Irish language as the ordinary language of the Irish people and rather little else in the form of education for most people. The damage done to the educational system was enormous, but at least the Irish Celticists themselves certainly repaid the support that they undoubtedly received with an impressive intellectual harvest. This came both in the form of the rediscovery and reconstitution of much of Ireland's Celtic past and a very significant contribution to the country's intellectual life. It was a contribution greatly appreciated by an intelligentsia much put upon by Church and State in the early years after independence. Political instability, economic depression and political isolation during the war years almost certainly damaged the mobilised intelligence of the entire country very seriously. Intellectual bullying by the authorities of church and state silenced many voices. One person who clearly saw it more or less this way was a rather younger scholar, Daniel Binchy.

As time went by, Daniel Binchy became perhaps the senior Celtic Studies scholar of his day in Ireland, an expert on Nazism, an analyst of Italian fascism, a medieval historian and the master of at least nine languages, ancient and modern. Sometime in the early 1950s, a gangling and talkative Dublin schoolgirl called Maeve Binchy went to visit her uncle Dan. Daniel Binchy was just back in the Georgian buildings of the Dublin Institute for Advanced Studies on Merrion Square in the centre of the city after a five-year stint in Oxford, and already absorbed in what was destined to be a thirty-year-long study of ancient Irish law tracts. He was an austere and rather distant, if benign, figure. After half an hour of her cheerful chatter, Professor Binchy looked at her genially and said: 'My dear Maeve; I have a ten-shilling note in my pocket. If I give you this princely sum, will you promise never to enter this room again?' It is believed she took the money.[18] Maybe she went home and wrote a story about it. He was a man who, like many others in that era, was captured by the Irish past.

In as much as this is Binchy's story it is also the story of a whole group of intellectuals whose impressive body of work on Ireland's cultural inheritance has informed and influenced our modern view.

Notes

1   Austin Clarke, 'Anglo-Irish Poetry', in J. E. Caerwyn Williams (ed.), *Literature in Celtic Countries*, Cardiff: University of Wales Press, 1971, pp.153–174, quote from p.155.

2   Roderick O'Flaherty, *Ogygia*, Dublin: McKenzie, two vols., 1773, original Latin version written circa 1668; Charles Vallancey, *A Grammar of the Iberno-Celtic or Irish Language*, Dublin: Marchbank et al., 1773.

3   John Hutchinson, *The Dynamics of Cultural Nationalism*, London: Allen & Unwin, 1987, p.14.

4   George Moore, *Letters to Lady Cunard, 1895–1933*, Westport, Conn., Greenwood, 1979, p.30.

5   Eugene O'Curry, *Manners and Customs of the Ancient Irish*, London: Williams and Norgate, three vols., 1873.

6   See Hutchinson, pp.117–19.

7   Sean O Luing, *Kuno Meyer*, Dublin: Geography, 1991, p.1.

8   Ibid., p.27.

9   NLI Richard Best Papers, MS11, 008, (1), (2), (3).

10 An important pioneering text of John Strachan's remained unpublished until it was resurrected and edited by Osborn Bergin in 1944. Cf. *Stories from the Táin*, Dublin: Royal Irish Academy, 1944, reprinted 1976.

11 RIA Eleanor Knott Papers, 12021/78–102, J. G. O'Keefe, 7 February 1924.

12 See O Luing, pp.71–2. '*Narrenschiff*': Ship of Fools.

13 Ibid., p.70.

14 Ibid., p.115.

15 As cited in Tom Garvin, *Nationalist Revolutionaries in Ireland*, second edition, Dublin: Gill and Macmillan, 2005, p.102.
16 Philip O'Leary, *Writing beyond the Revival: Facing the Future in Gaelic Prose*, Dublin: UCD Press, 2011, p.387.
17 I am indebted to an old colleague for this insight.
18 There are various versions of this anecdote, mainly varying in the amount of money. I have guessed a very generous amount.

MISE-EN-SCÈNE

When Binchy belatedly joined Ireland's intellectual movement of the twentieth century, it was nothing if not distinguished and included a significant cross-section of the small educated public of the time. The context in which we must view Binchy's contributions is populated by the giants of Celtic studies of the time as well as individuals whose opinions had a huge influence on Irish politics and culture. The biographies which follow pay tribute to the achievements of these characters as well as affording us a fuller understanding of the life and work of Daniel Binchy.

Rudolf Thurneysen (1857–1940) was born in Basel in 1857. He had a formidable education in the Swiss-German tradition, Jacob Burckhardt, the famous historian of the Italian renaissance, being amongst his university teachers along with Friedrich Nietzsche, the rather notorious German philosopher. Nietzsche was apparently a family friend, who dandled young Thurneysen on his knee. Young Rudolf went on to study in Jena and Leipzig in Germany and finished up his studies in Paris. Eventually he worked in Freiburg and in Bonn. In 1911, he lectured at the School of Irish Learning (SIL) in Dublin. His Grammar of Old Irish, first published in German in 1909, was eventually translated into English and revised by Osborn Bergin and Daniel Binchy during the years of the Second World War, to be published by the Dublin Institute for Advanced Studies (DIAS) in 1946, six years after Thurneysen's death. Whether he knew it or not, he was, in many ways, to be the father of academic study of the Irish linguistic past; Binchy, who studied under him, quite clearly idolised him. However, he was disconcerted to find that the learned Swiss tried to speak modern Irish, which he did not know as a spoken language, as though it were German in pronunciation.[1] Binchy and Bergin, in a jointly written obituary, recognised him as their intellectual father. They commented that he was Swiss, and bilingual in French and German. Binchy remarked:

This dualism was also reflected in the quality of his scholarship, which combined the finest elements of both national temperaments, the limpid clarity of the French mind and the thoroughness of the German. Those who have had the privilege of being taught by him – and they include a number of Irish scholars – will remember him as the most inspiring of teachers. But they will remember even more vividly the man himself, the soul of kindness and courtesy, ever interested in the work of others, ever eager to put at their disposal his enormous store of learning. My own debt to his generous encouragement and assistance is indeed unlimited, but everyone who sought his help must have had a similar experience.[2]

Douglas Hyde (1860–1949) was born in Castlerea, Co. Roscommon, in 1860, son of a Church of Ireland rector in an area where a handful of Protestants lived surrounded by a sea of Catholic peasants which was gradually morphing into a community of owner-occupier farmers. If Thurneysen was, possibly unknowingly, the intellectual founder of the linguistic movement, Hyde was certainly the ideological leader and the political organiser of the movement. Hyde had considerable political ability and was able to lead people through persuasion, example and charm. He was a fluent Irish speaker, having picked up the language from local people. The language, although a dying one, was still spoken by poorer, less educated people in more remote areas, a relationship that persisted for the entire century of the language's long and slow decline. In Co. Sligo, next door, a common saying was that 'the Irish faded out of this place like the frost off the tops of the ditches in springtime'. Children in Sligo at that time had a little rhyme commenting quite humorously and shrewdly on this enormous change of language:

Broc and Badger ran a race.
Up the chimney was the chase.
Broc fell down and broke his face,
And that's how Badger won the race.

Hyde himself reminisced about speaking to a young boy in Sligo in Irish at the end of the nineteenth century and being answered by the lad in English. When Hyde asked him in English why he wasn't speaking Irish to him, the lad replied in English of a sort, 'Amn't I speaking to you in Irish?'

Hyde later became a passionate propagandist for the language, adhering to a strange, almost racialist theory to the effect that Irish people had spoken Irish for so long that speaking English was unnatural for them, and that learning English cost them their ancestral culture while being biologically inappropriate as well.

The allied idea that the English language was a corrupting influence on the minds of the people was quite widely held in late Victorian Ireland, almost to the point of there being a moral panic about it. Ireland was developing a reading public, and this public was doing its reading in English, that language being transmitted to the young through the National Schools. Books and magazines in English were commonly seen as pornographic or, even worse, as secularist and unbelieving. For obvious reasons, an opinion that could easily be described as barbaric and ridiculous was expressed more often in private than in public. Quite apart from nationalist and religious considerations, a snobbish contempt for what was seen as English low-class vulgarity was sometimes voiced.[3] Canon Peter O'Leary, author of several well-known Irish-language novels and an autobiographical memoir, believed that the English language threatened any remnant of piety or civic virtue that remained in the Irish people. Canon Patrick Sheehan, not a linguistic revivalist but a very well-known novelist, peddled similar rancid views of English commercialised popular culture. He also had the idea that one heroic individual could, by self-sacrifice, bring about a mortal transformation of a demoralised, Anglicised and morally corrupted people.

Hyde was politically acute. He understood that the kind of people who supported linguistic revival were commonly state or church employees who were discouraged, or even prohibited, from engaging in political action. The early Gaelic League, therefore, eschewed any kind of overt party politics and was, by and large, ignored by the police as a harmless cultural organisation, though Hyde himself got some public prominence in 1902 by objecting to British Israelites digging up the hill of Tara in search of the Ark of the Covenant and other relics of the lost tribes of Israel.[4]

For some years the League enjoyed a remarkable popularity, partly because it was one of the few organisations in rural Ireland where the young of both sexes could legitimately meet one another freely. Together, Hyde and his Catholic colleague, Eoin MacNeill, were a very formidable force. As de Valera said famously much later on, MacNeill was politically powerful – and useful to have on one's side – because the priests trusted him. Hyde, on the other hand, was the political intelligence of the movement and caused it to walk a tightrope between cultural activity and nationalism. Between 1911 and 1915, however, the organisation was thoroughly infiltrated. The mainline nationalists, led by John Redmond and John Dillon, did not know what to make of the League, correctly sensing a plot to undermine constitutional nationalism but not knowing what to do about it.

There was certainly a very unadmitted but strong dislike of main-line nationalist politicians among many members of the Gaelic League. By 1910 an Irish Party activist deputed to translate material from English to Irish for party literature complained of this somewhat weird political bias, observing that many members of the League:

> have a sort of 'strangeness' and narrow-minded distrust of politicians, no matter what their knowledge of Irish or how earnest their efforts towards its revival … in face of the supposed non-political shibboleth of the Gaelic League, the vast majority of its members and officials have up their sleeves a paltry prejudice against politicians of the Nationalist type, and, in fact, I myself have heard many of them freely preach that prejudice.[5]

Eventually these 'advanced' nationalists of the Irish Republican Brotherhood (IRB) and the League were to stage a rising in Dublin and elsewhere and take over most of the country politically in the 1920s.

Richard Irvine Best (1873–1959), librarian and partially self-taught linguist and Celticist, in many ways played a very quiet but central role in the formation of the academic study of Celtic civilisation in Ireland. Precisely because of his key position in the National Library of Ireland (NLI) during the first half of the twentieth century, he encountered and befriended almost every significant intellectual figure in the movement or even in the country. He was quite a squirrel of documents, and his lode of letters, deposited in the NLI, is a fascinating source of information and anecdote. Letters from Daniel Binchy, John Millington Synge, James Joyce, Carl Marstrander, Rudolf Thurneysen, Paul Grosjean, Myles Dillon, John

Eglinton (William K. Magee) and dozens of other rather clever people over a period of half a century jostle each other. The son of a customs officer, Best was born in 1873 in Derry city into a Protestant family, worked for a while in a bank in London as a very young man and lived for a while in Paris. There he knocked about with the young literary revival people, including John Millington Synge and Stephen MacKenna. He also attended lectures by the French Celticist, Henri d'Arbois de Joubainville. Later, in 1903, he translated de Joubainville's *Le cycle mythologique irlandais et la mythologie celtique* of 1884 into English.

According to the biographers, he never attended university and apparently never needed to, like so many other brilliant artists and intellectuals of that era. However, he mastered literatures in the English, Irish, German and French languages pretty much on his own. W. J. McCormack has him attending Trinity College in the company of his good friend Synge in the early 1890s.[6] It seems likely that, in reality, he probably spent time knocking about Trinity without ever registering for a degree. Things were pretty informal at that time, when the equivalent of the modern secondary school Leaving Certificate was regarded as a very good educational level. In any case, in those days, as far as modern and ancient languages and the humanities in general were concerned, the Leaving Certificate from an elite secondary school in Ireland approximated, intellectually, to a university bachelor's degree in Ireland attained, typically, at the age of 21. One potted biography in Irish observes:

> He was a great scholar in many ways. He was friendly with many unusual people: Joyce, Bergin, Father Peter O'Leary, George Moore, Stephen MacKenna, Synge, Meyer ... he was a great scholar, despite never attending a university. Without him, the School of Irish Learning would not have survived and possibly there would be no School of Advanced Celtic Studies and perhaps no School of Celtic Studies at the Institute of Advanced Studies.[7]

Whatever the details of his educational background, he was extremely able, his particular skill centring on palaeography and the dating of ancient texts. He did some acting, playing Ainle in W. B. Yeats' *Deirdre* in early 1901. In 1904 he joined the NLI in time to be allocated a walk-on part in

James Joyce's *Ulysses*. He appears in the Scylla and Charibdis episode at the National Library in Kildare Street. As Stephen Daedalus discusses Hamlet with Thomas Lyster, the Librarian, and W. K. Magee (John Eglinton), 'Mr. Best entered, tall, young, mild, light. He bore in his hand with grace a notebook, new, large, clean, bright.'[8] Ellmann remarks 'Best and Magee were well-read, intelligent men. Best had spent much time in Paris ... he spoke with a prissiness that Joyce mocked in *Ulysses*.'[9]

Best became a formidable scholar and was appointed senior professor at the Dublin Institute for Advanced Studies (DIAS) in his old age. In his youth, Best was, indeed, an attractive man, good-looking, very sociable and charming. He was famously described by George Moore in the early years of the century as being very attractive to women:

> Best is John [Eglinton's] coadjutor in the National Library: a young man with beautiful shining hair and features so fine and delicate that many a young girl must have dreamed of him at her casement window, and would have loved him if he had not been so passionately interested in the in-fixed pronoun – one of the great difficulties of ancient Irish. ...Best is Kuno Meyer's favourite lamb and Kuno Meyer is a great German scholar who comes over to Dublin from Liverpool occasionally to shepherd the little flock that browses about this Celtic erudition ...[10]

That alleged lack of interest in women, however, did not prevent Best marrying Edith Oldham, a noted pianist, singer and *Feis Ceoil* champion, and one of its founders.[11] She was a teacher at the Royal Irish Academy of Music (RIAM), an institution whose management was, like the Gaelic League, determinedly non-sectarian. The musical revival she and her colleagues at the RIAM were associated with, Harry White has argued, was appropriated by the academic, linguistic and political movements.[12] Oliver St. John Gogarty remembered at mid-century a recent encounter with Best (probably in 1948):

> Talking of things golden, I had just left Richard Best in the [Trinity] College Park. He was walking from the Library, probably. He was in a hurry, so he asked me to come to his house any evening

to continue our talk. Richard Best, the scholar. I remembered how, years ago, he confided to me that there was only one alternative: religion or scholarship. And I remembered, too, how George Moore had described his golden hair and his unageing, pink complexion, described him as one envious, for Moore's own hair that had been red once was yowden now.[13]

The Bests ran a household in Upper Leeson Street well-known for its hospitality to foreign visitors and for its gregariousness and *salons*. Oliver St. John Gogarty describes it:

> Best lives in 57, Upper Leeson Street, in one of those houses set far back from the highway with a garden in front and a garden at the rear. It belongs to a period when men insisted on space and privacy and life was unconfined.
>
> He saw me as I walked up the garden path, and he opened the door before I ascended the seven steps to the hall. The rooms on the right had the folding doors between them removed so that the rooms formed one long chamber with a view of flowering-trees and shrubs fore and aft. Laburnum and lilac leant over the path in the front garden. You could see fruit-trees flowering in the garden at the back. And the house was silent, as becomes a scholar's dwelling.[14]

For many decades Richard Best helped quietly in the background to further the work of a large number of Irish writers, in particular perhaps James Stephens, whose classic retellings, *Irish Fairy Tales*, published in a handsome edition with illustrations by Arthur Rackham in 1920, benefited from Best's expert advice on the selection of narratives.[15]

Osborn Joseph Bergin (1873–1950) came of a Quaker family in Cork city, his father being in insurance. He was educated locally and attended the Queen's College in Cork (QCC). He studied classics and then developed an interest in the Irish language. He learned excellent modern Irish in west Cork and Kerry, and all his professional life he insisted on the essential unity of the Irish language in all its many varieties since the sixth century. He argued persistently that the understanding of Old and Middle Irish depended completely on a good and instinctive grasp of the modern idiom. He lectured in QCC on the Irish language between 1897 and 1903. He sat at the feet of Thurneysen and Zimmer in Germany, getting a doctorate there in 1906. Kuno Meyer said of him to Richard Best, 'That man Bergin of Cork – he knows more Irish than any of us.'[16] Bergin was unusual intellectually in that he believed that the spoken language had to be learned first and the dead medieval versions afterwards. As Binchy put it with direct reference to Bergin's view:

> Virtually all these great scholars, then, approached the subject from one angle only. Or, if I may change the metaphor, they brought but one key to open the house, their knowledge of comparative linguistics. This is indeed a most valuable key, indispensable in fact for several rooms in the house, but there were other rooms which it could not open; for these a different key was necessary, familiarity with the modern spoken language of which, when all is said and done, Old Irish is but an earlier stage. This applies particularly to syntax and idiom. Irish has always been a highly idiomatic language, and idiom often persists where forms have been drastically changed. But unless one knows the idiom in modern speech one is unlikely to recognise it in its older dress.

Binchy goes on to point out that even Thurneysen often missed this point because of his lack of modern Irish. He construed a phrase in Old Irish as 'do something for X' when it really meant 'do something because X thinks you should do it'. Bergin believed that west Munster Irish was the best dialect to learn because it was the closest to the literary classical language of the seventeenth century.[17] He wrote up a text, *Pairlement Chloinne Tomáis*, in *Gadelica* in 1912–13. Nicholas Williams has remarked 'his text in *Gadelica* is full of careless slips'.

At any rate, he seems to have always been a one-man awkward squad. Yeats referred to him in late 1899 as 'The main person in *Fain an Lae* – I purposely blur the spelling of that word – the most argumentative person I ever met. Whatever the other Gaelic Leaguers said he objected to, with perfect good humour but with great obstinacy and seriousness.' The newspaper was *Fáinne an Lae* (the dawning of the day), the Gaelic

League weekly bilingual newspaper, which had pilloried Yeats' great friend George Russell (AE) for taking a job in the Gaeltacht without knowing any Irish. Russell was a well-known expert on agriculture and a co-worker with Plunkett.[18]

Because of the time he had spent in Germany before the First World War, Bergin seems to have had a strong grasp of German political culture and premonitions of that country's and Europe's tragic future. In early 1923, during the Irish Civil War, he wrote an avuncular letter in Irish to a very young Myles Dillon, then studying in Germany and having rather a good time according to himself. Because he had foreign currency, he could live rather high on the hog, describing the German collapse as leaving seething hatreds, anti-semitism and xenophobia. Myles had written to Bergin in late 1922 from Bonn where he was studying under Thurneysen:

> I have told Maria in my letter of the luxurious living which our English money makes possible for us. All around us are splendid restaurants with music and excellent service, and all filled with the Germans who are still rich, and with foreigners. The former class are of course largely Jews, and it is really instructive to observe the noses at each table, hundreds of Hebrew *Kriegsschieber* feeding well while many are hungry. 'K' is the word here for war profiteer, and the only thing that casts a shade over one's bliss is that one feels a bit Kriegsschieberish oneself. The war and after-war collapse has had a strange effect here, because it seems to have left many people very well off and well able to pay the huge sums of marks demanded, while others live on black bread and beer. War profiteers and business people and these sinister Jews have all flourished.[19]

Bergin wrote back presciently in Irish, giving what almost looks like a gentle reproof for his casual anti-semitism: 'It is likely that great evil will come upon Germany presently, and upon all the peoples of Europe. Look after yourself!'[20]

Gearóid O Murchadha (Gerard Murphy) reminisced about Bergin in the west of Ireland: 'The bearded professor who would lie in the shallow water on a day of July sunshine discussing etymologies, or suddenly quote

Dante as he climbed the hill to hear John the Bull tell in vivid Irish how he wrestled with the bear in America.'[21] Frank O'Connor remembered Bergin affectionately as he was in the thirties:

> He was a small man with a neat brown beard and a face that varied between the stern and precise and the vague and the vacuous. He usually wore a costume that had been fashionable among Irish nationalists at the time I was born – a tweed jacket, pantaloons and long cycling stockings – and he usually sat with his legs crossed and one eye half closed, making patterns in the air with his pipe. I used to follow the patterns with my eyes, feeling sure that his subconscious mind was writing messages of great significance in the air, if only I could interpret what they meant. Where Russell burbled, Bergin rasped. When he had a story to tell you he would pull his legs in under his chair, point at you with his pipe, and screw his face up. When we were alone in his house he would put down his pipe, pick up his old fiddle and play and sing *Gaudeamus Igitur* and other songs from his student days in Germany. His fiddling was worse than his voice, which was terrible.[22]

Bergin liked the Bible and disliked drink. Binchy, in his obituary lecture, described him rather absurdly as a Socrates, but he seems to have been a rather un-chatty Socrates most of the time. He would talk away happily in the Gaeltacht, but otherwise '...among his academic colleagues he had the reputation of being able, like Moltke, to be silent in seven languages.'[23] Throughout his life he was repeatedly seen by many different people as somewhat withdrawn in personality, reluctant to lead, a cat that walked alone and intensely private. At one stage he accused Best of speaking 'public house Irish'. Best retorted that he had never been in a public house in his life, and neither had Bergin.[24] Carl Marstrander wrote in 1929:

> [J. G. O'Keeffe] was very sharp in his criticism of the people in Dublin, and very bitter that the School of Irish Learning was discontinued and *Eriu* taken over by the Academy and that *Anecdota* had folded up. The criticism of Bergin was particularly strong. He completely lacks

initiative, cannot form a school, cannot educate new students. In his defence one has to say that he is overworked with university work. His Irish courses are attended by 300 students, who all have to take their exams at the end, and he has to correct all their papers. O'Rahilly, who for some time was in Trinity College where, however, he didn't seem to get on well with the other gentlemen, has gone to Cork...But I have strong doubts whether Irish linguistics or philology will ever grow strong on Irish soil without *outside* organisation.[25]

Thomas O'Rahilly wrote to Eleanor Knott in 1935 from Cork:

Dr. Bergin has been down here since the beginning of the month [of August 1935]. Why he doesn't take a decent holiday somewhere I cannot understand. He must be one of the most inert men alive. He is in the enviable position of having no commitments and no house-selling or house-hunting problems; and still he can think of nothing better than hanging around in a dreary place like Cork. Fortunately, Binchy wants to read some of the Laws with him at the beginning of next month, and so he has asked him to go to Schull with him at the beginning of next month – where also I understand the Bests are going.[26]

Bergin's almost aggressive privacy sometimes had unfortunate repercussions. W. J. Maloney, latterly a Reuters journalist and an extraordinary polyglot himself, a man who knew the world of Irish academic Celticists for many years, wrote to Eleanor Knott in 1954 about 'the sad ending' of a friendship between Bergin and Thomas O'Rahilly, a younger and rather ebullient man. By that date both men were dead.

I cannot conceive of Bergin as at any time unreasonable, but he had an impersonal quality about him which must have been an irritation to minds more attracted to emotion. It didn't prevent him from being a most steadfast friend, but it did set a boundary beyond which, I always felt, it would have been unwise to try to go ... O'Rahilly probably blundered across that threshold when he raised the temperature over the Institute appointment.[27]

Nevertheless, Bergin had given O'Rahilly a generous if critical review of his last book. Bergin was regarded internationally as a formidable scholar. He was not without whim; in 1922 he wrote a semi-popular song in Irish (*Maidean i mBéarra*) to the tune of the Derry Air, possibly to please that Derryman Richard Best. Certainly he was also seen as an attractive man among the University College Dublin students who included Máire Cruise O'Brien's mother, Margaret Browne. Margaret used apparently to flirt with him and addressed him as 'Osby' when they met on holidays in the Gaeltacht of Ballingeary in west Cork. He seems to have been receptive of these advances: his little book of poems in Irish published in 1922 was dedicated to Margaret: *Do Phéarla na mBrúnach ón té do cheap* (to the Pearl of the Brownes from the author).[28] Living in Leinster Road in later life, he was fond of watching Westerns in the Stella cinema a few perches away in Rathmines, often with George Russell in tow. Archbishop Donal Creed remarked 'It was nearly impossible to live in Dublin in the nineteen Forties without the spare figure of Osborn Bergin striding down the Rathmines Road, often towards the Stella Cinema where he took his relaxation watching cowboy films.'[29] He read Shakespeare's plays for fun and celebrated Cecile O'Rahilly's early academic triumphs with a poem. In 1944, William Magee could remember being somewhat baffled by him: 'I think of that extremely able, accomplished and somewhat enigmatic man with wistful curiosity.'[30] Máire MacEntee, later to be Máire Cruise O'Brien, being a fluent speaker and writer of the modern language, remembered his teaching style as it had been in the thirties and early forties:

> My relationship with the Institute's professors was peculiar, much as it had been in UCD, in particular with Professor Bergin, who had once dedicated poetry to my mother. ... I realised fully that we were at cross purposes, but could not think how to remedy this; some of it undoubtedly had roots in Civil War hostilities, but a major part of the difficulty was, I think, that I had always known Irish, never had to learn it, any more than I had to learn English. ... I loved the Old Irish poems and sagas, but never felt the need to master Old Irish – it was a course requisite – as a separate language, while my instinct made it easy for me to arrive at what I regarded as sufficient comprehension

by guesswork and reference to notes and vocabulary, and I could get
by without what was regarded as a 'thorough foundation'. Very early
on in Professor Bergin's class at UCD, he wrote on the blackboard, *In
t-ech gel* (the white steed, in Old Irish). 'Now,' he said, 'I want you all
to decline this phrase for me, I have given you three of the forms, so
you can only make twenty-seven mistakes.' I promptly wrote down,
In t-each geal (substituting two Modern Irish forms). 'Here.' Said
Professor Bergin, standing behind me, 'is a young woman who is
capable of making twenty-nine mistakes!'[31]

Of course, Bergin had fancied her Mammy in his own youth.

Bergin died in 1950, having just drafted that genial, complimentary,
very learned and occasionally devastatingly dismissive review of O'Rahilly's
magnum opus, *Early Irish History and Mythology*. Seen as a rather double-
edged intellectual sword, the review was not published until several years
had elapsed after both Bergin's and O'Rahilly's deaths. Frank O'Connor
wrote of him: 'Like other artists he identified himself with his subject, for
he was one of the last of a great generation of scholars in a country where
scholarship was no longer regarded.'[32] In 1938 he published a classic article
on the syntax of the verb in Old Irish, explaining why it often did not obey
the 'verb first' rule of modern Irish. E. G. Quin wrote admiringly: 'While
the argument continues about the Indo-European origins of the Irish verb,
Bergin's article is still imperturbably there in his coolly factual, analytical
and oddly exciting style for all to read who would read it with care.'[33]

As a larger-than-life eccentric figure, he attracted folklore. He was held
to have stared at the coffin of well-known Irish writer Peadar O Laoghaire
and remarked 'Disgraceful! That coffin plate contains seven grammatical
errors.' Binchy always insisted that this never happened.

Kuno Meyer (1858–1919) was, as we have seen, a moving force for a long
time in the micropolitics of Irish Celtic academia. A German, he first
encountered a Celtic language in the form of Scottish Gaelic on the Isle
of Arran. In Ireland he was heavily involved with the Gaelic League in
its early, most enthusiastic years. He had a huge influence on W. B. Yeats
and others in the Irish literary revival in the English language. Arguably,
Meyer was himself a key figure in the literary movement as he had prowess

as a translator of Old Irish poetry *into English*, neither of these languages being his native tongue, even though he was a master of both. He suffered throughout his later life from a form of chronic rheumatism.[34] During the First World War he naturally took the German side openly which, of course, cut across his involvement in Irish cultural affairs. He died suddenly in 1919, again a serious loss to the Gaelic revival movement.

Carl Marstrander ('Charlie') (1883–1965) was another pioneering Celticist at the beginning of the twentieth century. A Norwegian, he became interested in the Celtic languages as an undergraduate at what was later entitled the University of Oslo. He was possibly influenced by his father's extensive library of comparative linguistics and history. Norwegian nationalism, coinciding with the coming of Norwegian independence in 1905, could also have been a conditioning factor. There was an obvious linguistic dimension to Norwegian nationalism, two standards of the language (*Nynorsk* and *Bokmal*, or 'New Norwegian' and Norwegian Danish) competing against each other, a little like Irish versus English in Ireland. Unlike the Irish case, however, speakers of each of the two languages did not find the other language so impenetrable as to force the abandonment of one for the other. As a young man, 'Charlie' Marstrander was awarded a scholarship to go to west Kerry and learn Irish. He soon discovered the Great Blasket and met Tomás O Criomhthain, later to be the author of *An tOileánach* (*The Islandman*). O Criomhthain (O'Crohan) was impressed by *An Lochlannach* (the Norseman) himself, admiring the rapidity with which he learned Irish and his athletic ability. Marstrander was on the Norwegian Olympic team and was wont to pole-vault over the cottages on the island, much impressing the locals. O Criomhthain remembered from the early years of the century (probably 1909) the young Norwegian coming to the Great Blasket Island in a currach, having only a smattering of Irish. This was at a time when many scholars were investigating the language, and teaching these gentlefolk from half-a-dozen countries evolved into a kind of cottage industry in the Gaeltacht areas of western Ireland. Marstrander was not the first but was perhaps one of the more exotic of its visitors.

> He was a fine man, with a gentle, humble style that, of course, is common amongst many like him who are well-educated. He spent

five months in the Blaskets. We had a two- or three-hour session every day for half the time, and then he got news that he couldn't stay as long as he had intended to because he had too much to do back where he was employed. And so the two of us had to work out a change of plan. The gentleman asked me if I could spend two sessions every day with him. 'And', says he, 'you'll get as much from me for the second session as you got for the first'.[35]

Marstrander went on to teach at that hedge university, the School of Irish Learning in Dublin, replacing Bergin in 1910. At about the same time, Kuno Meyer had taken over an ambitious project of the Royal Irish Academy (RIA), the production of a scholarly dictionary of Old and Middle Irish. Meyer took Marstrander on to assist with the dictionary, presumably because, unlike many of the Irish scholars, Marstrander had an academic training that matched the formidable German academic tradition. Marstrander used to correspond with Best in English, German and even in perfect Kerry Irish in the old script and the old unreformed spelling. His ideas about the dictionary got him into conflict with the Irish scholars and with Meyer; these colleagues saw his proposals as far too ambitious and impractical. To be fair to them, they had a valid point; the completion of the dictionary took well over half a century, using Marstrander's template and general ideas.

Due in part to health problems (he contracted pleurisy) Marstrander went back to Norway in 1911 and later severed his connection with the dictionary project, partly as a result of that row. He taught in Oslo and eventually commanded an extraordinary range of Indo-European languages, including Hittite, Breton and Manx. During the Second World War he was involved in the Norwegian national resistance to the German occupation and was locked up for a while by the forces of occupation. He kept a diary in Old Irish in prison, apparently written on toilet paper. The diary was confiscated by the Gestapo, who sent it to Berlin. The dons in Berlin certified that in the territory controlled by the Reich, only a certain Professor Carl Marstrander of Oslo could translate it.

Eoin MacNeill (1867–1945), an older man and, in many ways, the intellectual leader of the movement, was born John MacNeill in Glenarm in the Glens of Antrim in 1867, the year of the Fenian rising. His father was a shopkeeper and veteran sailor. The family was a large one, and they lived in a Catholic enclave which still had memories of a recent Irish-speaking past. He was a brilliant student at St Malachy's secondary school in Belfast and eventually became a law clerk at the Four Courts in Dublin. As we have seen, he became a founding member of the Gaelic League in 1893 and, under the guidance of Edmund Hogan, developed a fascination with the early history of Ireland. He befriended the future revolutionary Patrick Pearse a few years later. He married Agnes Moore in 1898 and they had four sons and four daughters, founding a dynasty of sorts that is still very much around in Dublin.

MacNeill, despite Meyer's scepticism, developed into a very successful and creative Celtic scholar. Many of his ideas were received with suspicion, and some of them appear rather fantastical to modern eyes, but some of them have been vindicated in whole or in part in the long run. He was one of the first to point out that much of the dating of Irish history was untrustworthy, being the creation of later propagandists trying to establish a pseudo-historical pedigree for the Uí Néill dynasty's claims to the High-Kingship of Tara. He argued that all Irish historical narratives prior to the fifth century were mythical and should be discounted. Unionist views of Celtic Ireland, as being without any concept of the state and being generally hopelessly primitive and in need of English civilising, were aggressively rebutted by him, sometimes in public polemic.

However, MacNeill was very eager to prove that Celtic society as it had existed in the British Isles and Gaul before the Roman invasions was harmonious, had civic order and no pathological level of violence or anarchy. In a lecture written before 1913 he wrote about local 'parliaments' allegedly existing in medieval Celtic society.

> In these assemblies laws were enacted, modified or confirmed, taxes and tribute were regulated. The men of lore came there with their poems in praise of the living and their stories of the olden times and their genealogies. Musicians came, and clowns with their antics, and slight-of-hand men. The men of military age came with their arms for weapon-show and then laid their arms aside till the assembly ended. Traders from distant countries came to sell and

buy. Horse-races and other games were held. The general public, at least in the larger assemblies, was ranged and classed in divisions, and wooden galleries were set up to seat them. Street booths were set up for eating and sleeping, giving the place of assembly the temporary aspect of a town, and such towns were, I think, the cities named and placed in Ptolemy's description of Ireland. The detailed account that is extant of the Leinster assembly at Carman, and the rare references in the annals to disturbances of assemblies show that order and peace were in general characteristic of these occasions.[36]

In another lecture written at the same time he made it evident that he felt that the character of ancient Irish society was not completely extinct. He was a determined denier of the idea that modern Ireland had not the potential to be a worthy cultural successor to Gaelic Ireland. Donal McCartney has written:

MacNeill's definition of 'nation' and of 'state' was closely related to his view of Irish history. He strongly denied what, he said, critics of Irish nationhood ignorantly asserted, namely, that the idea of an Irish nationality was a modern figment. Irish nationality, he often reiterated, was not invented or discovered or created by Grattan or Tone or by any other politician or patriot of modern times. An Irish nation had existed from antiquity. And in early Irish literature could be found 'a positive conscious nationality', 'more real and concrete' than was ever the conception of nationality in ancient Hellas. He shared, if he had not inspired, the view expressed in Alice Stopford Green's influential little book, *Irish Nationality*, that whereas the Roman Empire was a state held together by the power of a central ruler, in the Gaelic idea the forces of union were not material but spiritual – the language, literature, law, traditions and religion of the people. It is not surprising, therefore, that for MacNeill the greatest age in Irish history was the early Christian period when, as he put it, 'the Irish were the schoolmasters of Europe'. 'This', he wrote, 'will always appeal to me as the crowning glory and the greatest pride of our nation.'[37]

MacNeill argued that, before the First World War, 'The Irish were and are fiercely democratic, but instead of abolishing one-man rule as the Gauls and Galatians did, they maintained it in a very ancient form down to the last days of their freedom, and even at present their politics appear to consist in votes of confidence in this man or that man.'[38]

MacNeill had a political career of some fame in parallel with his academic career, and it certainly could be argued that the two activities interfered with each other. In 1913 he wrote a famous pamphlet ('The North Began') arguing that nationalist Ireland should emulate unionist Ireland by raising a volunteer armed force to defend Ireland and the country's right to self-government. The IRB, the nationalist secret society, backed him and he became president of the Irish Volunteers later in the year. He seems to have persistently underrated the strength of unionist resistance to Home Rule and thought nationalists and unionists could unite in an all-Ireland alliance against such British policies as the alleged over-taxation of Ireland. He was opposed to any armed insurrection against the British government, and was systematically undermined by Pearse and a cabal led by Diarmuid Lynch within the IRB: a secret society inside a secret society. This cabal was to organise the 1916 rising in Dublin and elsewhere, even though MacNeill had desperately tried to call it off. Lynch used to refer to Patrick Pearse as the only martyr ever appointed by a committee; that committee was Lynch's cabal.

MacNeill became elected to the first Dáil Éireann in 1918 and supported the Anglo-Irish Treaty of 1921. One of his sons, Brian, was killed in murky circumstances on Ben Bulben mountain in Co. Sligo while fighting on the anti-Treaty side in the subsequent Civil War; he seems to have been murdered. MacNeill was the Irish Free State's first Minister for Education between 1923 and 1925, and was the Dublin representative on the Boundary Commission set up under the Treaty to delimit the border between British Ireland and Independent Ireland. In 1925 the report was suppressed by both the British and Irish governments as being unfavourable to Dublin. In 1927 MacNeill's political career came to an end. He returned to academic life in UCD, working on place names, early Irish law and the controversy over the historicity of St Patrick. He died in 1945. In many ways, his work has lived on after him and many of the modern arguments in Irish Celtic studies go back to initiatives taken by him. Daniel Binchy, in so many ways the senior, if somewhat wayward, heir to this cultural heritage, spoke admiringly of his 'uncanny sense of communion with a long-dead past'. Francis John Byrne commented on MacNeill that most previous historians knew little or no Irish, and certainly not the medieval forms of the language. Even if they were not myth-makers, they were 'helplessly dependent on the "Irishians"' once the Latin sources dried up.

> To MacNeill belongs the credit of having dragged Ireland practically single-handed from the antiquarian mists into the light of history. He came to the study of the Gaelic world, as all must, through the philological disciplines, and throughout his scholarly life he was never to remain exclusively a historian. To be more exact, he realised how barren such a limitation must have been. Since all historians are dependent upon written records, the decipherment, edition and interpretation of texts must constitute the indispensable preliminaries to their work.[39]

Eleanor Knott (1886–1975) was born in Dublin in about 1886 and lived in the tranquil inner Dublin suburb of Ranelagh (No. 2 Sallymount Place) throughout most of her long life. Her father was a medical man and her mother was Cornish and they encouraged her nascent interest in things Celtic. She never went to a university; the only one available, Trinity College, although it taught 'Celtic' did not admit women students. Through the Gaelic League she became interested in the Irish language and in Irish nationalism. Best encouraged her to progress to the study of the older form of the language at the School of Irish Learning in 1907. She wrote a considerable amount of nationalist journalism for the *Irish Peasant* and for Arthur Griffith's *Sinn Féin*. She did an apparently heroic amount of lexicographical work for the RIA amounting to a permanent achievement of great importance, working with Marstrander and his successors on the Dictionary for many years. She became an acknowledged expert in Irish medieval poetry, with particular emphasis on the bardic tradition. She became a lecturer in Trinity College in 1928, getting a Chair in 1939. Rather like Richard Best, Knott corresponded with a large number of colleagues internationally, and her correspondence, preserved in the RIA, gives many insights into Irish cultural life in the early twentieth century. In 1949 she was finally admitted into membership of the RIA, as the bizarre rule forbidding women members was finally abolished. Blindness forced her retirement in 1955 and she died in 1975. She never married. David Greene felt that she deserved most of the credit for the continuation of the RIA's Dictionary of the Irish Language after the departure of Marstrander in 1911: '... to those who worked on that great project during the last half-century she was its living embodiment'.[40] Daniel Binchy, in a gracious obituary in *Eriu*, wrote:

> She was not only a splendid scholar: she was also a most remarkable personality. In many ways she reminded me of Bergin: the same initial reserve (to some extent, perhaps, due to shyness), followed by a lavish helpfulness once she saw you were in earnest, and culminating in a friendship which was all the more precious because it was not lightly bestowed; the same absolute integrity in scholarship as in life; the same dislike of publicity-seeking and self-advertisement. What she wrote in her obituary notice of Bergin at the beginning of *Eriu* Vol. XVI may be equally well applied to herself: 'His critical standards had their own sure basis in his unshakeable love of truth and justice and honesty, and his contempt for speciousness, humbug and sloppy pretentiousness in any connexion.' Again like Bergin, she had a keen sense of humour, and her witticisms, though never unkind, could be caustic at the expense of those who in her view were guilty of 'sloppy pretentiousness' in their work.[41]

James Carney (1914–1989) was a lively and well-read scholar. His father was a customs officer in the Irish midlands who died young. Carney attended Synge Street Christian Brothers School and UCD, where Bergin and Gerard Murphy taught him Celtic Studies. He took a First Honours degree and followed the usual German route to Thurneysen in Bonn. Later he was appointed to the DIAS where he remained until his retirement. He died in 1989. He was a well-known figure internationally, and held lectureships and professorships in Uppsala and at the University of California. In Uppsala he founded a Department of Anglo-Irish Studies. His publishing record was formidable, but the work for which he is best known is his *Studies in*

Irish Literature and History (Dublin: DIAS, 1955). In it he criticised 'nativist' tendencies in Irish Celtic Studies, possibly unfairly, as it seems almost impossible to keep political argument out of the teaching of Irish history and even prehistory; the influence of modern political ideology on Irish archaeology, for example, is sometimes grotesquely obvious. It should be remembered that this phenomenon is not unique to Ireland. *The Problem of Saint Patrick* (1961) suggested that the saint had arrived in Ireland not in 432 but in 457. Entertainingly, it also argued that many places traditionally associated with Patrick were designated thus for purposes akin to modern tourism. He was not a believer in the revival of the Irish language as the ordinary spoken language of the people. Binchy's trenchant criticism of his work in 1962, among that of others, stung him grievously.

Thomas Francis O'Rahilly (1882–1953), born in Listowel, Co. Kerry, in 1882, O'Rahilly was a member of one of the famous clans associated with Ballylongford, Co Kerry, a town well-known for producing academics, poets and larger-than-life public figures of all sorts. His older brother was Alfred O'Rahilly, later president of University College Cork (UCC), and a sister, Cecile, was also a prominent Celtic scholar. He was educated by the Holy Ghost Fathers at Blackrock and read Classics and Celtic Studies in what was becoming UCD. He became a law clerk in 1906 and later applied for the Chair in Modern Irish at UCC and was rejected. This caused something of a flurry, as he was already held in high respect by many established scholars of the time. Robin Flower, the English Celticist and later to be the translator of *Fiche Bliain ag Fás* wrote to Best from London in 1911 expressing regret at the rejection, commenting 'But wisdom is not found in Universities, and Windle is Windle.'[42] Sir Bertram Windle, an Englishman, was President of UCC at the time and, understandably, distrusted the extreme nationalist movement. After all, the Fenians were busily hijacking various cultural and social organisations at the time.

O'Rahilly eventually earned a Chair in Modern Irish at Trinity College Dublin (TCD) in 1919 and subsequently had a meteoric career around Irish academia, serving in both UCC and UCD for periods, held a senior position at the DIAS and finally returned to TCD as an honorary professor just before his death.

One of his early works was a marvellous study of Irish traditional proverbs published in 1922, focusing in particular on the work of Michael Og O Longáin, a late-eighteenth-century collector, hedge schoolmaster and admirer of the United Irishmen and their rising of 1798. This was his *A Miscellany of Irish Proverbs*. He was an accomplished textual analyst, published a pioneering study in 1942 entitled *The Two Patricks* and, a few years later, produced an extraordinary long work, *Early Irish History and Mythology* (Dublin: DIAS, 1946). Much of his sometimes over-imaginative argumentation of 1946 has been dismissed or refuted in detail since then. However, it would be difficult not to admire the energy and audacity with which he attacked abstruse linguistic and historical problems. He had a considerable reputation for being an extraordinarily industrious worker. He lived in Highfield Road in the salubrious suburb of Dartry in his later years.

His *amour propre* seems to have been very well developed, somewhat like that of his well-known brother 'Alfie', noted for his absence of a sense of humour. Myles na Gopaleen's guying of the DIAS in the pages of the *Irish Times* in the late forties enraged him ('offensive clowning'). Erwin Schroedinger, the famous physicist, had sat out the War in the DIAS and had given a lecture that apparently dismissed the idea of there being a First Cause to the universe. Similarly, O'Rahilly was inaccurately credited with inventing the idea of there being two St Patricks. Myles inevitably congratulated the Institute for spending five years of lucubration at the taxpayers' expense only to conclude that there was no God but two St Patricks.[43] In a letter to Eleanor Knott in 1942 O'Rahilly pointed out that the idea that there were several figures lurking behind the semi-legendary figure of Patrick was not his own invention but went back at least to George Petrie's 'The History and Antiquities of Tara Hill' in 1839.

> Petrie suggests that there were at least two Patricks, an early Patrick, who preceded Palladius, was the author of the *Confessio* and died circa 461, and a late Patrick, who died circa 492 and who may have been identical with Palladius. This is the nearest to my own views that I have met; but as you will observe, the difference is as striking as the resemblance.[44]

O'Rahilly corresponded a lot with Knott over the years and expressed indignation at the scandalous veto on women in the RIA, congratulating Knott on her much delayed membership.[45] He died suddenly in 1953. Apparently much of his paperwork was destroyed after his death by his wife, who was convinced, probably rightly, that overwork had hastened his end. Proinsias mac Cana wrote in Irish: 'O'Rahilly wrote the most important book existing about Gaelic literature and I am able to give a high rating without any misgivings and say he was the man with the most and the widest knowledge of the Irish language in all its long history.'[46] Eleanor Knott evidently knew much of his personal circumstances. She wrote:

> His unsurpassed knowledge of modern Irish dialects and manuscript literature was acquired in his early manhood when as a civil servant his chosen studies had perforce to be relegated to evenings, weekends and vacations. Unceasing application during this period together with recurrent attacks of influenza brought about a definite decline in his health and this should be taken into account in considering a characteristic asperity in criticising the work of other scholars.[47]

Cecile O'Rahilly (1894–1980) was born in Listowel, Co. Kerry, and was Thomas's sister. Rather like Knott, she was a gifted Celticist in a pretty sexist academic world. The entire family was of distinguished descent; among their ancestors were the famous eighteenth-century poet, Aodhagan O Rathaille and the nineteenth-century pioneering Celticist, Eugene O'Curry. Michael Joseph O'Rahilly, killed in the 1916 rising, was their uncle. Again a brilliant student, gaining a First in Celtic Studies in UCD in 1912, she moved to the University of Wales at Bangor. Her Welsh became fluent and she taught at a school in Beaumaris on Anglesea Island (*Inis Móna*) for some years, later expanding her scholarly work into a study of the relationships between medieval Ireland and Wales. Joining the DIAS in 1946, she became the Institute's first woman professor in 1956. Her last important projects were a definitive study of the *Tain Bo Cuailnge* and a study of *Cath Fionntrá* (*The Battle of Ventry*). She published an extraordinary range of articles in international journals, including the world-famous *Zeitschrift Für celtische Philologie*. She never married, but had a long-enduring relationship with a Welsh scholar, Myfanwy Williams, who came to Ireland to look after her in her later years. Not always fully acknowledged, she was, in some ways, the best published Irish Celticist of her age-group, a group characterised, by and large, by formidable academic achievement.

Myles Dillon (1900–1972) was the brother of James Dillon, future prominent dissident Irish politician and son of John Dillon, the prominent Home Rule leader. He was educated by the Jesuits at Belvedere College, Dublin and Mount Saint Benedict in Gorey. He went on to study comparative linguistics in UCD and was introduced to Sanskrit by Bergin. A travelling studentship brought him to Berlin, Bonn, Heidelberg and Paris between 1922 and 1927: the usual itinerary. Thurneysen taught him in Bonn, where he received his doctorate. Bergin evidently had a high regard for him and wrote to him from Dublin in November 1922. 'But here am I giving you advice, when you are in the head centre of *Wissenschaft*, and I am hundreds of miles away, and years behind the times. If you aren't able to teach me in a couple of years I shall be surprised. Still, you asked for it.'[48]

He lectured in UCD subsequently and did not succeed to Hyde's Chair in 1932, allegedly because he opposed the government's educational policy on compulsory Irish and, like his father and brother, held openly that a peaceful Home Rule settlement in Ireland would have been far preferable to the violence and partition that actually transpired. He was appointed to a new Chair in Celtic Studies at the University of Wisconsin. In 1946 he transferred to Chicago and, shortly afterwards, to Edinburgh. He was a prolific scholar and ended his career as Director of the School of Celtic Studies at the DIAS. He was, for two years, a scholar at the Indian Institute for Advanced Studies. A well-liked figure, he died in 1972.[49]

James Hamilton Delargy (1899–1980) was born in Cushendall, Co. Antrim, his father being a publican and the family having a strong seafaring tradition. He was taught in UCD by both Hyde and Bergin. In the twenties he went to Uíbh Ráthach in southwest Kerry to perfect his Irish and encountered a famous local story-teller (*seanachaí*) Seán O Conaill. He worked in UCD and realised quickly that he was looking at a doomed culture. Consequently, he set up the Folklore of Ireland Society in 1926, which quickly morphed into the Irish Folklore Institute in 1930. Government money was forthcoming and eventually the government-backed Irish Folklore Commission was set up in 1935. His cultural achievement was monumental, and has been memorialised by the vast folklore collection in UCD. This is described later on in the narrative. He was famously parodied by Myles na gCopaleen in his Irish-language satire of 1941, *An Béal Bocht*.

Notes

1 D. A. Binchy, *Osborn Bergin*, Dublin: UCD, 1970, p.11.
2 Daniel A Binchy and Osborn Bergin, Obituary of Rudolf Thurneysen, *Eigse*, 2, 1940, pp.285–88.
3 Tom Garvin, *Nationalist Revolutionaries in Ireland 1858-1928*, Clarendon Press, pp.82–107.
4 W. B. Yeats, Collected Letters of W. B. Yeats, Vol. III, pp.213–4.
5 *Freeman's Journal*, 30 August 1910.
6 W. J. Mc Cormack, *Fool of the Family: A Life of J. M. Synge*, Weidenfeld and Nicholson, 2000, pp.84–86.
7 Diarmuid Breatnach and Máire ní Murchú, 1882–1982: Beathaisnéis a Dó, BAC: An Clóchomhar, 1990, pp.19–20, quote at p.20. My translation from Irish.
8 James Joyce, *Ulysses*, Harmondsworth: Penguin, 1969 (first published 1922), p.186.
9 Richard Ellmann, *James Joyce*, New York: Oxford University Press, 1983 (first published 1959), p.118.
10 George Moore, *Hail and Farewell*, Colin Smythe, Gerrards Cross: 1985, p. 377. First published 1911, 1914, 1925 as *Ave, Salve, Vale*.
11 NLI MS 8824,/ 16, H. F. Norman Papers.
12 I owe this information to W. J. Mc Cormack, *Fool of the Family: A Life of J. M. Synge*, London: Weidenfeld and Nicholson, 2000, p. 84, and to conversations with Harry White.
13 Oliver St. John Gogarty, *Rolling Down the Lea*, London: Constable, 1950, p.34.
14 See ibid., p.106.
15 NLI MS 11,004 (2), Richard Best Papers, 20 February 1919.
16 See Binchy, *Osborn Bergin*, p.11.
17 Ibid., pp.11, 13.
18 Yeats, W. B., *Collected Letters of W. B. Yeats*, Vol. II: 1896–1900, on Bergin; on AE, see Peter Kuch, *Yeats and AE*, Tatawa N. J., 1986, p.157.
19 Joachim Fischer and John Dillon, *The Correspondence of Myles Dillon, 1922–25*, Dublin: Four Courts Press, 1999, p.33.
20 Ibid.,p.95. My translation.
21 Diarmuid Breathnach agus Máire ní Mhurchú, *1882—1982: Beathaisnéis a Dó*, BAC: Clóchomhar, 1990, p.19.
22 Frank O'Connor, *My Father's Son*, London: Pan Books, 1971 (first published 1968), p.81.

23 See Binchy, *Osborn Bergin*, p.3.

24 Seán O Lúing, 'The Scholar's Path to Kerry's West', *Cork Holly Bough*, Christmas 1982, p.2. As in NLI MS 47,763, Tim Enright Papers.

25 Carl Marstrander, *Dagbok*, Diary of Visit to Man 1929–30, DIAS 1983, 914.289 M, p.3. June 1929. (Manx Museum, MM MS 5258B). Liam Breathnach pointed this material out to me.

26 RIA Eleanor Knott Papers 12021/78 (LXX), 24 August 1935.

27 RIA Eleanor Knott Papers 12021/ M. J. Maloney to Knott 11 March 1954.

28 Máire Cruise O'Brien (*née* MacEntee), *The Same Age as the State*, Dublin: O'Brien Press, 2003, p.44.

29 Breathnach agus ní Mhurchú, *1882-1982: Beathaisnéis a Dó*, p.19.

30 NLI, Richard Best Papers, MS 11,001 (27), 1 January 1944.

31 See Cruise O'Brien, *The Same Age as the State*, pp.161–162.

32 See O'Connor, *My Father's Son*, p.91.

33 E, G, Quin, 'Irish Studies', in T. O Raifeartaigh (ed.), *The Royal Irish Academy, 1785–1985*, Dublin, RIA, 1985, pp.166–187, quote at pp.173–4.

34 See Moore, *Hail and Farewell*, pp.377–83.

35 Tomas O Crohan, *The Islander*, a new translation of *An tOileáanach* by Garry Bannister and David Sowby, Dublin: Gill and Macmillan, 2012, p.270.

36 NLI MS 10,452, Alice Stopford Green Papers; lecture by MacNeill, 'The Norman Conquest'.

37 Donal McCartney, 'MacNeill and Irish-Ireland', in F. X. Martin and Francis John Byrne (eds.), *The Scholar Revolutionary*, Shannon: Irish University Press, 1973, pp.77–97, quote at p.84.

38 Ibid.

39 Francis John Byrne, 'MacNeill the Historian', in F. X. Martin and Francis John Byrne (eds.), The Scholar Revolutionary, Shannon: Irish University Press, 1973, pp.17–36, quote at p.17.

40 Breathnach agus ní Mhurchú, *1882-1982: Beathaisnéis a Dó*, pp.46–47.

41 *Eriu*, Volume 26, (1975), pp.182–185.

42 NLI Richard Best Papers, MS 11,000 (22).

43 Anthony Cronin, *No Laughing Matter: the Life and Times of Flann O'Brien*, Dublin: Grafton, 1989, pp.177–78.

44 RIA Eleanor Knott Papers, 12021/78 (xxi), Myles comment 16 October, 1950; two Patricks note 25 August, 1942.

45 RIA Eleanor Knott Papers, 12021/90(i), n. d. (1949).

46 Breathnach agus Ní Mhurchú, 1882-1982: Beathaisnéis, p.132.

47 Ibid., p.133.

48 Joachim Fischer and John Dillon, *The Correspondence of Myles Dillon, 1922-1925*, Dublin: Four Courts Press, p.34.

49 DIB, Vol. 3, 311–312; See Fischer and Dillon, *The Correspondence of Myles Dillon*.

CHAPTER ONE

UNCERTAIN BEGINNINGS, 1899–1929

According to apparently reliable academic folklore in Dublin, Daniel Anthony Binchy was born in Charleville, Co. Cork, in 1899. Biographical sources usually give us 1900, a few give 1899. All his very long life of about ninety years he asserted that he had been born in 1900, so that he could claim to have been 'born with the century'. Why this harmless fib (if it was a fib) was persisted in for so long is something of a mystery. One possibility is that the Binchy family invented the alleged fib to protect young Daniel from possible conscription into the British Army in 1917–18. This is merely my own surmise; the Victorian Irish practically made a custom out of lying about their age, or keeping this important datum a deeply held secret; this was particularly true of farmers, terrified of losing their authority over their holdings to their juniors. Furthermore, it sometimes worked the other way; when the Lloyd George Budget of 1909 brought in the Old Age Pension, payable at seventy, every oldster in the country suddenly remembered the Night of the Big Wind of 1839, a night when, at least in folklore, the gales took the roofs off one-third of the houses in the country. It was also known among the more traditionally minded as the Night the Fairies left Ireland.

Binchy's family was very well-off, and had a well-known tradition of producing doctors and lawyers practising mainly in the Charleville area in north Cork, near the border with Co. Limerick. His father was a shopkeeper, and there were five children in the family: Owen, Mary, Daniel, Rita and William. All his life he was closest to Mary, a little older than he was. Their father died young. There was also landed property in the family. Although plentiful around Charleville, the name Binchy is an unusual one in Ireland, and their ancestors were said to have come across with Cromwell, presumably mainly turning Catholic after the repeal of the Penal Laws. Charles-Edwards comments '[The Binchy family] belonged to a section of Irish society whose loyalty had to be maintained if British rule was to endure – Cromwellian settlers who had prospered under the Union.'[1] The family was generally conservative Catholic and nationalist in the Parnellite or Redmondite 'Home Rule' tradition. Daniel was to hold with pro-Treaty and 'Commonwealth' politics all his life, and had little sympathy with de Valera's republicanism. As is common in electoral polities, his political opinions were, in part, inherited. Some of the Binchys had a shop on the main street in Charleville and refused to keep jobs for republican soldiers on the anti-Treaty side in 1922–23. One of them, John Higgins, lost a job he had held there and 'Old Binchy' left a note to say that when all this 'blackguardism' of the Irish Civil War was over 'there would be no jobs for [anti-Treaty] Republicans in this firm, or anywhere else for that matter.' Higgins was a poor man for the rest of his life, and was the father of Michael D. Higgins, later to be a well-known academic, Labour politician and President of Ireland.[2]

Daniel's father seems to have had scholarly inclinations, but his mother, apparently famously bossy, had taken him out of University College Dublin (UCD) to run the shop.[3]

Daniel's early schooling was with *La Sainte Union*, an order of French nuns in the picturesque little town of Banagher by the banks of the Shannon in Co. Offaly. All his life he boasted of his good oral grasp of French as having been given to him by this early teaching by native speakers. Later he attended the Jesuit secondary school, Clongowes Wood College in Co. Kildare, from 1910 to 1916. Whilst, apparently, Binchy's memories of Clongowes were not as happy as those of the preparatory school in Banagher, interestingly, his stay here coincided with Joseph Walshe's time as a scholastic or trainee Jesuit on the teaching staff.

Walshe was later to be an influential senior civil servant. He came from Killenaule in Tipperary, not too far from Binchy's home town, and was quite a scholar in his own right. He had been sent to the Netherlands during his novitiate and had studied philosophy there. Decades later he was to support the French far right and was something of an admirer of Pétain. In spite of this, he disliked Hitler, apparently for religious rather than political reasons, though he had a sneaking regard for Nazi 'reforms' in the early thirties. He distrusted the populism of electoral democracy. He was a fluent Irish speaker, had excellent French, Dutch, some German and also taught Latin, Greek and English in Clongowes. Among his first students was John Charles McQuaid, later to be Archbishop of Dublin, notoriously conservative, sectarian and one of the most powerful people in the entire country.

Dermot Keogh reports that Binchy was taught by Walshe.[4] It is highly unlikely that young Binchy was unknown to him, and Walshe very probably imparted some of his linguistic skills to the boy. Certainly later they were on cordial and familiar terms, despite their wildly differing political opinions. Young Dan was in Second Preparatory in 1910–11, while Walshe was teaching Latin, Greek, English and mathematics at that time. In 1911, Dan won an English prize at Christmas, Walshe apparently being his teacher. In 1916, young Binchy won a not too impressive third prize in Religious Knowledge.[5]

Walshe had left the Jesuits aged 29 in 1915 before ordination, reportedly for health reasons. He was recruited by Seán T. O'Kelly as a competent linguist to serve in the Paris office of Sinn Féin in 1919 while being part of a nominally illegal shadow government of Ireland during the Anglo-Irish War. He became a civil servant in the Irish Government's new Department of External Affairs a few years later, when the Irish Free State came into being in late 1922. He was then appointed Secretary of the new Department in succession to Robert Brennan in 1922, this promotion having been at Brennan's suggestion.[6] Walshe was a doughty bureaucratic infighter, and resisted attempts by the civil servants in both the Department of Finance and the Department of the President of the Executive Council to take over External Affairs and even close it down. A tiny Department, glamorous, privileged and therefore resented in a small and hungry country, Walshe's staff understood that he was their defender and there was usually a fair amount of *esprit de corps*. Many distinguished historical figures served in this Department: Conor Cruise O'Brien, Val Iremonger, Máire MacEntee and Frederick Boland were among its many well-known veterans.

Walshe was to become Binchy's boss for a few years 15 years later during the latter's brief tenure as Irish Minister (ambassador) to Germany, 1929–32. It is most likely that Walshe, well-apprised of Binchy's abilities, tapped the young man for the job. The learned middle class of the new Catholic Ireland was small and tended to be interlinked by family connections and school ties. It was also much resented, particularly in the twenties by the coming forces of de Valera's Fianna Fáil, built on the ruins of the defeated Irish Republican Army (IRA) after the Irish Civil War and supported by the poorer farmers, landless labourers and what little there was of a classic working class.

After Clongowes, Binchy attended UCD as a student. His university education was wide ranging and completed with astonishing speed; his first degree was a BA in legal and political science (1920), followed by an MA in Irish history the following year. He collected a string of first-honours results. For his Master's degree he concentrated on aspects of the sixteenth-century Desmond Rebellion, a very Cork-centred topic and an interest reflected in Binchy's first book, a small volume on aspects of sixteenth-century political history made up of a series of articles written between 1921 and 1925.

Over the next three years he attended the University of Munich on a National University of Ireland (NUI) Travelling Scholarship and while he was here, studying medieval law, history and language, Binchy found time to complete a doctoral dissertation for the University of Munich on the Irish Benedictine monastery of Ratisbon (modern-day Regensburg).[7] His thesis was over 70,000 words and written in good German, though, decades later, when reviewing a similar study of Ratisbon by Pádraig Breathnach, he referred to his own apprentice piece as an *opusculum*, remarking that Breathnach 'treats it far more tenderly than it deserves'. He reminisced that it had been 'wished upon' him and was:

> a 'scamped' piece of research, crammed into the intervals when I was not imbibing knowledge from Lehmann, Baumker and Grabmann, and I am so far from proud of it that I have sedulously avoided it ever since and even parted with the solitary typescript of it that remained in my possession; neither have I kept up with the abundant *Fachliteratur* on the subject that has appeared over the past half-century.[8]

Strange Encounter

Curiously, during his time in Munich, Binchy had an encounter with a young ex-soldier and agitator called Adolf Hitler and his observations of him were to generate a minor explosion in Ireland when they were finally published in an extraordinary article in the Irish Jesuit scholarly periodical *Studies* twelve years later, in 1933. This publication came just in time for Hitler's finalising his grip on supreme power in Germany and was full of the insights of a man who had watched Hitler's stilted rise to power from close quarters. Binchy's 1921 encounter provides us with his first impressions.

According to this article, in November 1921 a German friend from the University of Munich invited Binchy to come along to a meeting of a new political party (the National Socialist German Workers' Party or NSDAP) in the Bürgerbräukeller in Munich. The attendance was drawn from the poorest inhabitants of the city, sprinkled with a few war veterans. This latter detail was the only feature that marked the attendance off from that at a similar Communist Party meeting he had attended a few days previously. Hitler was the principal speaker, and as the young Austrian emigré with the black cowlick and the moustache waited his turn to speak, the young Daniel Binchy observed him with a fair amount of Corkonian disdain:

> Hitler was the principal speaker, and as he sat on the platform waiting for the very prosy chairman to conclude, I remember wondering idly if it would be possible to find a more commonplace-looking man. His countenance was opaque, his complexion pasty, his hair plastered down with some glistening unguent, and – as if to accentuate the impression of insignificance – he wore a carefully docked 'toothbrush' moustache. I felt willing to bet that in private life he was a plumber: a whispered query to my friend brought the information that he was a housepainter.[9]

Actually he was a war veteran and mediocre artist as well as a part-time housepainter; Binchy's somewhat snobbish reactions dissipated rapidly once Hitler started to speak. He realised that Hitler might be a half-educated man, not too intelligent and possibly a fool, but he was also a 'born natural orator'. His reaction to Hitler's rhetoric was precisely the same as that of Anton Drexler a little earlier in the decade. Drexler, the first leader of the German National Socialist Workers' Party, had reacted to Hitler's speech at a party meeting by exclaiming famously '*Dieser Kerl, er hat es!'* ('This fellow really has it!'). Drexler promptly ceded leadership of the tiny NSDAP party to the unknown orator. Binchy observed that Hitler started hesitantly, having trouble with grammar like any ordinary man unaccustomed to public speaking; he had a heavy Austrian accent. Then suddenly 'he seemed to take fire'. His eyes blazed with conviction and he somehow transcended his own provincial origins and handicaps. He became exalted, he began to shout and he waved his arms about wildly: 'As his exaltation increased, his voice rose almost to a scream, his gesticulation became a wild pantomime, and I noticed traces of foam at the corners of his mouth.' He spoke of the betrayal of Germany in 1918, the victorious German Army stabbed in the back by the communists, the social democrats, the capitalists and, of course, the Jews, who were to be seen as being behind every evil thing that had occurred to a putatively heroic and undefeated Germany. Hitler's *Dolchstosslegende* (myth of the stab in the back) flattered the humiliated Germans, unable or unwilling to grasp the fact of their own military and economic defeat. The audience was captivated by him. 'His purple passages were greeted with roars of applause' and when he finished and sat down exhausted he left behind him an indescribable scene of hysterical enthusiasm. With 'all the arrogance of twenty-one' Binchy remarked to his friend that Hitler was 'a harmless lunatic with the gift of oratory'. The unforgettable retort of his German friend to this piece of silliness was to the effect that in the conditions of the Germany of 1921 'no lunatic with the gift of oratory is harmless'.[10]

Binchy next saw Hitler nine years later in 1930, and found him to be unchanged, except he had become fatter and more prosperous-looking; his ideas and rhetoric were exactly the same. 'I found little change in his appearance beyond a marked increase in his waistline: "the twentieth century Siegfried", as one of his followers called him, had developed a very unheroic *embonpoint*.' He had turned out to be in at least one way a quite common type of successful politician working with an electorate in a democratic system: one who has one story or argument that hits a nerve among ordinary people and who repeats it endlessly, year in and year out. Heinrich Himmler used to say that once you had heard one of Hitler's speeches, you had heard them all. Later academic judgements of the man were to describe him as 'history's most terrifying bore'. Despite this commonplace characteristic, his intellectual mediocrity, in many other ways Hitler was, to say the least of it, a very unusual politician indeed. He clearly had that elusive quality famously described by Max Weber and labelled 'charisma'. Binchy certainly spotted this characteristic: Hitler's ability to get and keep the attention of the crowd. Another development since 1921, of course, was that Hitler had gone to prison for participating in an attempted coup in Munich in 1923. In a very comfortable jail surrounded by admiring warders, he had written a big fat book: *Mein Kampf* (My Struggle). It is written in a dull, monotonous and wearisomely repetitive German. Binchy doubted if even many of his own most devoted followers had actually read it.

> It certainly has given more ammunition to Hitler's enemies than to his friends, and any unprejudiced outsider who has the patience to finish the work is bound to conclude that its author is a man of very limited intelligence. Written in a maddeningly wooden style, in which hackneyed *clichés* alternate with windy rhetoric, full of rambling digressions and hysterical denunciations, it affords no insight whatever into Hitler's own life and development. Anything he tells us about himself is merely introduced as a peg on which to hang some political or ethnological dissertation. Commonplaces of history, politics and sociology are paraded as new and epoch-making discoveries; long discarded theories are rescued from the lumber rooms of science and enunciated with all the pompous omniscience of a village schoolmaster. At times one is almost disarmed by the author's *naiveté*; occasionally, too, one meets a gem of entirely unconscious humour. But for the most part the book makes sad reading, and anyone who has even attempted the task will readily understand why Hitler exalts the spoken over the written word.[11]

Binchy supplemented his reading of Hitler's book with information about this strange man's actual life. He found that Hitler was indeed Austrian, from the back-country of Upper Austria, and that his father was a minor customs officer. His father was a brute, and young Adolf was very attached to his mother. His parents had died when Adolf was a teenager, and young Adolf had absorbed the idea that he had some genius as an artist.

The few years he had spent at a *Realschule* near Linz had been utterly wasted, either because (as Hitler says) he was too high spirited to learn anything except what interested him, or because (his enemies' version) he was too stupid to learn anything at all. His great ambition was to become an artist or an architect, and he believed that he had a marked talent for sketching. This belief was not shared, however, by the examiners of the Vienna Academy of Art (were they, perhaps, Jews?), who rejected his candidature for admission. The fifty gulden, a respectable sum in Braunau on the Inn, were quickly spent in Vienna, and Hitler had to abandon his artistic ambitions and seek work as an unskilled labourer. For four years he belonged to the poorest stratum of the Viennese proletariat, living in grinding poverty, frequently unemployed, always unhappy. Yet they were not wasted years, for during them he obtained that insight into the social problem and the psychology of the proletariat which has since stood him and his movement in good stead

He was mainly self-educated, reading widely if unsystematically from the public libraries and little books that he bought with his hoarded pennies. 'For, he tells us proudly, his complete philosophy of life was formed during this period, and since then he has found "nothing to subtract from and little to add to it".[12] Having been turned down by the Academy as having little natural talent he had to take up manual work of various kinds, and spent the next few years living in rented accommodation, house-painting and earning a few extra pennies by painting postcards and peddling them on the streets. He was not very popular with his fellows, as they found him haughty and distant. In 1912 he moved to Munich and set himself up as a housepainter and decorator. He considered Munich to be the best city in Germany; Binchy remarked 'probably the only preference which he shares with the present writer.'[13] He welcomed the coming of war in 1914 wholeheartedly, and served in the Bavarian Army with distinction, earning the Iron Cross Second Class for bravery as a messenger along the front line. The officer who presented the award to him was Jewish. Towards the end of the war, Hitler was invalided out, suffering from hysterical blindness, a common condition of soldiers exposed to continuous conflict and horror. He soon recovered, having been treated by hypnosis in an experimental procedure of the period.

Binchy spotted Hitler's obsession with racial purity and the claimed necessity to avoid the mongrelisation of the 'higher' white types of human being by miscegenation with black, yellow or, above all, Jewish racial types. The pseudo-scientific ideas of Gobineau and Houston Chamberlain were recycled by Hitler and his Nazis in the 1920s, and the demonisation of the Jews became a central tenet of official Nazi doctrine. There was nothing new in German political racism; in reading Gobineau's draft book on the biological inequality of the human races, Alexis de Tocqueville, the great French social analyst, had advised the writer back in the 1850s never to let it be published in German, 'as our friends across the Rhine might take it literally'. Tocqueville often seems to have had an eerie gift of prophecy, almost as if he could smell the future and its frightfulness.

As late as 1933, Binchy still seems to have thought, or at least hoped against hope, that Hitler was a passing phenomenon, and that his own admired heroes, Hindenburg and Brüning, would be able to clip the orator's wings at the eleventh hour. The idea that Hitler 'could not last' was a natural one, and it has been argued that, had the German elites resisted him for another year or so, his magic moment might have passed. Stein Rokkan, the Norwegian political scientist, argued as much in private in the 1970s; Nazism was a potentially temporary phenomenon which was permitted by foolish and snobbish elites to institutionalise itself. Rainer Lepsius, the well-known German political scientist, has made a similar diagnosis. Like many another, Binchy fatally underestimated Hitler's cunning, ruthlessness and energy; his hysterical determination was perhaps beyond the range of Binchy's rather cool and rationalist mind. He just refused at some level to take Hitler seriously, again an understandable mental condition. Hitler was grotesque, and that itself helped to put people off their guard; far from being some kind of clown prince as many people felt, he was the most dangerous man in Europe. The Nazi leader was nobody's man, and he was about to bend the entire German super-power to his crazy purposes. However, in other respects Binchy's assessment of Hitler is perceptive, wise and almost unconsciously prophetic.

There are only two barriers to megalomania in public life: intelligence and humour. I believe Hitler to be lacking in both, and thus faith in himself and his mission has become for him a kind of religion. Such fanatical belief can be easily communicated to the masses, especially when it is accompanied, as in his case, by the gift of eloquence. It is not merely the right sort of faith which is capable of moving mountains.[14]

Hitler, Binchy wrote, was in complete control of Germany and he wanted a war. However, in March 1933, Hitler still depended on others who could get rid of him. Binchy could not quite believe in Hitler's ascent to complete power, or did not want to believe in it.

When Binchy's *Studies* article on Hitler was published in March 1933, one year after Binchy had left the Irish embassy in Berlin, he was warned by a British friend never to go back to Germany while the Nazis were in power, as he would certainly be murdered by the regime, many of whose minions regarded Hitler as a god and would have certainly regarded Binchy's article as blasphemous.[15] The article was to have had a wide circulation in Ireland, particularly among political elites.

Return to Ireland

Like many young academics, Binchy had to search for a while before deciding where his intellectual vocation lay. Back in 1921, he had not yet, it seems, decided to become a medievalist and a Celtic scholar, and throughout his life he repeatedly displayed a willingness to take up subjects sometimes very removed from his avowed intellectual vocation. Sixty years later, in 1981, he recalled that, at this stage, as a young man, he had known no Irish '… which was to me a book sealed with seven seals!'

After his spell in Munich, Binchy attended the *École des Chartes* in Paris, and not long after he was appointed to the part-time Chair of Roman Law, Jurisprudence and Legal History in UCD, despite his own protestations that he knew little about Roman law. There seems to have been a curious and rather casual practice in the NUI colleges of that time of very young professorial appointments; Binchy's was not that unusual a case. Dublin folklore tells of one case in the 1920s when a governmental appointment was made during an apparently chance meeting in Stephen's Green park in central Dublin: John Marcus O'Sullivan's meeting with William T. Cosgrave, the President (prime minister; this office was later renamed Taoiseach) of the country. Binchy's own account of his appointment, which proved so formative, was recalled by him fondly in old age:

> [In 1925] from a background in classics, history and law, I had gone over to general medieval studies. Having spent three years at the University of Munich, I was already halfway through a further year in Paris at the *Ecole des Chartes*, when I received news of my appointment to the part-time Chair of Roman Law and Jurisprudence in University College Dublin.

In response to his appointment Binchy shifted abruptly to the Faculty of Law in Paris. He had the advantage of his UCD law degree and the legal tradition in his own family. Sir Paul Vinogradoff, Professor of Jurisprudence in Oxford, got in touch and urged him to take up the study of ancient Irish law.[16]

Eoin MacNeill, co-founder of the Gaelic League at the end of the nineteenth century, pointed out to him that if he followed Vinogradoff's advice he would have to know not only modern Irish, but medieval and ancient Irish as well.

> … you must realise that the main problem is a philological one, and it will remain so for many years to come. So unless you can first learn enough Old and Middle Irish to make you able to correct me, and even to correct Thurneysen, your medieval and legal qualifications won't be much use.[17]

Accordingly, back in Ireland in 1925 to take up his Chair in Law, Binchy was to befriend Osborn Bergin and enter into the strange universe of medieval Irish studies, one in which he was to dwell as a rather original resident for the next 65 years. He reminisced in the middle of an academic argument involving comparative linguistics:

> Some years later when (at the age of 26) I took up the study of Irish and Irish law, both Bergin and MacNeill made it very clear

to me that I should read as widely as possible in Old and Middle Irish literature before tackling the obscure and sometimes archaic language of the legal tracts. Apart, then, from Greek, Latin and Irish, together with some knowledge of Middle Welsh and a minimum of Sanskrit (which I also owe to Bergin), I am very ill-equipped to confront the vast array of languages which [Heinrich] Wagner has laid under contribution.[18]

Many years later, he wrote of that time:

After my return to Dublin I read right through the English translation in the five volumes published by the Rolls Commission under the title *Ancient Laws of Ireland* (1865–1901). It was a discouraging experience which left me with a sense of bewilderment and frustration. The matter printed in large type seemed to be incoherent as well as disjointed; that in smaller type was much more voluminous (in every sense of the word) and much easier to follow, but it was even less likely to attract a prospective student. For the elaborate, often alternative and sometimes contradictory 'explanations' offered in the glosses did little or nothing to lighten my darkness; worse still, the long-winded, repetitive and schematic commentaries with their rabbinical distinctions and pseudo-mathematical jugglery, seemed to lead nowhere. I began to wonder uneasily whether these later scholiasts had any real understanding of the text they were supposed to interpret. Later, when I had read MacNeill's two books as well as his revised translation of the two tracts on status, [Charles] Plummer's useful series of 'Notes on Some passages in the Brehon Laws' … and above all [Rudolf] Thurneysen's masterly edition of *Cáin Aigillne* … the article to which Vinogradoff had given such high praise, I found that my suspicions had been anticipated and amply confirmed by these three scholars.[19]

This period from 1925 onwards is significant in allowing us to understand Binchy's burgeoning interest in the Irish language, but there is one further endeavour which occupied Binchy up to 1925 which contextualises his later work.

Historian: Spies in Ireland, Diplomats in Madrid

Whilst Binchy began to pursue his linguistic studies and develop his interest in Irish legal history, he maintained his interest in political history through a series of articles which were to become his first published book. Somewhat remote from his later interest in Nazism or German politics in the early twentieth century and also unconnected with the historian's and legal career outlined for him by Thurneysen, Vinogradoff and others of his teachers, whether Irish, English, French, German or Swiss, it was a study in political history. Oddly, in view of Binchy's later career, it was also a study in primitive Irish diplomacy. It consisted of a series of articles published in *Studies* between 1921 and 1925, amounting in all to a short book, on sixteenth-century Irish efforts to mount a diplomatic presence in the Madrid of Philip II.[20] This curious pattern of writing long journal articles that amounted to short books was one that was to characterise much of his learned work throughout his long academic career.

The book itself, 'An Irish Ambassador at the Spanish Court, 1569–1574', reads somewhat like an adventure story of derring-do by pre-war writers like Jeffrey Farnol or Raphael Sabatini. It is an intriguing story in its own right and deals with the efforts of the Norman and Gaelic Catholic aristocrats of Munster to persuade the Spaniards to mount an invasion of Ireland to displace English power and, presumably, set up a separate Irish Catholic monarchy under Spanish protection. Led by the Desmond ('Geraldine') clan which was associated with the area more or less corresponding with the modern county of Cork, the Catholic Archbishop of Cashel, Maurice MacGibbon, became the *de facto* Irish Ambassador to Spain on behalf of a rebel Irish Catholic state-in-formation centred on Munster. Two Desmond chieftains were immured in London, and James Fitzmaurice, a cousin, acted as their agent and as the leader of the Irish grandees and clerics. MacGibbon was himself a bar-sinister connection of the Desmonds.

At this time this was not a quixotic or hopeless mission, as Spanish agents of the Duke of Alva were active in Ireland, trying to stir up trouble for the English administration in Dublin. Furthermore, persecuted priests and friars as well as agents of Catholic Palesmen and landowners passed fairly freely from Ireland to Spain and back. Ireland remained very much a restless and unsubdued Catholic country under a determinedly Protestant English queen. There was great support from the four Catholic archbishops and the chieftains for the proposed embassy, which *de facto* became representative of native and Norman Catholic Ireland. A document listing the complaints of the Catholics of Ireland, and expressing a wish that Ireland be taken under the wing of the Spanish sovereign, was drawn up by Fitzmaurice. A Catholic king would be established under Spanish protection, it was proposed. From the English point of view this was, of course, an act of treason.

Philip was a crafty monarch, but was also actually an innately cautious man and was notoriously slow in coming to a decision. In this case he was, perhaps, particularly slow. Madrid was riddled with English spies and there were English, French and Irish double agents of all sorts as one might expect at the Renaissance court of a great power such as Spain was at that time. England was not yet really a major power. MacGibbon was, in effect, being treated as a representative of Ireland as a legitimate foreign power, presumably much to the fury of the English. Elizabeth had legitimacy problems of her own, and an internal challenge to her right to rule still existed in the form of her own prisoner, Mary Queen of Scots, locked up in the Tower of London. However, even Mary would not take kindly to an Irish secession from the realms that she claimed the right to rule any more than Elizabeth would. MacGibbon was embarrassed by Philip's inactivity, and the Irish leaders at home became increasingly impatient with the archbishop as the desire for complete secession from the English kingdom grew among them. The idea of making Philip's brother, Don John of Austria, king of Ireland grew among them by 1570. At about the same time the Pope decided out of the blue in July 1570 to excommunicate Elizabeth without checking with Philip first; the Pope and Philip were not on good terms.

In the midst of all this intrigue and cross-purpose, an English adventurer, Thomas Stukely, arrived at the port of Vivero in Galicia. Stukely was the man MacGibbon was persuaded should lead a Spanish expedition to Ireland. He was also one of the most extraordinary of many con-men to intervene in Irish affairs over the centuries. As Binchy commented:

> The story of Thomas Stukely's connection with Irish foreign relations reads like a grotesque romance, the truth of which might well be doubted, were it not authenticated from the most reliable sources. In

the light of after events, now that the full record of his discreditable life has been revealed to us, it is but natural that we should wonder at the apparent folly of the Irish in using, even indirectly, such an unworthy instrument.[21]

Stukely would, in modern times, be simply regarded as a criminal. Like Drake and Hawkins, he had been a notorious pirate or 'privateer', technically in the service of the English Crown. He had betrayed the secrets of the King of France, conspired against the English with the Spanish ambassador in London, dissipated his wife's fortune, coined money and, bankrupt, had arrived in Ireland in 1565. Here he had befriended the Lord Deputy and won the trust of Shane O'Neill, then at the height of his power in Ulster. Elizabeth put a halt to his gallop when he attempted to buy the high office of Marshal in Ireland in 1566. This finally turned Stukely against her. Nonetheless, he had one last try at office under the Crown in 1567 and bought the office of seneschal of Wexford. Elizabeth got wind of this and tried to fire him in 1568, finally succeeding. He was jailed for a short while afterwards. Somehow or other he got away, and ended up throwing in his lot with the dissident Irish. Binchy wrote:

And so this strange man – a typical child of Elizabethan England in his pride, his haughty ambition, his agreeable presence, and his utter lack of moral sense – was at last driven into the arms of the insurgent Irish. He came to them, not of his own free-will or through any honest sympathy with their cause, but through motives of personal pique and hopes of personal aggrandisement, goaded by the faithlessness of Elizabeth and her minister into joining hands with their opponents. These were the causes of his association with Irish nationalism; and a connection based on such reasons could be neither happy or lasting.[22]

The Archbishop of Cashel, still working in Madrid as Irish envoy, eventually saw through Stukely and warned the Vatican against him in 1571. However, Stukely had, by this time, insinuated himself into the confidence of Philip and was accepted, rather strangely, as the incumbent military leader of the Irish. He seems to have fooled a Jesuit or two as well. Philip, however, was no fool, despite his future destiny to become an Elizabethan version of Xerxes watching his military might being destroyed on the sea by a despised foreign power allied with nature in 1588. He seems to have calculated that he could use this unscrupulous but possibly useful English desperado to foment a rebellion in Ireland which, with Spanish military assistance, might lead to the attachment of Ireland to the Spanish crown as a permanent block to English western expansionism into the Atlantic. At the very least, such an adventure would give the English a headache and was, therefore, worth trying. Of course, the English would move heaven and earth to prevent any such enterprise in what they thought of as their own back yard. Archbishop MacGibbon realised that Stukely had by-passed and outsmarted him, and all he himself could do was to return home discredited in the eyes of his own people in Munster. However, first he went to Paris and contacted the English embassy there. Francis Walsingham was the ambassador; a famous secret service agent, he was also extremely shrewd and ruthless when he deemed it necessary to defend his Queen against domestic, foreign, Catholic or Irish enemies. MacGibbon attempted to mend a fence with the English authorities, but the ambassador was not deceived by the Irishman's lame excuses for leaving Ireland for two years to engage in what was obviously an elaborate anti-English intrigue in Spain. The Archbishop offered to inform the English of the details of Stukely's treachery and treasons. He was, of course, angling for a pardon from the Queen.

He was unsuccessful, returned briefly to Ireland, and then made his return to Spain through Scotland, a normal route for Irish people who felt they were anathema to the English. He presumably used independent Scotland like many another at that time to avoid being taken by the English. He settled eventually in Oporto in Portugal, then about to come under the Spanish crown for a period of 60 years, between 1580 and 1640. He seems to have died around 1578. Meanwhile Stukely came to be seen quite rightly by Elizabeth as a dangerous traitor, and a menace to any political settlement between England and Spain. However, he soon fell out of favour with Philip also and his dreams of being Spain's viceroy in Ireland faded. For Binchy, a very young scholar in the uncertain beginnings of his career, this study of Irish diplomacy in the sixteenth century was extraordinarily mature, thoroughgoing and shrewd.

Binchy promised a further article on the rogue's subsequent adventures, but seems to have lost interest in Stukely and Spain at this juncture; the article never appeared. Pressure of work could have been a factor; John Marcus O'Sullivan, his fellow Germanophile, took leave of absence from his professorship in UCD to become Minister for Education in November 1925, and Binchy acted in his place until the middle of 1929, when he transferred on leave of absence to the government's Department of External Affairs. During this year Binchy also attended the lectures of Rudolf Thurneysen at the RIA, describing it afterwards as a turning-point in his intellectual career.

The Spell of the Irish Language, 1925–1929

Daniel's political opinions at this time are revealing of the young man that he then was. As his youthful choice of sixteenth-century Irish political history indicates obliquely, he was quite the Catholic clerical nationalist, as were so many Irish Catholic intellectuals of the time. One of his themes later on in the late 1930s was to be that of the priest as hero, which becomes obvious in his work on Pius XI and Italian politics under fascism. He remained a firm upholder of the rights of the Catholic Church in modern society, but came rapidly to see through the claims of authoritarian systems of government such as Italian Fascism or German Nazism. Nazism he came to abhor in particular, which emotion was to mark him out from many in the Ireland of that time; some among the Irish leaders and intellectuals had a sort of uncomprehending admiration for Hitler and his reorganisation of Germany under the Nazi dictatorship from 1932 onwards. Joseph Walshe was a fringe member of this group. This mood was particularly strong among some people in Fianna Fáil, de Valera's party, due to come to power in early 1932. People on the Fine Gael side of the political divide sometimes had a similar uncomprehending admiration for Mussolini, Franco and Salazar as Catholic anti-communist heroes. Binchy was to be somewhat isolated politically by his anti-Nazism and he came to sympathise passionately with the determined resistance to Germany which was to be led by Winston Churchill ten years later. Communism he condemned immediately, and seems never to have worshiped that particular god that failed. As a believing and committed Catholic, he was presumably immunised against any avowedly anti-Christian and atheistic system of ideas. He was equally rapidly to come down in favour of democracy as an essentially anti-extremist and tolerant form of government, and one that should be readily compatible with the claims to autonomy and freedom of various religions, including that of the Catholic Church. He seems to have been free of that Platonist contempt for democratic procedures which was common among Irish Catholic thinkers of that era. Furthermore, he disliked Catholic clerical high-handedness in Ireland, of which there was plenty to disapprove.

Whilst political thinking was clearly of interest to Binchy, from 1925 onwards he entered more fully into the world of medieval Irish studies and encountered more closely many of the characters who were to shape his own life and the life of intellectual Ireland at the time. Binchy realised that John O'Donovan and Eugene O'Curry knew far more Modern Irish and Middle Irish than Old Irish, and the very early language had not really been properly studied by grammarians at the time; they did the best they could with the intellectual instruments they had available to them. Old Irish had to await the coming of the great German comparative grammarians of the late nineteenth century. It was at this time that Binchy's association with Osborn Bergin became significant and he, apparently, fell under the spell of this formidable older intellectual, attending his lectures in UCD. He was also taught by MacNeill, who encouraged the young man, and Binchy was always fond of the two older men. 'Thanks to … [MacNeill] I learned from the outset that to understand Irish law (or for that matter any branch of early Irish history) one needs much more than a training in historical method: a sound linguistic basis is equally essential.'

Bergin, a rather reserved and solitary man, befriended the younger Binchy, and Binchy spent long periods in Dunquin and on the Great Blasket to perfect his west Kerry Irish, which he certainly wrote perfectly all his life. A particular rendezvous was the O Dálaigh house in Coumeenole at Slea Head, one of the most dramatic pieces of landscape in Ireland. There he met, besides the locals, James Stephens, the well-known Irish writer and friend of James Joyce, who insisted on speaking bad French so as not to pollute the local pool of pure Gaelic. This was despite the fact that most people in the house understood English, while Stephens knew no Irish at all.[23] Binchy evidently fell in love with west Kerry and the

Dingle Gaeltacht, as many another has done over the decades. The cultural importance of Dingle as a last stronghold of Gaelic culture, combined with the spectacular natural beauty of its landscape, seas and cliffs, the Blasket islands and the dramatic pyramids of the Skelligs further out on the western sea has commonly made people undergo an experience akin to religious conversion. The charm and hospitality of its people are almost proverbial. The area has commonly been used in modern films, often with subject matter quite unconnected with Ireland and the Irish. Young people were perhaps particularly vulnerable to the spell of that western peninsula. Bergin was his mentor. In Coumeenole to the west of Dingle, according to himself, under Bergin's guidance he started with *Séadna* and finished with *Amra Coluim Chille*, thereby covering one and a half millennia of the Irish language by going backwards in time.

In August 1926 Bergin wrote good-humouredly about this enthusiastic young man: 'I came here on Wednesday bringing a new bicycle, as Binchy wrote rapturously entreating me to join him in Dunquin and offering to meet me anywhere in his car.'[24] All his life Binchy was fond of sports cars. Years later, after a flying visit to Ireland and Dunquin from the Irish Embassy in Berlin in 1930, Binchy wrote to Richard Best from Berlin 'You can imagine what a relief Dunquin was after the snobbish artificiality of Berlin!'[25]

Bergin was, of course, a believer in the essential historical unity of the Irish language over 2,000 years; to him, the modern and ancient languages were one. To learn the old language you had to first learn the modern one. There was something of a tradition of disregarding the modern language as a debased *patois*, and quite often scholars went straight to the medieval language and more or less ignored the living language; Bergin set his face against that curious custom, always arguing that many of the idioms in the modern language were echoes of similar turns of phrase in the older versions of the language. If you were unfamiliar with the modern tongue, you were in danger of engaging in a wildly inaccurate translation of the older language.

Binchy always remembered Bergin's great intellectual generosity to younger scholars; he recalled many years later that everything Binchy wrote, Bergin checked up on for him and criticised positively. Bergin, quite the purist, was rather appalled by the amateurish English-language writings of literary people such as W. B. Yeats, whose free way with Irish myth and legend he found to be wrong in almost every conceivable way. Yeats knew no Irish, and his writing makes that fact very obvious even to the layman; he routinely misspells the names of characters in the sagas and stories, and plays fast and loose with the myths. However, according to Binchy himself in old age, 'It must be confessed that Bergin transmitted the cult of certainty, the reluctance to commit oneself to print, to a number of his disciples, myself included.'[26]

Binchy, despite his claimed modesty, was not reluctant to publish. What is striking is the astonishing range of his subject matter: he came to be an internationally recognised master of medieval Irish history and language, but he also wrote biography, political science and political history. He was quite willing to engage in public comment on contemporary political affairs. Bergin was somewhat reclusive, as we have seen, and that privacy of personality may have been partly responsible for Binchy's own growing reclusiveness in later life. Binchy was liable to something akin to hero worship of older men. Reverence for the old was probably much more common then than it is nowadays; it was a mark of a rather static, unchanging society, much as was famously described by two American anthropologists of that time, Arensberg and Kimball. Vinogradoff and Thurneysen were two of the older people who had originally suggested to Binchy that he take up the study of ancient Irish, or Brehon law. Bergin was clearly one of the main and more immediate influences on the young man's decision to take up Celtic Studies rather than becoming a mainline historian, legal scholar or even lawyer. Binchy reminisced later, with nostalgia for a well-remembered youthful enthusiasm:

> Every summer during our time in Dunquin, we would read a series of Old and Middle Irish texts … and I can imagine no pupil can ever have been so fortunate both in his teacher and environment. To be taught Old Irish by such a master, with the sound of the modern language all around us, was surely a blessing for which I can never be sufficiently grateful.[27]

It should be remembered that the 'little band' of Celtic scholars and other medievalists in Ireland and elsewhere were facing a gargantuan task far beyond the capacity of their small numbers. The well-known

English medievalist, H. M. Chadwick, author of classic studies of Celtic and medieval Britain, while on a visit to Dublin before the First World War, looked at the collections housed in the Royal Irish Academy and Trinity College Dublin and seems to have been somewhat intimidated by their richness. They include various versions of old heroic epics such as the *Táin Bó Cúailnge,* many versions of the *Fiannaíochta,* or the exploits of Fionn mac Cumhaill, Caoilte Mac Rónáin, Oisín, Oscar, Bricriú of the Bitter Tongue and the rest of the Fianna, dozens of other tales and romances and, not least, huge tracts of law codes. The collections cover 1,000 years of literature, history, mythology, pseudo-history, religious texts, legal codes in various varieties of Irish and Latin: the impressive detritus of an entire dead civilisation. They are supplemented by extensive holdings in the British Library, the Bodleian in Oxford and by further holdings in Irish, British and continental monasteries. Chadwick remarked somewhat ruefully in a long footnote in his classic cross-cultural study *The Heroic Age,* 'On the other hand I have no doubt that many interesting features are to be found in the Irish Heroic Era (or rather perhaps Heroic Eras). This subject is beset with such extreme difficulties of every kind that I dare not touch it.'[28]

This is an extraordinary remark from someone who was spectacularly accomplished and quite capable of discussing the mythological systems of Celtic Britain, classical Greece and Rome, Germany, various eastern European cultures and others even further afield. It almost certainly reflects the unconscious and almost pathological disregard many modern British scholars had for the Irish past, a disregard that had deep political and sectarian roots commonly unrecognised even by British scholars of great goodwill. This, in turn, had led them to ignore it, and Chadwick was possibly an unsuspecting participant in that neglect.

Binchy himself gradually developed an attitude to historical and linguistic enquiry in Ireland which was characteristic of the best scholars of his generation. This consisted of a determined aspiration toward scientific history, partly in reaction to the highly romanticised pseudo-historical accounts which abounded in the Ireland of that time. Ireland had, of course, been going through a phase of exaggerated popular nationalism, which had driven a torrent of amateur studies and popular retellings. In June 1927, in the course of a review of a new study by Edmund Curtis,

Richard II in Ireland (1394–5) and the Submissions of the Irish Chiefs, he remarked 'There are too many general histories of Ireland (most of them, incidentally, strange compounds of *Dichtung* and *Wahrheit*) and too few source-books. This is a source-book and a very valuable one.'[29] The casual use of assertion unsupported by positive evidence was, he felt, an Irish intellectual vice which would have to be eradicated if a scientific understanding of the history of the island was ever to be achieved. In this he was, interestingly, at one with the group of young men, younger even than Binchy, who were trying to set up a tradition of scientific history in the Irish Universities, led by Theo Moody in TCD, Robin Dudley Edwards in UCD and David Quinn in Queen's University Belfast. All three young men had experienced postgraduate training at the University of London. It seems that the cultural disaster of the destruction of the Four Courts at the beginning of the Irish Civil War in June 1922, which involved the complete destruction of the National State Archive of Ireland for the second time in two centuries, was being echoed in academia by an emphasis on whatever other archives might have survived the vandalism of the IRA.[30]

However, Binchy was always something of an intellectual wanderer. He spoke fluent German, French and Italian. Charles-Edwards recalled how 'The sudden shifts of direction, from his Munich doctoral thesis on the *Schottenkloster* of medieval Germany to Roman law, and then to the history of fascist Italy, undoubtedly betray a certain restlessness of spirit.'[31]

Another key characteristic of Binchy's intellectual development was, of course, his legal training. The rules of evidence in modern law are very different from those in history or the social sciences, partly because the consequences of acceptance of argument in a court of law are generally so much more momentous than those of (say) historical enquiry. One can speculate learnedly on the identities and motives of the murderers of Julius Caesar, but if one is on a jury in a modern murder trial, one must not speculate too much on who murdered whom. Legal rules of evidence, as Ciaran Brady has often pointed out, are so severe and demanding of high levels of probability as to make much history writing impossible, were they to be insisted on.

It was at around this time that Binchy met another Corkman, Michael O'Donovan, who was shortly to become famous under his *nom de plume* of Frank O'Connor, author of such classic short stories as 'Guests of the Nation', 'My Oedipus Complex' and 'In the Train'. O'Connor was also the author in later life of popular and very lively studies of Irish cultural history of a kind that brought the fruits of academic research to the attention of the ordinary Irish reader (*Kings, Lords and Commons* and *The Backward Look*). He was a gifted translator of poetry. O'Connor had virtually no formal education and, in contrast to Binchy, came from a very deprived Cork city background. George Russell ('AE'), the well-known writer and painter, who acted as a kind of Maecenas to the young writers of the time, said to Binchy about O'Donovan some time in 1927, 'You *must* meet him. You'll find him most exciting.' As Binchy remembered decades later, a few days later AE entertained them both to 'weak tea and stale biscuits' in the Dublin office of the *Irish Statesman*. The two Corkmen scowled at each other; they had been on opposite sides in the Civil War a few years earlier and O'Donovan had spent time in an Irish government prison camp. O'Donovan, although he repudiated political violence and repented of his military past, was insistent on the sincerity of the IRA's resistance to the Treaty. They disagreed violently 'on every subject, from the Irish Civil War to Heine's poetry'. Poor George Russell, who was a famously kind man, looked on in a mixture of dismay and amusement at this cockfight; Binchy remembered 'even his unique capacity to spread sweetness and light was powerless against two very angry and very youthful know-alls'. From this rather unpromising beginning in a Corkmen's cockfight the two young men gradually became great friends, partly because of the filial affection they both felt for Bergin and AE. Binchy wrote many years later:

> I remember it was Bergin who first called my attention to 'Guests of the Nation' ('Read that story,' he said, 'it's one that deserves to live.') But more important was the fact that, after a number of false starts in different directions, I had just settled down to work at Celtic Studies under Bergin's direction. And that in itself was a sure passport to Michael's goodwill.[32]

The love they shared for the Irish language awakened a respect for Binchy in the other young man. O'Connor had learned modern Irish as an adolescent, while under the influence of Daniel Corkery, but the ancient language seems to have been a closed book to him as it is to the vast majority of Irish people. On and off over the following decades, from the thirties through to the late fifties and the early sixties, Binchy was to try to teach O'Connor Old Irish, and, perhaps unknowingly, became a kind of intellectual godfather to O'Connor's last book, *The Backward Look*, a magnificent series of lectures on the Irish literary tradition delivered in TCD just before his death in the sixties. The book was published posthumously. Interestingly, it was during these efforts to teach his friend the old language that Binchy found that O'Connor had an innate talent for appropriate translation of ancient Irish poetry into modern English. He spotted that his friend had a natural eye for a poetically valid line. Binchy commented:

> Bergin used to lament that Michael had not been 'caught young' and put through the mill of scholastic discipline. But surely his temperament would have revolted against what Germans call *die Zunftwissenschaft*; indeed this might only have blunted the edge of his genius. For his approach to scholarship was primarily intuitive, and his intuition was at times so overwhelming as to leave a professional scholar gasping with amazement.

> It was this that made collaboration with him an unforgettable experience. It was not only his power to make you share his own excitement and enthusiasm. There was the fascination of watching him wrestle with a problem which had baffled the professionals, and after a number of wildly false starts, produce the right solution. 'Nonsense!' he would cry out against the received translation. 'No poet would ever have said a thing like that. It must be –' and he would propose something quite off the beam. 'Impossible, Michael, the grammar would be all wrong.' 'Well, what about this?' And so on until, suddenly, the lightning struck and you said to yourself half-incredulously: 'He's done it again.'[33]

Binchy's admiration for O'Donovan's intuitive if untutored brilliance is revealing, both of his own intellectual generosity and his own more disciplined 'scientific' temperament. At times this austere cast of mind must have prevented him from following his instincts in intellectual inquiry, and at some level he must have had an uneasy sense that this might be the case. He writes almost shamefacedly: '[Michael] worked tirelessly at Old and Middle Irish, so much so in fact that professional scholars such as myself were shamed by his wholly disinterested pursuit of the subject we were paid to study.'[34] In the late 1920s O'Connor and Sean O'Faolain were already friends and had started writing. Binchy got to know O'Faolain later on, and they also became lifelong friends, forming, under the distant auspices of Bergin, perhaps the academic equivalent of a crack Cork team. Interestingly, O'Faolain's description of O'Connor's style of argument echoes Binchy's rather eerily. O'Faolain wrote in the mid-1960s:

> I do not know what I would have done for intimate companionship in those years [of the thirties in Dublin] without Michael, as I called Frank O'Connor … his imagination was a ball of fire, mine was less combustible but steadier; his memory was infallible, his interests more confined; his brain was first-class but completely untrained, and discipline was a word he had never heard; his intuitive processes were something to marvel at, to distrust and, if one was wise, to respect profoundly, because if you were patient enough to discard the old boots and bits of seaweed that he would bring up from his deep diving he was certain, sooner or later, to surface with a piece of pure gold. I do not think he ever reasoned out anything. He was like a man who takes a machine gun to a shooting gallery. Everyone falls flat on his face, the proprietor takes to the hills, and when it is all over you cautiously peep up and find that he has wrecked the place but got three perfect bull's-eyes.[35]

The Scholar turns Diplomat, 1929–1932

Back in the late 1920s Daniel seemed to be all set for a happy career in Irish academe. By 1929 he was already busying himself with a task that was to become his life's work, slowed up though it was by multifarious other activities. In 1929 an academic conference involving Rudolf Thurneysen took place in Dublin which became remembered as a landmark in the development of academic Celtic Studies in Ireland by confirming its international appeal. Thurneysen, whom Daniel evidently loved, conducted the seminar, which took place at the RIA, then as now the centre for academic research for all of Ireland.[36] However, in the same year Binchy was tapped to become the Irish Free State's first Minister (ambassador) to Germany. He was obviously qualified, his mastery of German was an unusual skill in the Ireland of that time, and it is probable that Walshe had had his eye on the young man for some time. Had Walshe been more aware of Binchy's incipient hostility to Nazism he just might have looked elsewhere; Walshe, like quite a number of the educated elites of the time, was sceptical about the merits of democracy and developed an admiration for authoritarian government which spilled over into an obvious and rather myopic sympathy for Hitler's regime in the 1930s. He used to advise de Valera, prime minister from February 1932 on, to 'give parliament a holiday' so that he could concentrate on governing the country without worrying too much about the trivialities of democratic governance. Walshe, since becoming Secretary of the infant Department of External Affairs in 1922 had, with the personal support of Prime Minister William T. Cosgrave, been enabled to expand the Department rapidly in 1929 while fending off the attempts of the civil servants in the Department of Finance to take it over and, perhaps, close it down. The Berlin post was created at the same time as similar posts in Paris, Rome and at the Vatican. A United States post already existed.

Even before he was appointed to Berlin, Binchy, in his new capacity as trainee diplomat, was already displaying expertise of yet another kind: as constitutional theorist. In October 1929 he wrote a highly technical and well-informed long essay on kingship and regnal succession as it operated in the United Kingdom and the British Commonwealth and affected the constitutional status of the Irish Free State. This was, at that time, a matter of considerable public controversy and, of course, an issue which had been one of the causes of the Irish Civil War of 1922–23. In particular he focused on the religion of the king and the possibility of removing the requirement that the king be Protestant by religion. He made the point that there were far more Catholics in the United Kingdom now than there had been in 1700, the date of the Act of Settlement, and the British Empire and Commonwealth itself contained many Catholics. Therefore, this was a likely future issue in matters of regnal succession. Prophetically, he contemplated the possibility of a future regency in the case of the monarch having a chronic illness, much like that of George III, handing an Irish government the possibility of having a different regency council to that of the United Kingdom. A somewhat similar situation did indeed materialise with the abdication of Edward VIII a few years later; he might easily have found himself as Edward I, King of the Twenty-Six Counties.[37] Dev (as de Valera was sometimes known) was, however, prepared for such an undesirable, if comical, outcome.

Immediately afterwards Binchy departed for Berlin, apparently being expected to abandon his academic vocation and take on the role of professional diplomat. Binchy was rather reluctant to undergo this particularly drastic metamorphosis and remained an academic deep down. During his two and a half years in Berlin he tried to continue his legal and mediaeval studies in his own time with some assistance from a few fellow Celticists in Berlin while continuing a voluble correspondence with his academic colleagues in Ireland, Germany and elsewhere. Nonetheless, he took up his diplomatic post on 10 October 1929. He turned out to be an excellent choice, submitting to the Irish government perceptive, accurate and wise assessments of the toxic politics that marked the dying years of the Weimar Republic.

Notes

1 T. M. Charles-Edwards, Obituary of Daniel Binchy, *The Pelican*, 1988–89, pp.68–72. Copy found in Maeve Binchy papers, Special Collections, University College Dublin, MB 2011, Folio 31, Obituaries.
2 *Sunday Business Post*, 13 April 2014.
3 Interview, Helen Burke née Binchy, 11 July 2014.
4 Dermot Keogh, 'Profile of Joseph Walshe', *Irish Studies in America*, Vol. 3, No. 2, 1990, pp.59–80, 62.
5 Information provided by Bruce Bradley S. J., from Clongowes records.
6 *DIB*, Vol. 9, pp.774–777; Louis McRedmond, *Modern Irish Lives*, Dublin: Gill and Macmillan, 1998, p.317.
7 There is a copy of the thesis in DIAS, Binchy Papers, BIN/P/31.
8 *Celtica*, Vol. 14, 1981, pp.155–164, quote at p.155.
9 Daniel A. Binchy, 'Adolf Hitler', *Studies*, XXI, March 1933, pp.29–47, quote at p.29.
10 Ibid., p.30.

11 Ibid., pp.31–2.

12 Ibid., p.33.

13 Ibid., p.35.

14 As quoted in 'Daniel Anthony Binchy, 1900–1989', Obituary, *Studia Celtica*, 1989–90, pp.153–157, at 154.

15 I owe this information to Liam Breatnach.

16 'Irish History and Irish Law', *Studia Hibernica*, Vol. XV, pp.7–37, quote from p.7.

17 Ibid., p.10.

18 DIAS, Binchy Papers, BIN/P/45.

19 Daniel A. Binchy, 'Irish History and Irish Law I', *Studia Hibernica*, XV, 1975, pp.7–15, quote at p.8.

20 'An Irish Ambassador at the Spanish Court, 1569–1574' in *Studies* X (1921) pp.353–74, pp.573–84; XI (1922) pp.199–214; XII (1923) pp.83–105, pp.461–80; XIII (1924) pp.115–28; XIV (1925) pp.102–19.

21 Ibid., *Studies*, XI, p.199.

22 Ibid., p.212.

23 Donnchadh O Corráin, interview, 28 June 2014.

24 NLI Best Papers, MS 11,000 (7), 6 August 1926.

25 NLI Best Papers, MS 11,000 (10), 15 August 1930.

26 Daniel A. Binchy, *Osborn Bergin*, Dublin: National Library of Ireland, 1970, lecture, 18.

27 Diarmuid Breathnach agus Máire ní Mhurchu, *Beathaisneis a Dó*, BAC: An Clóchomhar TTA 1990, 19.

28 H. M. Chadwick, *The Heroic Age*, Cambridge: Cambridge University Press, 1912, p.431.

29 Daniel A. Binchy, 'Review' of Curtis, *Studies*, XVI (June 1927), pp.344–6, at p.344. The German means 'Art and Truth'.

30 This suggestion was originally made to me by Ciaran Brady.

31 Charles-Edwards, Obituary, p.70.

32 D. A. Binchy, 'The Scholar-Gipsy', in Maurice Sheehy (ed.), *Michael/Frank: Studies on Frank O'Connor*, Dublin: Gill and Macmillan, 1969, pp.16–22, at pp.16–17.

33 Ibid., pp.18–19.

34 Ibid., p.19.

35 Sean O'Faolain, *Vive Moi!*, London: Rupert Hart-Davis, 1967, p.284.

36 D. A. Binchy and Myles Dillon (eds.), *Studies in Irish Law*, Dublin: 1936, a report on the 1929 'Thurneysen Conference'.

37 Ronan Fanning, Michael Kennedy, Dermot Keogh, Eunan O'Halpin (eds), *Documents on Irish Foreign Policy, Vol. III, 1926–32*, pp.393–401, 5 October 1929.

CHAPTER TWO

A LUNATIC WITH A GIFT FOR RHETORIC, 1929–1932

The government of the newly independent and somewhat inexperienced Irish Free State, having finally made its own Department of Finance, beat a retreat on the issue and embarked on establishing a real diplomatic corps in 1929. At the beginning of Irish independence in 1922, leaving aside relationships with the old metropolitan power Great Britain, the two countries favoured because of special historical relationships were two very different ones: the Vatican and the United States of America. Germany, France and Italy now followed.

On Binchy's appointment to the post of Ambassador to Germany he moved to Berlin in 1929 and Dublin treated its new envoy to Germany very generously. Binchy was provided with a hotel reservation and later a residence with servants and an office close to the Tiergarten, the large public park in central Berlin. Binchy must have been pleased; the Tiergarten was, and is, ideal for horse-riding, and the new envoy was a lifelong horse-lover. The residential apartment was apparently quite stylish and even luxurious by German standards, standards which were, at that time, quite Spartan; Germany had been impoverished by the war, the semi-revolutionary struggles which ensued in the defeated country and by the debauching of its currency in 1923. The Irish were using the Irish sterling-backed pound and found Berlin prices very low.

Binchy's time in Berlin was not altogether happy. Mildly depressed, he reported to his friend, classical scholar Michael Tierney:

> For me the round of social activities is an unceasing torment, I dodge them with increasing unscrupulousness when at all possible … Even worse is my own entertaining, I don't know whether the dinner to the British Embassy or the Patrick's Day function (given a week late because of 'flu) to the Irish Colony was the worse – I'm inclined to

think the latter. Fortunately the flat is a dream of beauty, and people spend most of their time admiring it. Germans think it is '*eine typische Irische wohnung*'; whereas I doubt if there is anything like it in the whole of Dublin, with its Dun Emer carpets, Hicks furniture, Carrickmacross lace, and pictures (mostly lent by friends) by Lamb, Paul Henry, Jack Yeats, AE and Nathaniel Hone.[1]

At that time Berlin was a relatively small and compact city, laid out on an ambitious scale in administrative reforms made in the mid-1920s. Long before Hitler, the German authorities were clearly planning for a much bigger city, more than twice its actual size in 1929 of about three million, and had provided it during and after the *Kaiserreich* with an elaborate underground railway (*U-Bahn*) as well as an *S-Bahn* or overhead commuter railway, again designed for a far bigger population. A London-sized Berlin was fantasised about though it was never to happen, but the city retains an air of spaciousness and *rus in urbe* to the present day. It was this accidental enclosure of so much green space, forest and lakeland that made the besieged half-city of West Berlin a reasonably tolerable place to live and work in during the near half-century of being bombed-out and partitioned during the stand-off of the Cold War after Germany's defeat in 1945. Even after reunification in 1990, the entire city had only about four million people.

Binchy had some difficulty in 1929 convincing the Germans that Ireland was actually an independent country, with its own history and cultural traditions; he often characterised the German attitude to his country as one of an uninformed and vague sympathy. Unsurprisingly, nobody was all that terribly interested, and the only use the Germans had for the Irish Free State was the rather tentative possibility of using its membership of the British Commonwealth to influence British policies in some unimagined way. Oddly, Ireland's status as an English-speaking country and its very inaccurately imagined aristocratic rurality was rather an advantage. In his first general report to Joseph Walshe in May 1930 Binchy wrote wryly:

...I think I may sum up German public opinion towards Ireland as one of uninformed sympathy. I must deal first with the people among whom my present position compels me to move, that is to say the so-called members of 'society'. Berlin post-war society is a strange body. One of its chief characteristics is a cult of English ways and English fashions which amounts almost to a religion. I think that this cult existed in aristocratic circles before the war, but their successors of the revolution have carried it to crazy lengths. In society nowadays it is a test of respectability to speak English, which is occasionally very trying for native speakers of that language. The Englishman is regarded as the very essence of good breeding and smartness, the *beau idéal* of social life ...The average member of Berlin society regards Ireland as a country where English is also spoken, where people play bridge, drink Whiskey, hunt, golf, shoot etc. and therefore a kind of 'next best thing' to England.[2]

As the representative of a small, new and disregarded country, Binchy had only one real ace up his sleeve: his fluent German, learned in Munich in the early 1920s, combined with his close acquaintance with German academia and its intellectual tradition. Envoys from the Anglo-Saxon world commonly spoke no German and had to rely on translators, although the Americans usually had a few German scholars. The French apparently sometimes made a point of not speaking the language of their hated enemy, preferring instead to shout at them in French, which was, after all, the diplomatic international language of the era; the bitterness of the Armistice or *Waffenstillstand*, with its strange and even ominous suggestion of temporariness, never faded during the inter-war years.

A Reluctant Diplomat

Michael Kennedy has pointed out that Walshe's central idea was that Irish diplomats should, of course, represent the Irish nation, further its interests and assert its independent stance in international affairs. However, a related central purpose was to gather information about the host country, its political life, cultural movements and future intentions and possibilities. A further related purpose was to double as trade attaché, and Binchy was fortunate to have Leo McCauley as a highly competent number two to look after economic matters in particular. McCauley, from

Derry city, was a University College Dublin classics graduate and a lawyer, coming from an intellectual background not dissimilar to that of Binchy himself.

German nonchalance about small and faraway countries was expressed in the long delay Binchy experienced in waiting for an invitation to present his letter of credence as ambassador to the President of the Republic, Paul von Hindenburg. Then in his early eighties, the President was an old cavalryman, ex-Chief of Staff of the Reichswehr and also a veteran of the wars of 60 years earlier who knew nothing about Ireland other than that the island bred good military horses. Eventually the routine invitation came through, and Binchy hurried to the presidential palace, so flustered that he forgot his letter of credence and had to go back to the hotel to get it, thereby keeping the President of Germany waiting for ten minutes. In a little speech he made in German he mentioned his own experiences of German universities.

> ... The establishment of full diplomatic relations between Germany and Ireland affords deep satisfaction to the Irish Government and people. In the past there has been close association between our countries in many spheres. To mention but one of them, Ireland owes a deep debt of gratitude to a long and brilliant line of German Celtic scholars (under some of whom I myself have had the privilege of studying) whose researches have thrown much light on our ancient language and literature.
>
> In the new Irish State, German science and German industry have played a considerable part. I need only refer to the great national scheme for the electrification of the River Shannon, now nearing completion, the construction of which has been entrusted to a leading German firm.[3]

He seems by his own account to have been somewhat overawed by the old soldier at first, but the President's undoubted charm won him over very quickly, and when Binchy was taking his leave more than two years later in March 1932, the old man gave him an autographed photograph of himself with the message that it would help the young man to remember the old chap in Berlin long after he had died. This was apparently an honour of sorts only given to very highly regarded representatives and rarely to unimportant representatives coming from insignificant countries. Binchy himself thought he had been favoured because he was very much the junior among the diplomatic group. It is clear also, however, that they actually liked each other. One thing they both had in common was a love of riding; Binchy rode all his life, rather like his ultimate boss and political guardian William T. Cosgrave, President of the Irish Free State, and it seems the old cavalryman shared at least that common interest in horses. During that first meeting Hindenburg mentioned the German transatlantic flight from Ireland to the United States, an Irish Army Air Corps officer, James Fitzmaurice, being part of the crew. The German aviators had mentioned to him the remarkable friendliness of the Irish toward Germany; there seemed to be no post-war bitterness in the country. This apparently displayed a lack of awareness of Ireland's historical difficulties with Britain. However, during the same meeting Hindenburg departed from any official script and asked Binchy about the Irish horse-breeding industry. 'He said that in all his [cavalry] career as a soldier his best horses were invariably Irish bred. Of some of these horses he told stories at considerable length.' It seemed to Binchy that some of these stories were rather difficult to believe.[4]

Whatever shortcomings Hindenburg might have had as a statesman, as a human being he was attractive, Binchy thought, writing with hindsight wisdom in 1937. Hindenburg had been reviled for many alleged failings, particularly being accused of never taking responsibility for his own actions and passing that burden on to his subordinates or civilians. Here, of course, the pinning of the military defeat of October 1918 on to the unfortunate civilian politicians who had been, in effect, forced to sign the Treaty of Versailles is the unspoken prime example of such behaviour. Binchy passionately defended the old man's behaviour in 1918, arguing that he had no control over events and behaved correctly throughout. Erich Ludendorff, his principle colleague, certainly did not behave as well as the old Prussian. The new republican government of 1918 requested Hindenburg to lead his soldiers home, and he obeyed out of loyalty to his country and a Prussian sense of soldierly discipline. Binchy describes the old man's behaviour admiringly:

He carried through the bitter task without flinching. At times it must have been agony. It is true that his selfless conduct had won him the esteem of the Republican government and of thousands of convinced revolutionaries. But there were many others to whom Hindenburg and his armies were the hated symbols of a hated régime.

The soldiers, whose heroic courage even in defeat had saved Germany from invasion, were jeered at and insulted by irresponsible hooligans on their weary journey home. Officers were stoned and beaten, their epaulettes and decorations torn off, and even the Government, in a weak attempt to conciliate the extremists, decreed the removal of all emblems of rank. Hindenburg marched grimly on, giving no sign of the rage and despair with which such things must have filled his heart. When the withdrawal of the western armies had been completed with an efficiency which has won tributes from all military historians, he moved General Headquarters to Pomerania, and there awaited release from his uncongenial post.[5]

Binchy does not mention this, but by way of contrast, Ludendorff had scuttled abroad and later curried favour with the revanchist militarists, including the Nazis. He was involved, along with Hitler, in the attempted *putsch* in Munich in 1923 and received a slap on the wrist from the authorities. He repented his alliance with Hitler later. After the Armistice, Hindenburg stayed away resolutely from public life for a long time. The death of his wife in 1921 was another blow to the old man. However, on the death of President Ebert in 1925 he was apparently persuaded by that crafty old Admiral von Tirpitz to return to politics despite his unofficial motto, which was '*Ich will meine Ruhe haben!*' (Leave me in peace!). The presidential election of 1925 was filthy, even by Weimar standards. Binchy remarked privately that Weimar Germany was a country 'where defamation of one's opponents is regarded as a branch of political science.' Hindenburg himself continued to behave correctly, and had a narrow victory which gave him a seven-year term as head of state. Hindenburg was no Nazi and was in fact a royalist who would have liked a restoration of the Hohenzollern monarchy. He despised Hitler, and wished to keep the 'Bohemian corporal', as he contemptuously referred to young Adolf, out of power. He beat

Hitler handily in the presidential election of 1932, and it seemed that an alliance between the old man and Heinrich Brüning, the *Zentrum* leader and Chancellor, would stop Hitler at the last minute. Then, strangely, Brüning was suddenly dismissed by Hindenburg, for reasons that Binchy had difficulty defending later on. It seems that Von Papen, Schleicher with the army and his fellow barons put the old man up to it. Certainly the old man disliked Brüning's plans for land reform in the east of the country. It also seems that Hindenburg's inherited dislike of Catholicism and those shiftless southern Germans, possibly combined with an incipient senility, were the reasons for this strange and fatal move. By the end of January 1933 the Bohemian corporal was Chancellor of the Reich.

> Hindenburg was now very old and very tired. In the preceding months he had aged greatly. I can confirm this at first hand, for he received me in farewell audience at the time when Brüning's fate hung in the balance. Not having seen him since the beginning of the year, I was shocked at the change, physical and mental, that had occurred in the interval. The massive frame was bowed and shrunken; the alert and jovial manner had been succeeded by a weary listlessness. At long last nature was claiming her toll of that iron constitution, and in effect the days of his active participation in state affairs were drawing to a close.[6]

Curiously, this description of Binchy's in 1937 of Hindenburg in extreme old age is flatly contradicted by his own admiring and affectionate dispatch to Joseph Walshe in March 1932. In it he described the President as fully alert and clear-minded.

> In view of the statements circulated by his opponents in the Presidential election that he had aged beyond recognition in recent months, I was amazed at his bodily and mental vigour. Even his hearing is quite perfect; he did not miss a single word that I said. Indeed, despite his 84 years, he seemed to be just as vigorous as the first day I saw him.[7]

Perhaps Binchy's loyal apologia for the old man in 1937 needed the hypothesis of senility to excuse his appalling behaviour, and a confidential dispatch to Walshe written by himself five years earlier could presumably never be resurrected in public to contradict him. Very probably he had forgotten what he had written earlier. However, for a man who was, in later years, in an almost exaggerated way a stickler for the truth in scholarly matters, this lapse is distinctly odd. Ludendorff, probably far more intelligent than Hindenburg, woke up to the evil of Hitler later on, and wrote to Hindenburg: 'By appointing Hitler as Chancellor of the Reich, you have delivered our holy German fatherland into the hands of one of the greatest demagogues of all time. I solemnly prophesy to you that this unholy man will cast our nation into the abyss ... Future generations will curse you in your grave for what you have done.'[8] This was from a man who had allied himself with Hitler in 1923.

Andreas Roth questions Binchy's high opinion of Brüning, which seems to have been driven by his evident liking for Catholic democratic leaders as a species, de Valera being a conspicuous exception to this generalisation until he made peace of sorts with the new Irish prime minister in the mid-thirties.[9] According to Binchy's 1937 piece, Hindenburg's 'tragic incomprehension' of political realities drove him into the hands of a 'cabinet of barons' led by the notoriously slippery Franz von Papen, a cabinet which lasted five months and led to Hitler's appointment as Chancellor. Von Papen and his aristocratic friends felt that as highly educated and extremely arrogant grandees they would easily control the Austrian 'lunatic with a gift for rhetoric'. The catastrophe was to occur, with the unfortunate Hindenburg turned into a Nazi idol by Goebbels' propaganda machine, passive, possibly not really knowing what was going on, and already dying. Several of these grandees, including Schleicher and his wife, were to be murdered. However, von Papen, despite his treachery a survivor of everything rather like the legendary Vicar of Bray or the almost equally legendary Talleyrand, was sent off to Austria by the Hitlerites to betray some more political leaders. Hindenburg's name ended up being remembered mainly as that of a swastika-bedecked airship lifted on inflammable hydrogen gas that was burned to ashes dramatically in Lakehurst, New York a few years later in 1938. Somehow, it seemed to be a symbol of both Nazi arrogance and the invincible ignorance implicit in Nazism.

Binchy's persistent habit of finding heroes, particularly Catholic heroes, certainly coloured his perception of Brüning among others. Heinrich

Brüning was a Catholic, born in Westphalia in western Germany. In September 1932, as the German crisis reached its peak, Binchy wrote of his quiet and very determined steadfastness as Chancellor in the face of almost intolerable stresses and deep treachery. Unlike many Germans of that time, and certainly unlike Adolf Hitler, Brüning was quite the cosmopolitan. He had a deep knowledge of both France and England, having lived in Normandy, where he had family connections, for a long time and in England for two years. He had served on the western front for three years, being promoted several times and ending up as a lieutenant. After the War he became involved in the German version of Catholic Action and eventually the *Zentrum*, the Catholic party and the predecessor to both the Christian Democrat Party and the Bavarian Christian Social Party in modern Germany. Binchy saw this party as the crucial 'centre' party in German politics, steady, enduring and resisting the attacks of both left and right. This view of the essential sanity of Catholic democratic action was to remain with him throughout his life.

> Ever since the revolution [of 1918] – and now more than ever – the *Zentrum* holds the key position in Germany. Alone of the middle parties it has weathered all the storms of political radicalism, both from the left and the right; and even after the recent elections, during which it was attacked more fiercely and unscrupulously than any other party by the Hitlerites, it stands 'like Teneriffe or Atlas unmoved.' This key position carries with it the responsibility of deciding (at least under the parliamentary system) what coalition is to govern Germany.[10]

After the 1930 general election, in which the Nazis had made an electoral breakthrough, Brüning became Chancellor (appointed by Hindenburg) and ruled Germany increasingly by decree for two years, forced to do so by the constitutional situation. This was the year the Great Depression hit Germany in full force, with the collapse of the Austrian *Kreditanstalt* Bank, an institution most people had never heard of. A run on the German banks forced Brüning to give a government guarantee to certain banks, which staunched the flow. Fatally, he put his support behind plans to break up bankrupt estates in the east of the country and convert them into viable smallholdings.

Binchy thought Brüning rather resembled Kevin O'Higgins in his thoughtfulness and his ability to adopt an unpopular but logical policy and see it through to the end. He also had the ability to resist violent personal attacks on his motivations and purposes and had 'an utter indifference to popularity'. Ironically, both of his heroes were to be destroyed, O'Higgins murdered by the Irish Republican Army (IRA) and Brüning's political career ended by the Nazis.

Binchy does not seem to have foreseen Hitler's power grab even at this late date. However, perhaps this was natural. As M. Rainer Lepsius has put it, the experience of the Nazi Party in the November elections of 1932 had weakened Hitler's magic to quite an extent, and the Nazis were also running out of money. 'Had it not been for his seizure of power at the last moment, in January 1933, elections in 1933 and 1934 would most likely have seen a severe defection of NSDAP voters.'

Charismatic authority and a charismatic community rest on the belief in the extraordinary gifts of the leader. The destruction of such a movement will be unavoidable if the charisma of the leader can no longer be proved in the perception of his followers....

Charismatic authority needs a situation in which extraordinary capacities are expected: ordinary situations do not call for extraordinary means or personal gifts. It was the combination of a political and economic crisis in Germany in the years 1929–33 that created an atmosphere conductive to belief in extraordinary gifts. Hitler's chances consisted in his capacity to define the situations as doomed and his leadership as the last chance for salvation. These chances would have been limited by improvement in the economic situation, which was expected in 1933, and by governmental stability as provided by the Brüning government on the basis of emergency decrees. However, developments in 1932 reduced politics to a single issue: chaos or regeneration of Germany. This allowed Hitler to gain support from very divergent segments of the population with heterogeneous interests and aspirations on the level of ultimate values. The eschatological character of Nazism had a peculiar pseudo-religious fascination, extremely favourable for the belief in charismatic authority.[11]

As it happened, the Nazis avoided their probable electoral fading by stealing the election of March 1933; by disenfranchising the Communists, locking their leaders up and threatening everyone else. Hitler's henchmen had taken control of the Prussian police. Contrary to the prevailing myth, Hitler was not elected democratically. However, he certainly was popular, and possessed a winning combination of charisma, cunning and ruthlessness. Essentially he was a streetfighter rather than a statesman. Having gained power, he proceeded to purge the universities of anyone who was Jewish, even by remote descent. This was merely the first phase of his systemic wrecking of Germany, and few grasped the thoroughness of his hate-fuelled vision. According to Heisenberg, Max Planck argued with him in 1933 in support of those academics who stayed behind in the country and did not join the general exodus:

> You have come to get my advice on political questions, but I am afraid I can no longer advise you. I see no hope of stopping the catastrophe that is about to engulf all our universities, indeed our whole country. ... I would like to apprise you of my conversation with Hitler a few days ago. I had hoped to convince him that he was doing enormous damage to the German universities, and particularly to physical research, by expelling our Jewish colleagues; to show him how senseless and utterly immoral it was to victimise men who have always thought of themselves as Germans, and who had offered up their lives for Germany like everyone else. But I failed to make myself understood – or worse, there is no language in which one can talk to such a man. He has lost all contact with reality. What others say to him is at best an annoying interruption, which he immediately drowns by incessant repetitions of the same old phrases about the decay of healthy intellectual life during the last fourteen years, about the need to stop the rot even at this late hour, and so on. All the time one has the fatal impression that he believes all the nonsense he pours forth, and that he indulges his own delusions by ignoring all outside influences. He is so possessed by his so-called ideas that he is no longer open to argument. A man like that can only lead Germany into disaster.[12]

Planck saw the universities as helpless, and his own role as simply hanging on in the university system until the catastrophe was over, so that after Hitler Germany could rebuild from the ruins left by the Nazis. Presumably even he could not imagine how colossal the disaster was going to be.

Learning the Job

Back in 1929, all this was in the unknown future. Binchy was doing a good job, writing able and perceptive reports on German political life and on public opinion in the country. He was also going around the country drumming up trade contacts of a kind Ireland so clearly needed. At that time Irish foreign trade was non-existent, nearly all of her external trade being with the United Kingdom. The extraordinarily successful Industrial Development Authority and Córas Tráchtála (Irish Foreign Trade Board) did not come about until some years after the Second World War, mainly as a project of John A. Costello's Fine Gael party in 1948–51. The Irish Government was naturally very concerned about Ireland's historical economic entrapment in the British Isles and enjoined its envoys to concern themselves with gaining most favoured nation trade status with the United States, Canada, France and Italy as well as, of course, Germany. Binchy was being very much ahead of his time without realising it, and was seen to be doing a sterling job by his Minister of External Affairs in Dublin, Patrick McGilligan and by William T. Cosgrave. A theme of his reports, his later ones in particular, was the growing menace of Hitler and his own personal hatred of the man.

Binchy sometimes wrote personal letters to Walshe, addressing him as 'my dear Joe', apparently reflecting a personal friendship of long standing, perhaps going back to Clongowes days. In January 1930, he wrote to Walshe denying any intention of resigning from his job in Berlin.

> I was … very surprised to hear from Leo [McCauley] that [Timothy] Cleary had given some of you [in External Affairs in Dublin] the impression that I was contemplating resignation. I cannot see where he got such an extraordinary and unfounded impression. I did not exchange a single word with him except in Leo's presence and both

of us are perfectly clear that resignation was never mentioned. I once alluded to the possible difficulty of getting my pictures through the customs when returning to Ireland and this can be the only conceivable source from what his imagination has drawn.[13]

However, Cleary's guess turned out eventually to have been a shrewd one, as Binchy's sense of being personally unsuited for the duties of a diplomat became evident a few months later in April 1930 in a private letter to Michael Tierney cited below.

Walshe wrote an official letter from Dublin in late February 1930, congratulating his protégé on his work and his extraordinarily rapid adjustment to a very different work environment. He also thanked Binchy on standing in for the Minister at the League of Nations and for his promulgation of cultural nationalism Irish style on German soil.

> The Minister is exceedingly gratified with the success of your Irish publicity campaign in Berlin during the last three months. Your article in the *Berliner Tagesblatt* on the Language revival so impressed him that he wants to have it reproduced in the United States, France and Italy …The Minister was pleased with the way in which you attacked the idea that we are a sort of bastard English nation with no distinctive ancestry or civilisation of our own. Unfortunately, outside the learned few, Germany seems to be just as ignorant as France on all Irish affairs, except the purely political. The general attitude of the Press since your arrival is most hopeful.[14]

Binchy wrote a lot of personal letters home, and evidently missed his native acres, which included Dublin, despite his Cork origins. Furthermore, the political situation in Germany disturbed him increasingly during the next two years. However, the bottom line for Binchy was that he was, as he said himself, 'temperamentally a complete misfit for my job'. He hated the round of compulsory social engagements, the huge dinners, the formalities, the false friendliness and the need to dress for dinner in the evenings. He tried to dodge these obligations whenever he felt he could get away with it. Above all, he missed the scholarly life: '… my heart is all the time wrung thinking of the number of [Charles] Plummer's slips I could have verified and checked, during those wasted hours.'[15] He and McCauley had to put up with some hostility from some of the British diplomats, which he seems to have been rather amused by as much as anything else. He took to one of them, Harold Nicholson, immediately, as Nicholson was careless in dress and actually interested in literature, unlike the bulk of his colleagues. Nicholson had some Irish connections ('Shanganagh Castle') the strength of which he probably exaggerated, and Binchy tended to discount them. He saw Nicholson as shrewd, charming and dangerous. Binchy studied his *modus operandi* very carefully. Nicholson affected a complete openness in conversation and told Binchy during Sunday walks in the Tiergarten details of apparently confidential matters. However, he told him nothing Binchy could not have found out easily for himself, as Binchy himself spotted immediately. Unfortunately, the Englishman left soon after, having resigned from the British diplomatic service to go into politics with Mosley's New Party in Britain, dropping out of it pretty promptly when Mosley turned fascist. He later attached himself to Anthony Eden and Winston Churchill in an anti-Hitler caucus in parliament. Binchy had had only a few weeks at most to study him, apparently to some profit.[16] There is something odd about this; Nicholson resigned from the British Foreign Service in September 1929. Binchy took up his own post in October; possibly Nicholson had to work out his notice.

By way of contrast, the American delegation was very well disposed toward the Irish, and Binchy could draw on personal connections with some of the Americans who had studied earlier in Germany and had had some of the same teachers as himself.

In late July 1931, Binchy could see that political instability in Germany was getting worse. Brüning could only govern by using what he called 'dictatorial methods' in a chronically split parliamentary assembly, using a notorious flaw in the Weimar constitution which handed large emergency powers to the President. Brüning's alliance of 'red and black' (*Zentrum* plus the Social Democrats) was precarious, involving clericals trying to get on with anti-clericals.

> It remains to be seen whether he can still command their toleration
> by holding the threat of a general election over their heads, at which
> they must lose heavily to the Communists, and which would result in

a very formidable increase of the parties of disorder, both Right and Left.[17]

Binchy amid the Alien Corn

It is rumoured in Irish academia that Binchy actually spent a fair amount of his time in the Berlin years in Bonn, talking with his old mentor Rudolf Thurneysen and drinking white wine in the shadow of the Drachenfels, while letting the secretary mind the office in Berlin.[18] In May 1930, Binchy wrote plaintively to Richard Best, apologising profusely for not answering his letters from Ireland and complaining that the only Celticist he could talk to regularly was Professor Julius Pokorny, a Viennese scholar who had succeeded Kuno Meyer to the Chair of Celtic in the University of Berlin in 1920. Meyer, a moving force for a long time in the micropolitics of Irish Celtic academia, with a prowess for translating Old Irish poetry *into English*, neither of these languages being his native tongue, had died suddenly in 1919, a serious loss to the Gaelic revival movement. Pokorny had participated in the School of Irish Learning in 1908 and 1910, and knew the Dublin Gaelic league scene very well. It was there that he got the nickname '*Póigín*' (little kiss) because of his amorous approaches to young women. Pokorny had distinctly anti-English political attitudes, apparently derived from pro-Boer sentiment in his native Austria during his youth. It seems that it was from this early antagonism that he developed his political sympathy with Irish nationalism. 'He supported modern Irish and was thus firmly on the side of those who pursued the study of Celtic as a living language rather than an antiquarian subject.'[19] Binchy wrote from Berlin to Bergin in Dublin:

> I tremble to think of the way in which I have treated your last letter, which for every reason merited an immediate reply. I feel I deserve no pity and that you would be perfectly justified in never writing me a line again. Yet I have full confidence in your kindest of hearts: you will, I know, treat my disgraceful silence with magnanimity. After all, a letter from me cannot mean a thousandth part of what a letter from you does to me: your spiritual home is not Berlin and you are little interested in the struttings and frettings of diplomatic marionettes,

whereas my roots are in Dublin and all my real interests in Celtic Studies. So bear this in mind, and please write again in spite of my *cinla anfoit*! … [Julius] Pokorny (again *entre nous*) I find somewhat of a trial. He is kind and helpful but his conversation is inclined to converge unfailingly on a single topic! No use trying to get him off it with verbal forms. He is interested merely in Indo-European, and pre-Indo-European: I dare say he will yet give us a grammar of *Die Ursprache*! As for Old Irish, despite his wonderful theories, his practical knowledge I regard as surprisingly slight …Now I must hasten to dine with His Excellency the Bolshevik Ambassador – to eat the bread of sacrilege in fact! Be sure you don't tell the *Catholic Bulletin*![20]

Some other people thought equally little of Pokorny's mind or his scholarship. The Dutch Celticist, Anton van Hamel, was one of these, feeling that Rudolf Thurneysen, the father-figure of European Celticists, should have got the Meyer Chair in Berlin in 1920. The young Myles Dillon, writing from Germany in early 1923, held the same opinion. Carl Marstrander felt that Pokorny was not to be taken seriously.[21]

Best had taken Pokorny under his wing in the 1900s, but Bergin disliked him. But then Bergin disliked a lot of people, sometimes quite unfairly. Back in 1909, when Irish academic Celticism was getting off the ground, van Hamel commented about Pokorny 'If the fellow has no methodical instinct in him he badly wants someone to impart it to him; for without it he will stay an amateur all his life and never bring out anything of real importance.' In his pretty exhaustive biography of Pokorny, Pól Ó Dochartaigh points out correctly that Van Hamel had sniped at Pokorny for a generation; there was some personal feud going on, perhaps.[22] Alternatively, simple anti-semitism might have been at work. Perhaps the low opinion of his abilities was deserved. At any rate, in the tiny academic world of Celtic Studies there seems to have been a chronic propensity for perennial enmities as well as lifelong friendships.

A year later, in early 1931, Best finally agreed to go to Berlin to see his old friend and younger colleague. Binchy wrote 'Pokorny is overjoyed at the idea of seeing you, and is staying on in Berlin during the holidays.'

Do not think it is necessary to bring too much luggage. I have set my face against the custom of changing for dinner here (probably to the scandal of the servants!), except when there are a number of people invited, so there is no need to burden yourselves with too many dress shirts etc.[23]

Pokorny, who had been introduced to the study of Irish by Best in Dublin nearly thirty years previously and had been, to some extent, Best's protégé, expressed delight at the prospect of seeing his old friend. Rudolf Thurneysen, now a very old man, was to travel from Bonn to meet the Irish people. Binchy really wanted, in particular, to see Bergin, who was notoriously reluctant to travel anywhere. One way or another, Binchy joked, he had managed to put together a tiny Department of Celtic Studies in the capital of the Reich.

Any chance of your being able to bring dear Bergin along with you? There is ample room for him and I should love if he came. We could almost have an informal Celtic Congress!

I hope you continue very well. I fear I have done nothing much at the [Brehon] Laws since I returned. But I go to Pokorny's *Seminar* every Thursday; we are reading all the versions of the expulsion of the Dési, having commenced with the LU [*Leabhar na hUidhre*].[24]

According to Binchy, Pokorny had some very odd ideas, among them the notion that the Irish, or some of them at least, were descended from Eskimos. Like Binchy he was a confirmed bachelor. He was later to be dismissed by the Nazis from the Chair in 1933; there is a story that he had tried quite bravely to defend a Jewish colleague, Ernst Lewy, and demanded his release from prison in 1935. This is asserted by 'C. R. C.' (Conn O Cléirigh) in an obituary of Pokorny in *Studia Celtica* in 1971, after his death at the age of 84, and suggests that this stand may have brought him to the attention of the racists and the Gestapo.[25] However, O Dochartaigh, in his study, a work which is generally sympathetic to Pokorny, reports that he could find no evidence for the story.

The official Nazi genealogists ascertained that he had Jewish grandparents, a circumstance Pokorny insisted he had been unaware of. He was restored to his Chair subsequently, and believed that an informal intervention of the Irish government at de Valera's suggestion had brought about this happy event. Pokorny was fired again finally under the Nuremberg Laws in 1935, however, and was convinced that Charles Bewley, Binchy's pro-Nazi successor as Irish Minister, had undermined him.[26] This intuition was probably correct, as Bewley had a pathological hatred of Jews. In July 1932 in his position as Irish Minister to Germany, he recommended that the Irish government do nothing to help Pokorny as to do so 'might do us harm'. The unfortunate professor wrote to Eoin MacNeill in November 1935 concerning his loss of not only his job, but also his German citizenship. Could MacNeill do anything? 'I am a true Catholic, have always been one and also my parents before me. My grandparents, no less, are the unfortunate culprits.'[27] He seems not to have been aware that his life was actually in danger. There was a fair amount of sympathy for him in Ireland. Seán A' Chóta in western Kerry had befriended Pokorny as a young man and taught him Irish; he remarked fondly about the Austrian that he had 'never wanted for courage'.[28] Pokorny certainly needed bravery; he survived for eight more years in the Third Reich for reasons which are somewhat mysterious, and it is possible that the Irish succeeded in shielding him once Bewley had liquidated himself in spectacular fashion as far as his diplomatic career was concerned in 1939. Eventually Pokorny had to flee the Gestapo in July 1943 and achieved asylum in Switzerland; by that time the Germans had lost the battle of Kursk and it was evident that the war was probably lost; the Russians had broken the back of the Wehrmacht in the greatest tank battle that has ever been fought. Therefore, Hitler's pre-war promise to avenge himself on the Jews of Europe by murdering them all was to be fulfilled. It further appears that under Bewley's Ministry, an Irish visa had not been forthcoming.

Bewley's successor, William Warnock, issued Pokorny with one immediately when he took over the mission in 1939, but Pokorny refused to leave Germany until 27 July 1943. De Valera personally approved yet another new visa in 1943 on the initiative, apparently, of Warnock. It is also possible that Pokorny had someone powerful in the German regime shielding him, someone who was well enough connected also to be able to know when to warn him finally to flee the country. This is a pure guess. Evidently Warnock did not know afterwards that the visa had worked; somehow Pokorny managed to dodge the German border guards and slipped into Switzerland, the Swiss evidently accepting the Irish visa. He even managed to take his library along as well, however he managed it. Warnock telegraphed Frederick H. Boland in the Department of Foreign Affairs in Dublin in September: 'Visa did not help. Police are averse to letting anybody out of Germany; they are afraid that information might leak out.'[29] Apparently irrepressible, Pokorny survived the war, giving lectures in Switzerland in several universities, visited Ireland after the war and was eventually reinstated in his university, with some compensation, by the Federal German Government.[30] He was to live to be of a very ripe old age, yet another long-lived Celticist and a very lucky man. He was killed in a traffic accident at the age of 84.

Departure

At the beginning of 1932, Binchy was clearly resolved to resign and return to Ireland by April. He seems to have expected a Cumann na nGaedheal victory in the Irish election scheduled for February. However, he wrote to Best:

> If the government are defeated I shall of course resign at once: it will be a grim pleasure writing to the Republican [Fianna Fáil] Foreign Minister requesting him to advise His Majesty to issue his Letter of Recall! On the other hand, if the Government are victorious, I shall have to consult their convenience as regards the date of my resignation, as they really have treated me with every consideration … I can't tell you how pleased I am to be returning to anonymity.[31]

The political situation in Germany deteriorated steadily during Binchy's sojourn. The elections of August 1930 produced eleven major parties represented in the Reichstag, many of which refused point-blank to engage in power-sharing. Even the 'Middle Parties' suffered from a no-compromise syndrome. 'It is little wonder that the average German citizen is disgusted with parliamentary institutions, and that many are driven to listen to the crazy counsels of Hitler and his followers, who are clamouring for a dictator.' Binchy felt that the proportional representation electoral rules were mainly responsible for this situation. The Germans were apparently intrigued that, despite having PR, the Irish had managed to have a two-party system.[32] No one seemed to realise that there was a crucial difference between the two political systems: the Irish had a *candidate* system rather than a party-list system and, therefore, the Irish rules were quite different from those in Germany. Ireland and Malta, who use similar PR-STV candidate systems, have always had stable two-bloc party systems. In other words, in Germany you voted a party ticket and had no choice of candidate, whereas in Ireland you were routinely encouraged to split the ticket in favour of individual candidates; at that time party labels were not even on the ballot paper. To put it slightly differently, these two post-British countries have always had Anglo-American proportional representation laws and not continental list systems.

A year later Binchy was again to display his skills as a constitutional lawyer and political scientist in an essay submitted to the Irish authorities on the German constitutional order. The bald fact that Germany was described as a federal state hid the truth that Prussia was overwhelmingly dominant in that federation. It could nearly be said that Germany without Austria was Prussia plus a few satellites, a little like England's predominant relationship with Scotland, Wales and Ireland in the old United Kingdom or Russia in the Soviet Union, though Binchy did not make either of these comparisons. 'Accordingly, no matter what the political complexion of the Reich Government may be, the Prussian Government remains the deciding factor in most important matters of internal politics.' There was, in fact, a catch-phrase, *Wer Preussen hat, hat das Reich* (he who has Prussia, has the country). At the moment the Socialists and the *Zentrum* shared the governance of Prussia. This 'black and red coalition' created by Brüning was vital to the stability of the entire Reich, Binchy argued. In particular, he argued, it had policed the state very competently and had sided neither with the Nazis nor the Communists in their street brawls.[33]

In one of his last dispatches from Berlin at the end of January 1932, Binchy praised the aging Hindenburg for his steadfastness and courage in the face of seven dreadful years of turmoil. Writing to Best at about the same time he wrote 'I can't tell you how pleased I am to be returning to anonymity … I have seen things out of cheap fiction.'[34] There was little sense of catastrophe, which might surprise a modern reader, naturally possessing so much apocalyptic hindsight wisdom. However, Binchy was quite clear that Hitler was completely hypocritical, pretending concern for democratic and legal principles when quite obviously he was looking for a personal dictatorship.[35] On 1 March he predicted, correctly, that Hindenburg would defeat Hitler for the Presidency by several million votes. He conceded that Hitler could win, but thought it was unlikely. He commented on the rudeness and 'utter incompetence' of the Nazis. He noted ironically that Hitler, being born in Austria, had no German citizenship, and that this technically disqualified him from high office. However, the Nazis got the German state of Brunswick to appoint the Bohemian Corporal attaché to its legation to the Reich Government. 'Accordingly since the day before yesterday, when he swore allegiance to the Constitution which he is forever denouncing, he is *Herr Regierungsrat Hitler*' as the appointment gave him German citizenship automatically.[36] In the same dispatch he described the Reichstag as a bear garden.

> The present Government, as you know, has only the most slender and unstable majority in the House. Indeed except for the 'toleration' of the Social democrats, it would be in a hopeless minority. As a result the Reichstag is almost on permanent holidays; its law-making functions are exercised dictatorially by the Government by means of the Emergency Decrees … It is only summoned in cases of dire necessity and then only for a very short time. It must be admitted that the behaviour of a large section of the House during the recent session makes most Germans feel that the more rarely it is convened the better for German prestige. The National Socialists and the Communists engaged in veritable competitions of rowdiness. During the Chancellor's great speech the Nazis maintained a continual howl of interruptions.[37]

Later that month Binchy resigned from the Department of External Affairs and returned to Dublin. It is hard not to suspect that the concrete situation in Germany provided something of a push factor in encouraging

Binchy's decision, although undoubtedly the 'pull' factor of Dublin, his studies and his friends was very powerful. As noted earlier, in one of his last letters to Walshe, he portrayed Hindenburg's farewell meeting with the departing Irish Minister in very different terms than in his 1937 article about the old man. He described Hindenburg as 'chaffing' him humorously about leaving Berlin unmarried, despite Hindenburg's joke about having ordered the officials to find the young Irishman a wife. He also presents a Hindenburg as a hale if hoary oldster, as we have seen. After all, the old man died a year later, of old age and, one suspects, in despair of his country. Incidentally, Binchy seems to have found a girlfriend in Berlin, one who was unwilling to leave Germany and go with him to a remote Atlantic island.[38]

Around that time, far away in Ireland, Bergin demonstrated a shrewd perception of Germany on the eve of Hitler's coming to power. Frank O'Connor remembered:

> Once in explaining to me his dislike of the Germans, he and a French student named Etienne went to register as aliens. 'Osborn Bergin' sounded a good Teutonic name, so he had no trouble, but when it came to the French boy's turn the policeman said flatly, '*Etienne, das ist kein Name.*' According to Bergin, this had given him a hatred of Germans that had lasted throughout his life. When I protested he said gloomily, 'there are only two tones in the German voice, the whine and the bellow. They're whining now; the bellow will come later.' (This was before Hitler.) I, having no culture at all except what I had picked up from German, protested again, but he crushed me brutally. 'Binchy' (then our ambassador in Germany) 'says the Germans are a people you keep trying to like.' That settled that, too. God alone knows what Binchy did say, but this is what Bergin felt he should have said, and it was said on his behalf.[39]

Leo McCauley took over from Binchy in Berlin and reported quite brilliantly on the frightening rise of Hitler, already obvious to both himself and Binchy before the latter's resignation. Hitler's defeat in the presidential race had not finished him as a political leader, and his shadow grew darker and larger in the ensuing months. At first, McCauley hoped, like many another, that Hitler would restore stability to Weimar, but gradually, and very early on, he realised that Hitler was a true revolutionary, a mass murderer and a danger to Germany and Europe. In a dispatch to Dublin in early 1933, he described quite astutely Hitler's extraordinary manipulative powers. Hitler, he wrote, was 'a mystical and mysterious figure: no one knows what his principles and true policy really are, and one can only speculate as to his statesmanship.'

> … when Hitler has put his house in order in Germany he will turn his own amazing energy and the enthusiasm of his followers to foreign affairs. It is said that the military attachés in the various embassies are already calculating the period in which Germany will be able to take the field against Poland.[40]

Another Irish observer, a young man named Owen Sheehy-Skeffington, would have agreed with McCauley, but was even more clear-eyed about the future of Germany. In Berlin for a short visit from his study-leave year in Paris, he wrote to his mother in Dublin in July 1933, predicting war in four or five years, and that Germany would 'be beaten again'. 'They don't seem to have any feeling for peace. Victory is what they want. The latest [claim] is that they really won the war, I told Froman that I had a lot of sympathy for Germany before I went there.' The swaggering storm-troopers bullying people in the street, the anti-Jewish ranting and the general atmosphere disgusted him.[41] Skeffington was to become a noted public figure in Ireland during the post-war period. During the same year, under the new Fianna Fáil government in Dublin, McCauley the prophet was without honour in his own land, being transferred to the Vatican when Charles Bewley, that admirer of the Nazis, became Irish Minister to Germany. Bewley commented acidly that the Vatican rated far higher in Walshe's estimation than did Berlin.[42] O'Driscoll comments, 'The first two Irish Ministers to Germany found themselves on opposite sides of the conflict [in Germany] while de Valera tried to maintain "the middle way" symbolising the dilemmas which many Irish citizens had.'[43] It should be remembered that the Fianna Fáil party had a strong pro-German wing of a kind that was traditional among Irish republican nationalists, going back to a 'my enemy's enemy is my friend' psychology which had existed in the country for several centuries, attaching itself successively to a series of anti-British great powers historically, starting with Spain in the sixteenth century, as documented by Binchy in his early book.

De Valera, as he was wont to do repeatedly, had caught a Tartar in Charles Bewley, who was to be a major embarrassment for the new Irish Government during his six-year tenure. Rather like Henderson, his British opposite number, Bewley tended to go native and became ever more noisily pro-Nazi and openly anti-semitic particularly from 1936 on. Joseph Walshe, together with others in External Affairs, were rather lukewarm at best in their support for democracy, as we have seen, and Bewley did not at first seem to them to have opinions or behaviour that were too outlandish. Walshe spent time at a health spa in Cologne in mid-1933 and was very impressed by the Hitler government's reforms and modernisation projects. He was quite enthused about Nazi arguments about the ineffectiveness of democracy and felt the Irish had a lot to learn from the Hitler regime. Most strange of all, Bewley the out-and-out Nazi fan said in February 1935 that he believed firmly that Germany would be incapable of waging war for 'generations' at least.[44] Here he went against the predictions of a host of observers, many of them Irish. A month later, almost as though Hitler wished to refute Bewley's silly prediction, the Reich reintroduced conscription and founded the Luftwaffe openly, thereby clearly violating the provisions of the Treaty of Versailles. At the last moment, in August 1939, Bewley was recalled to Dublin. Eventually de Valera fired Bewley, as Bewley had already announced his own resignation because of being offered a job as Principal Officer in the Department of External Affairs in Dublin; to Bewley this seemed an insulting demotion, which it possibly was intended to be.[45] However, by the standards of the time and place, such an appointment was not unattractive. Bewley flounced off to Berlin and his beloved Nazis and later proceeded to Rome. Later he wrote a self-serving memoir, which refrained from mentioning Binchy by name. '... missing from Bewley's recollections is any reference to Daniel A. Binchy, his predecessor at the Irish legation in Berlin. Binchy of course was a brilliant Celtic scholar, a shrewd analyst of Fascism, and an admirer of many aspects of British policy – three adequate grounds upon which Bewley could exclude him.' Bewley's levels of accuracy are exemplified by the following unpleasant assessment of Binchy whom he evidently did not know well if at all: 'I applied for the post of Minister to Germany; the former Minister, moved by an equal dislike of Hitler and de Valera, had sent in his resignation after the accession to power of the Hosts of Destiny (i. e. Fianna Fáil).' There was no competition for the post.[46] Ironically Binchy and de Valera were to develop a cordial relationship later in the decade, the Irish language again operating as a solvent between people who had been bitter enemies over the issue of the Treaty. But that's another story. Many years later an anonymous obituary tackled the subject of the German episode by stating of Binchy:

> His innate courtesy and cant-stripping wryness – a combination of Charleville sharpness and Kilmallock insouciance – brought a breath of fresh air to turgid liturgies in Berlin. He was a brilliant diplomat because he was a brilliant endearing man. He touched nothing he did not adorn.[47]

Kennedy gives a more detached view. In his 1999 article he 'sets out to look at the three diplomats who served Ireland in Berlin from 1929 to 1939 and how they fitted into the role of information gatherer, a style defined for them as a diplomatic standard by their chief, Joseph Walshe'. Binchy he characterises as a 'conscientious and highly professional diplomat'. This was so despite his being, so to speak, 'thrown in the deep end'. The quality of his reports, his connections with the Berlin diplomatic corps and his relations with the German Foreign Office show an extraordinary maturity in a complete neophyte at the job. Roth claims that he exaggerated his influence in senior German government circles and amongst foreign envoys in Berlin from other countries. However, starting from scratch as he did as a complete tyro, he was unusually successful. McCauley, Kennedy says, was, in his own way, as good as Binchy, and certainly saw through the Nazis even more perceptively than Binchy, but during his year in office Hitler was showing his hand more openly and the monstrousness of Nazism was becoming blatantly obvious. Bewley started out quite well, giving informative, if sympathetic, reports up to 1936 but was eventually completely seduced by the Nazis.[48]

Binchy, then, was a brilliant, if amateur, and stable diplomat who regarded himself as unsuited to the job. Bewley, a snobbish and rather conceited man, thought himself to be some kind of a genius and was actually totally unsuited to the job. An acquaintance described him as 'peevish, clever, self-important, snobbish and not really very nice.'[49] The real question is why he was put there in the first place, and when he mutated into a fan of the Nazis after a few years, why on earth was he left in such a sensitive and even dangerous position, capable of damaging Ireland's international reputation so much and thus undoing Binchy's and McCauley's good work. Andreas Roth suggests that de Valera realised that to replace Bewley would require the permission of the King and therefore decided to leave him in Berlin. That suggests in turn that Dev was still hung up on the monarchy issue and also somewhat innocent about foreign affairs, particularly with regard to Nazism and how dangerous it was.[50] My own surmise is that he valued loyalty to the anti-Treaty position and to himself more than anything else, and in 1932 had not really found his feet. He was only beginning to realise that 'Free Staters' were generally just as patriotic Irish separatists as he was himself; he remarked as much privately to his son Vivion a few years later. He had been partly deceived by his own propaganda which had demonised the pro-Treatyites back in 1922–23. Joseph Walshe also probably favoured a representative who would be sympathetic to the new German government. After the February election of 1932, de Valera was so immersed in domestic affairs and in particular, in winning elections, that Germany came to seem very far away, hidden as it was by Britain and the sea, as indeed it was in those days before air travel on any serious scale. At that time, international travel was mainly done by surface transport; when Neville Chamberlain flew to Germany during the Munich crisis of 1938, it was the first occasion he had ever been on an aeroplane. It was eventually to dawn on de Valera that Hitler's Germany was the real danger and a much greater enemy than Britain could ever be. This realisation was to materialise as a tacit but unspoken British–Irish alliance during the Second World War, an alliance which could never be openly acknowledged, and has never been admitted to officially.

A long-term consequence of the Binchy 'interlude' in Germany was his own politicisation during the thirties. He evolved from being an Irish constitutional nationalist and convinced Catholic towards being an organised and highly articulate anti-racist combined with a convinced public commitment to democratic forms of government. He also became passionately anti-German and anti-Nazi, and wrote about the stupidity and evil of racialist thought in Irish journals, most conspicuously in *Studies*. He despised anti-semitism. The intellectual incoherence of Hitler's Jew-hatred made the Nazis an easy target for the analytical powers of someone like Binchy. His was something of an unorthodox position at the time, when newspapers such as the *Daily Mail* in England were openly pro-Nazi and in Ireland only a small and fractious left was automatically anti-fascist. As Bryan Fanning puts it perceptively, after Binchy's Hitler article and other articles about German politics expressing contempt for Nazism:

> A number of subsequent articles on Nazi Germany published in *Studies* took their tone and analysis from Binchy. One in 1938 by the reverend Denis O'Keefe, then Professor of Ethics and Politics at UCD, rubbished Nazi racial theories and argued that their real importance were as psychological tools of nation-building. 'It is a natural tendency for nations to seek an escape from the inadequacies of the present in a mythical past. This is a common experience in all countries. But it requires a portentous absence of humour to accept the theory in the form given to it in Nazi literature – in this form it is altogether pathological. A certain minimum of self-esteem is, no doubt, as necessary for the nation as for the individual. And unsuccessful peoples, in moments of stress, may have difficulty in reaching it. This is the purpose of mass-propaganda. It aims at restoring self-respect to a defeated people. In moderation racial feeling may be at the worst an amiable weakness, at best a proper pride. The Greek, with much justice, thought himself superior to the barbarian. And, in a negative way we have all heard, nearer home, of 'lesser breeds without the law' and of 'the wild hysterics of the Celt'.[51]

In some ways Binchy took the lead, along with Sean O'Faolain and a few others, in the demolition of racist thought in Ireland. They were helped by the fact that the Catholic Church, despite its many shortcomings, had always stuck to a traditional and well-founded insistence on the ineradicable unity of the human species and distanced itself from Old

Testament hints that the human race might have been created in unequal races by a wise Deity in the form of the descendants of Ham, Shem and Japhet. Catholicism, unlike some strains of Protestantism, regards the New Testament as an amendment or revision of the Old Testament, and where the two contradict each other the New Testament is to prevail. In 1938, all this public argument sparked off a symposium on Irish nationalism in *Studies*.[52] Participants included Michael Tierney, the well-known UCD classical scholar, who argued for a noble lie: a partially fake but therapeutic historicist nationalism and Gaelic revivalism. On the other hand, O'Faolain, fresh from his impassioned defence of the political legacy of Daniel O'Connell in *King of the Beggars*, essentially argued against Gaelic revivalism and for a secularised and English-speaking liberal democracy. What they were really attacking was not Adolf Hitler, but Daniel Corkery, author of several primary texts in neo-Gaelic nationalism, *The Hidden Ireland* and *Synge and Anglo-Irish Literature*. Corkery was, of course, a professor of literature in University College Cork and the old patron and teacher of that terrible twosome, Sean O'Faolain and Frank O'Connor. Binchy contributed to the symposium, pointing out that the Irish people had been loyal to the Gaelic lords to the end, thought much like them themselves, and gently questioned O'Faolain's impassioned rejection of the Gaelic past; after all, it was obvious that his fellow Corkman and good friend was completely fascinated by the very history that he railed against in his book about O'Connell.

However, the German dictator, and the perceptive take on him of an Irish academic turned diplomat, was the figure whose malign existence had started a domestic intellectual ball rolling in faraway Ireland. Certainly, it probably strengthened the hand of those in the Fianna Fáil governing party who were increasingly uneasy about the pro-German sentiment of a considerable proportion of their own activists across the country, a sentiment vividly articulated by Tipperary rebel Dan Breen. A few years later, during the Second World War, this old gunman was rebuked by an old comrade, Bob Briscoe, for attending parties at the German and Italian embassies in Dublin. Briscoe, being Jewish and having German connections, was well aware of the evils of Nazism and was personally naturally pro-Ally, even though he had been running guns into Ireland for the IRA in 1920, incidentally running them from Hamburg in between having rows with a young Charles Bewley. Breen retorted to Briscoe with an ancient fierceness:

> I hold the old Irish view and that one is very plain and simple and it has not changed – 'you can't serve Ireland well without a hatred of England.' That is old, but it is as true today as when it was first spoken …The Germans and the Italians are not the people that murdered and robbed my people for 700 years. It took your good English friends to do that and they continue to do it.[53]

Breen, a completely uneducated man with an ancestral hatred of British power, obsessed by the admittedly grim past of his own little country, seemed to be utterly unaware of the hideous world war that was tearing civilisation apart across the entire planet. All his life he had a picture of Hitler on the wall in his home, and wept bitterly when he heard of the Führer's death in 1945.[54]

Joseph Lee has commented on the 'intellectual inertia of the surrounding society' in the Ireland of the thirties. He has suggested that, for Irish republicans of that time, whether of the Fianna Fáil variety or the die-hard variety, intellectual 'solipsism' was the only diagnosis.[55] This was the kind of mentality de Valera had to deal with and, in many ways, he was personally trapped by it. It is a mentality that is nowadays rapidly being forgotten, but at that time it was an important residue of the political revolution that had occurred in Ireland. Binchy was also going to have to do his bit to combat it or simply endure its consequences. Even in his own area, politicised thinking about language and history distorted intellectual life and popularised a highly romantic fantasy vision of Celtic Ireland. Later in his academic career he and his students were to argue passionately against nationalist romanticisation of a medieval Ireland which was innately foreign to modern minds and in many ways grim, cruel, politically underdeveloped and profoundly undemocratic. Curiously, this view was to be very much at odds with that of his beloved mentor and teacher, Eoin MacNeill. However, first Binchy was going to tackle another political phenomenon of pre-war Europe: Italian fascism.

Notes

1   Fanning, Kennedy et al., *Documents in Irish Foreign Policy*, Vol. III, 1926–32, pp.521–22, 4 April 1930, reprinted from UCD AD LA30/448 to Michael Tierney.

2   *Documents in Irish Foreign Policy*, Volume III. 1926–32, 27 May 1930, p.546.

3   *Documents on Irish Foreign Policy*, Volume III, 1926–1932, 27 October 1929, p.456.

4   Ibid., p.457, Letter to Joseph Walshe, 29 October 1929.

5   Daniel A. Binchy, 'Paul von Hindenburg', *Studies*, XXVI, June 1937, pp.223–42, quote from p.229.

6   Ibid., p.240. On the firing of Brüning, see Robert Gerwarth, *Hitler's Hangman: The Life of Heydrich*, New Haven and London: Yale University Press, p.60.

7   *Documents in Irish Foreign Policy,*Volume IV, 1932–1936, pp.15–16.

8   Jean Medawar and David Pyke, *Hitler's Gift*, London: Piatkus, 2001, pp.22–23.

9   Andreas Roth, *Mr. Bewley in Berlin*, Dublin: Four Courts Press, 2000, pp.21–22.

10 Daniel A. Binchy, 'Heinrich Brüning', *Studies*, XX, September 1932, pp.385–403, quote at p.389.

11 M. Rainer Lepsius, 'From Fragmented Party Democracy to Government by Emergency Degree and National Socialist Takeover: Germany', in Juan J. Linz and Alfred Stepan (eds.), *The Breakdown of Democratic Regimes: Europe*, Baltimore and London: John Hopkins, 1978, pp.34–79, quote at p.69.

12 See Medawar and Pyke, *Hitler's Gift*, p.165.

13 *Documents on Irish Foreign Policy*, Volume III, 1926–32, pp.489–90, 15 January 1930.

14 *Documents on Irish Foreign Policy*, Volume III, 1926–32, p.510, 25 February 1930.

15 *Documents on Irish Foreign Policy*, Volume III, 1926–32, p.521, 4 April 1930, from UCDA LA30/448 to Michael Tierney.

16 *Documents in Irish Foreign Policy*, Volume III, 1926–1932, 27 May 1930, pp.540–555, quote at p.550.

17 *Documents in Irish Foreign Policy*, Volume III, 1926–1932, 29 July 1931.

18 Donnchadh O Corráin, interview, 28 June 2014.

19 Pól O Dochartaigh, *Julius Pokorny 1887–1970*, Dublin: Four Courts Press, 2004, pp.24, 32, 34.

20 NLI MS 11,000, Best Papers, 7 May, 1930, Binchy to Best.

21 Carl Marstrander, *Dagbok*, Diary of Visit to Man 1929–30, DIAS, 1983, 914.289 M, p.4. (Manx Museum MM. MS 5358B).

22 Quote from O Dochartaigh, Pól, *Julius Pokorny, 1887–1970*, Dublin: Four Courts Press, 2004, p.60. On Van Hamel, O Dochartaigh, op. cit., p.60. On Myles Dillon's opinion of Pokorny, Joachim Fischer and John Dillon, *The Correspondence of Myles Dillon, 1922–25* Dublin: Four Courts Press, 1999.

23 NLI MS 11,000, Best Papers, 5 March, 1931. Binchy to Best.

24 Ibid.

25 'C. R. C', Obituary of Julius Pokorny, *Studia Celtica,* Vol. IX, 1971, pp.343–345.

26 Mervyn O'Driscoll, *Ireland, Germany and the Nazis: Politics and Diplomacy, 1919–1939*, Dublin: Four Courts Press, 2004, p.172.
27 AD UCD, Eoin MacNeill Papers, LA1/K/70. 6 November 1935.
28 O Luing, 'The Scholar's Path to Kerry's West', *Cork Holly Bough*, p.4.
29 *Documents on Irish Foreign Policy*, Volume VII, 1941–1945, 3 September 1943, p.333.
30 Pol O Dochartaigh, *Julius Pokorny 1887–1970*, Dublin: Four Courts Press, 2004, pp.17, 83, 88, 119–120 and passim.
31 NLI MS 11,000, 22 January 1932, Binchy to Best.
32 *Documents in Irish Foreign Policy*, Volume III, 1926–1932,15 August 1930, pp.585–586.
33 *Documents in Irish Foreign Policy*, Volume III, 1926–1932, 5 August 1931, pp.809–814.
34 NLI Richard Best Papers, MS 1,000, 22 January 1932, Binchy to Best.
35 *Documents in Irish Foreign Policy*, Volume III, 1926–1932, 29 January 1932, pp.904–906.
36 *Documents in Irish Foreign Policy*, Volume III, 1926–1932, 1 March 1932, pp.15–16.
37 Ibid., p.15.
38 Myles Dillon, through his daughter, and Fergus Kelly, letter 28 August 2014.
39 Frank O'Connor, *My Father's Son*, London: Pan, 1968, p.83.
40 *DIB*, Vol. 5, p.832, February, 1933. Latter quote as in Michael Kennedy, 'Our Men in Berlin', pp.58–60.
41 NLI MS Sheehy-Skeffington Papers MS 40,482/6, 14 July 1933.
42 See O'Driscoll, *Ireland, Germany and the Nazis*, pp.100–102; Andreas Roth, *Mr. Bewley in Berlin: Aspects of the Career of an Irish Diplomat*, Dublin: Four Courts Press, 2000.
43 See O'Driscoll, *Ireland, Germany and the Nazis*, p.283.
44 Ibid., p.145.
45 Kennedy, 'Our Men in Berlin'. *Passim*.
46 Charles Bewley, *Memoirs of a Wild Goose*, Dublin: Lilliput, 1989, quotes from pp.291–2 and 117.
47 J. P. D., 'Obituary: Daniel A. Binchy', *Clongownian*, 1989, p.97.
48 See Kennedy, 'Our Men in Berlin', conclusion (no pagination).
49 See Bewley, *Memoirs of a Wild Goose*, p.286.
50 Andreas Roth, *Mr. Bewley in Berlin*, Dublin: Four Courts Press, 2000, p.21.
51 Bryan Fanning, 'Daniel Binchy and the Limits of Cultural Nationalism', in *Studies*, Vol. 102, 2013, pp.297–303, quote at pp.297–298.
52 *Studies*, September 1938, Vol. 27, 3, pp.353–80.
53 Philip Hannon and Jackie Gallagher (eds,), *Taking the Long View: Seventy Years of Fianna Fáil*, Dublin: Blackwater Press, 1996, p.107.
54 John Garvin, conversations, 1970s.
55 J. J. Lee, *Ireland, 1912–1985*, Cambridge: Cambridge University Press, 1985, p.198.

CHAPTER THREE

BETWEEN PAST AND PRESENT, 1932–1941

I n March 1932 Binchy returned to Dublin and resumed his duties in University College Dublin in Earlsfort Terrace. He also started to become a significant public figure, partly because of his growing international reputation as a Celtic scholar and partly because of his successful if short career as an Irish diplomat in Germany. Also he was becoming well-published. He had developed political contacts of a somewhat wider character than previously, including acquaintances in the British and American diplomatic services such as Harold Nicholson. He had acquired something of a reputation even among the republican anti-Treatyites who had taken office in February and who were, under de Valera's leadership, bent on uprooting the entire Treaty settlement of 1922. Their intention was to replace the Treaty and the Constitution of 1922 with a more definitely republican constitution even if that endangered the British Commonwealth connection so valued by Binchy and his colleagues. Binchy was also returning to a little learned world of rather original people, most of whom have survived in the collective memory of Ireland for far longer than they themselves might have imagined.

Sean O'Faolain returned to Ireland from England in 1933.

> … literary Dublin had meant little to me other than a night or two in Yeats's living room, a couple of clubs, such as the Arts Club and the P. E. N. Club, a couple of journalists' pubs, and gossip galore. When I now set out to explore it, I found that 'literary Dublin' meant the round dozen of Irish writers who lived there, and the occasional good play at the Abbey Theatre and the Gate Theatre. For the rest I could hear Mentor [Edward] Garnett saying it:

> 'Literature isn't produced by Dublin, London, Paris or anywhere else. It's produced by a few men sitting alone in their rooms before the

blank pages. You will find a few, and damn few, doing that in Dublin; a few more writing about literature; and a lot of fellows talking about those few. Stick to your desk, boy!'

All the same, Dublin, like any other city, has its atmosphere, and those groups can, if they are sophisticated, intelligent, informed and keen enough, work on it like a hotbed, forcing it, as a gardener would say, by a constant fermentation of criticism and discussion, not only about the arts, but about everything else surrounding the artist in his studio or his study. I would not go as far as to say that literary Dublin in the Thirties deserved all those adjectives, but for about five years or so I thought it a lively and stimulating place, and I was well pleased to be part of it.[1]

Frank O'Connor has given us a vivid pen portrait of the little clique of Celticists, poets, novelists, romantics and other intellectuals of thirties Dublin. They could be, he suggested, divided roughly into artists and scholars, and each set benefited from symbiosis with the other. Sometimes they quarrelled, but from the distance of three generations many of the quarrels look like those of old married couples rather than great philosophical or ideological differences. Another division was between those who had specific political agendas like nationalism or revivalism and those who did not. Dublin was a small city of a little over half a million at that time, and it was easy for the small number of educated and like-minded people to find each other to form a circle that met regularly. In fact, most of them lived within walking distance of each other in the middle-class 'leafy suburbs' (then not too leafy) of Rathgar, Rathmines and Ranelagh on the inner south side of the city. The city also had an efficient tram system at the time, the creation of William Martin Murphy, a figure much reviled by the Irish political left then and now. The tram system was later to be destroyed in the 1950s by an America-inspired civil service. The Abbey and Gate Theatres still provided a focus of sorts, and George Russell's regular open house institution on Rathgar Road, a series of salons of a sort, formed another. Bergin's home in Leinster Road in Lower Rathmines a few hundred yards away formed another, but reportedly rather Spartan, centre.

Russell had befriended O'Connor, who was now working as a librarian in the public library at Ballsbridge with a friend and fellow librarian, Dermot Foley. O'Connor had published a highly successful collection of short stories, *Guests of the Nation*, and he and Binchy had become friends after that bad start in 1927.

Russell, who was full of Hegelianism, used to argue that Irish literature developed in pairs. There were himself and Yeats, then Stephens and Colum, then Austin Clarke and F. R. Higgins, and now Geoffrey Phibbs and I.

But Russell was an example of another sort of Hegelianism, which he did not observe at all. The rediscovery of Old Irish, on which the whole literary movement was based, had been made by German scholars. When the discovery spread to Ireland the remarkable group of philologists, Irish and German, who worked here was probably the best group of scholars the country had known in modern times, and isolated by their very eminence. When Irish writers such as Yeats and Synge began to make use of the material they unearthed, and wrote as nobody in Ireland had written since the ninth century, they in their turn were isolated, and the two groups were drawn together and existed in an extraordinary love-hate relationship. There were the highly improbable friendships of George Moore and Kuno Meyer, of George Moore and Richard Best, of John Synge and Best.[2]

This scholar versus artist relationship is possibly best illustrated by anecdote. In the early years of the century Richard Best apparently explained to Moore, this being allegedly the first time it had ever been mentioned to him, the subjunctive mood as it exists in the English language. Thereupon Moore resolved to use no other grammatical mood than this particularly wonderful one when writing in English. Best and W. K. Magee did proofreading for Moore.[3] Best felt also that Synge, his old friend, had never really learned English properly. Best was also proud of the alleged fact that James Joyce had borrowed money from everyone in Dublin, but never got a penny out of him. He tended to be amused at the sight of American scholars writing huge books about Joyce which had been researched exhaustively and with an extraordinary literal-mindedness. In all probability he pretended to be noisily indignant about the alleged fact that he had little fame beyond having become a character in Ulysses.[4] In the thirties, a youthful R. A. Breatnach, later to be Professor of Irish Language and Literature in University College Cork, and who had earlier been a student of Bergin's at UCD,

> ... would regularly meet with him [i.e., Osborn Bergin] and two former teachers, Gerard Murphy and Daniel Binchy for leisurely luncheon sessions at which the discussion ranged over the entire history of the Irish language; these sessions formed part of the important but largely unrecorded oral tradition of the Irish-language scholarship of the period. This idyllic phase of his life would last only a few years.[5]

Bergin's intellectual severity was widely known and widely feared. In 1945, Breatnach departed to Cork. Bergin remarked laconically, 'I hear you're going to Cork. You won't like it. You'll have a good student every seven years or so; take care of him.'[6]

Bergin and Russell, two old bachelors (one a widower), formed one of these artist/scholar 'marriages'. According to O'Connor, W. B. Yeats, who was a kind of Archbishop to Russell's parish priest, envied Russell 'his' scholar. Bergin, as was notorious, disapproved of Yeats' playing fast and loose with the Irish language and Irish mythology; to Bergin, Yeats got everything *wrong*, which was certainly accurate enough. On one occasion in Bergin's house in Leinster Road in Lower Rathmines, Yeats made it evident that he wanted to befriend Bergin. The topic of George Moore came up, and Yeats became hopeful, as whatever Bergin thought of Yeats, he thought even less of Moore. '... and many a dear friendship has begun on nothing more than a common enmity.' This happy event failed to occur. Eventually Yeats marched out of the house with his nose out of joint, and O'Connor saw him to the tram. On his return, O'Connor remembered:

> 'Isn't he a great old card?' I said as enthusiastically as I could.

> 'He's a great old cod,' Bergin snapped, without looking at me, and for the rest of the evening I couldn't even get a civil answer out of him.[7]

This collision between Bergin and Yeats echoed old conflicts. As early as 1899, Yeats had written to Lady Gregory about the young Osborn Bergin 'the main person in *Fain an Lae* – I purposely blur the spelling of that word – the most argumentative person I have ever met. Whatever the other Gaelic Leaguers said he objected to, with perfect good humour but with great obstinacy and seriousness.'[8]

Despite his wish to have a scholar as friend and intellectual ally, Yeats himself seems to have been a very absent-minded colleague or ally. Sean O'Faolain writes:

> Here is Mrs. Padraic Colum telling us with asperity how she, just back from the United States, meets him unexpectedly in Nassau Street and says with delight, 'Why, good morning, Mr. Yeats!' – only to hear him intone:
>
> 'I hear a voice. It comes from beyond the sea. I know it not.'
>
> I can enjoy the impishness of that. But it is aloof. Here is his small daughter Anne walking or playing near his gate in Rathfarnham. She sees Papa approach, pause, look slowly at her and murmur: 'And what is your name?'
>
> In another man that could be pose or puckishness, not in him. It may well have been sheer absentmindedness. Here he is introducing Daniel Binchy, one of the finest Celtic scholars in the world, to his wife: 'This is Michael Tierney, the finest classical scholar in all Ireland.'[9]

Tierney, later to be President of UCD, was a respectable classicist, an able academic writer and cultural historian and also the prime mover behind the shift of the entire UCD operation from the city centre to a new campus in the south suburbs of the city in the 1960s. During the quiescent wartime years he rather cleverly built up a land bank in the Donnybrook area of the city which became the extensive campus of the university after 1963. I suspect that Yeats could not completely distinguish between different Catholic scholars for reasons of social caste. It should be recalled, however, that by the thirties Yeats was suffering from trouble with his sight.

Looking back to the thirties, O'Faolain thought that Yeats had been a bad builder of a cultural movement, because of this aloofness. Many years later Rebecca West remarked about him rather unkindly '…He wasn't a bit impressive and he wasn't my sort of a person at all. He boomed at you like a foghorn. … what he liked was solemnity and, if you were big enough, and strong enough, he loved you. He loved great big women. He would have been mad about Vanessa Redgrave.'[10] Stephen Spender felt that by the mid-thirties the poor man was going deaf and blind.[11] Certainly, he was a one-off; a genius who was irreplaceable, but no scholar. Perhaps that was his strength.

Old Laws and New Laws

It seems that Binchy's absence from academia as a young scholar generated different reactions. In March 1934, the Librarian of the Bodleian, H. H. E. Craster, wrote to Best in reply to an introductory letter, 'We are keeping a lookout for Dr. Binchy and will give him a warm welcome on your account and on that of Myles Dillon when he arrives. I wish it was you who were proposing to pay us a visit.'[12]

Binchy, meanwhile, was writing his memoirs of Hitler and Brüning as short articles for *Studies*, and published his first serious academic study of Brehon law in 1934, in two forms, as *Bretha Crólige*, a line-by line analysis of the ancient text in pamphlet form and as a short book containing an extended exegesis of the text, *Sick-Maintenance in Irish Law*, with Oxford University Press in the same year. This was to be reprinted finally as two characteristically long journal articles in *Eriu* some years later.[13] *Bretha Crólige* was a fairly recent discovery and, using Thurneysen's pioneering work, Binchy offered a word-for-word translation, with huge learned footnotes documenting obscurities and ambiguities. He referred to the MS as a fifteenth century '… legal tract here edited for the first time.' Most of the MS consisted of late Latin medical texts translated into Irish by anonymous medieval copyists. Binchy stated that it formed part of the famous collection of Irish customary law, the *Senchas Már*, accumulated in its original form during the first half of the eighth century. *Bretha Crólige* was rediscovered by Thurneysen and documented by him a generation earlier in the *Zeitschrift für Celtische Philologie*. Binchy thought it was the only surviving chunk of the 'lost third' of the *Senchas Már*. *Bretha Crólige* ('judgements of blood-lying') deals at great length with the customary laws concerning injuries inflicted on one individual by another either deliberately or by accident. In particular it deals with the obligation on the defendant to pay, one way or another, for the physical recovery of the victim either through his own efforts or through payment. Nursing the victim back to health is insisted on, according to the three great sources of justice: nature, scripture and conscience.[14] A central feature of the penalty system is the strict gradation by rank of the victim of the payments. The killing of a slave might only cost two *cumals* (female slaves), but the unintentional killing of a king might cost all of the estate of a well-to-do man.

A modern person might suppose that enforcement would have to be presumably by shaming and shunning, or the main force of the kinship group in the stateless society that Ireland was in the eighth century. However, Fergus Kelly of the Dublin Institute for Advanced Studies (DIAS) lists several pretty drastic methods of punishment for law-breaking. Often fines were exacted, but the system prescribed hanging, 'setting adrift', mutilation, flogging (only for slaves, wives, sons, pupils and younger brothers, of course) and outlawry. Kelly remarks that 'It is clear from linguistic evidence that many of the essentials of the early Irish legal system go back at least as far as the common Celtic period (circa 1,000 B.C.).'[15] Other modern scholars tend to accept this verdict. O Corráin, Breatnach and Breen have argued, however, that the contributions of Christian ideas and notions imported from Roman law have been understated.[16]

Bretha Crólige even lists specific and itemised entitlements to particular kinds of food and shelter, again graded by rank. This entire penalty system seems to apply to everyone in society, with some interesting exceptions which constitute a medieval shit-list. The text states:

There are three men in the territory [*tuath*] who have no right to either nursing or fines, unless *cáin* [tax] or treaty give it [to them]: a man who refuses [hospitality to] every class of person, a man who is false to his honour, a man who steals everybody's property ...

There are three women in the territory who have no right to either nursing or fines, although injury have been done to them: a woman

who cares not with whom she may sleep, a woman who robs
everybody, a sorceress who traffics in charms.[17]

In the accompanying interpretative article, *Sick-Maintenance in
Irish Law*, Binchy explained the intellectual importance of the tract. He
remarked:

> Students of comparative law realised that the rules governing
> compensation for personal injuries offer perhaps the most fruitful
> field for the work of drawing parallels between ancient legal systems.
> One of these rules seem to have been a feature of the criminal law of
> a great many peoples: I refer to the rule that, where one person has
> suffered physical injury at the hands of another, the latter is under
> certain circumstances, liable, not only for the normal legal mulct, but
> also for the medical expenses of the injured party.[18]

Binchy intended to demonstrate that the original somewhat Byzantine
maze of obligations of sick-maintenance (*folog n-othrusa*) was usually
eventually reduced over the centuries to a fixed payment, as in other
legal systems. These amounts continued to vary according to the rank
of the victim. In a society without currency, the payments were denoted
in slave-women (*cumal*). However, at its height, the ranking system was
very extensive: even diet was specified, the two highest non-royal ranks in
society being entitled to daily rations of ale or milk.[19] Binchy quoted the
text coolly:

> There are seven sick-maintenances most difficult to support in Irish
> law: maintenance of a king, maintenance of a hospitaller, maintenance
> of a poet, maintenance of an artificer, maintenance of a wise man,
> maintenance of an embroideress. For it is necessary [to get someone]
> to undertake their duties in their stead, so that the earnings of each of
> them may not be lacking in his house.[20]

Furthermore, if the victim died, naturally none of these provisos
applied, and the penalty skyrocketed. Instead the law of *éraic* or *corpdíre*
(body fine) applied. Binchy then summarised the system: the law gives

the 'leech' (physician) nine days to assess the seriousness of injury. If he says the case is hopeless, it is a mortal blood-lying (*crólige mbáis*) with its own rank-based system of fines. If the leech declares the patient to be curable, the defendant must supply *othrus*, payment for medical attention or what Binchy terms a 'leech fee.'[21] The text is inordinately difficult, partly because it had been copied so much into different versions of the Irish language over the centuries that commonly even the medieval glossators themselves were 'out of their depth' at times, as Binchy puts it, in trying to interpret the language and social rules of a society even more archaic than their own.[22] This was presumably aggravated by an early complexity being gradually replaced by a simpler system involving a system of exchange value approximating to a money system. Eventually coinage would be used. This gradual process of modernisation would, in turn, aggravate the bewilderment of later glossators.

The study was well-received. Eoin MacNeill, in a review in *Studies* in 1934, saw it as a truly pioneering investigation into medieval Irish society.

> To those who have known the editor as a specialist in jurisprudence, it may or may not be a surprise to find him here coming to the front as a specialist likewise in the handling of some of the oldest and most difficult material in the Irish language. It is mere justice to greet this work as a clear and promising advance in Irish historical and cultural studies.[23]

At about the same time, Binchy, wearing his lawyer's hat, found time to weigh in against de Valera's campaign to abolish the Irish Senate. The upper house, or Senate, of the Oireachtas (parliament) of the Irish Free State was the result of an understanding Arthur Griffith had reached with the British concerning the status of citizens traditionally of British loyalty in the newly independent Irish state. Therefore, the composition of the upper house tended to favour ex-unionists and the older upper classes of Irish society. It also contained several people of real academic or literary achievement, including Yeats himself, the author of several classic political speeches in the twenties. The ones on divorce and theories of education are of direct relevance even today, particularly perhaps his warning that education of children should never be bent to non-educational purposes like linguistic revival or religious or political indoctrination. Inevitably the Senate attracted the hostility of Fianna Fáil, being seen as a miniature House of Lords, a feeble echo of the hated House of Landlords that had stymied the development of an independent Irish democracy for so long. The fact that its debates tended to be interesting didn't help, neither did its propensity to delay the passage of government legislation.[24] Binchy's strictures did not move de Valera in any way, and the Senate duly disappeared in 1936, to be replaced by a new, more tractable version in 1938 under the new Constitution of 1937.

Also in the same year (1934) he commented on contemporary developments in the modern Irish language by giving a fulsome review in *Studies* to 'two Blasket autobiographies,' Tomás O Criomhthain's *An tOileánach* (The Islandman) and Muiris O Súileabháin's *Fiche Bliain ag Fás* (Twenty Years A-Growing), both of them to be recognised as instant classics of modern Irish literature which have never been out of print in either English or Irish ever since. The review clearly revealed Binchy's love of Dunquin, Coumeenole and the Blasket Islands, and his anger at the creeping Anglicisation of the Dingle peninsula. With regard to O'Sullivan he observed, 'Although born on the [Blasket] island, he spent the first five or six years of his life in Dingle, where the inhabitants are content to speak the worst English in the world in preference to the best Irish – and thus he has been bilingual since childhood.'[25] He faulted the Irish of *Fiche Bliain ag Fás* as against that of *An tOileánach* on these grounds, the latter book being less polluted by *Béarlachas* (anglicisms). It is true that the O Criomhthain book has a classic starkness and stoicism that the other book lacks. During these years Binchy spent much time on the Dingle peninsula, particularly in the O Dálaigh household at Cumeenole. On occasion he would go out with the Dunquin fishermen on their expeditions, the fare being a bottle of whiskey.[26]

The following year Binchy intervened in a controversy concerning constitutional change in the Free State and its possible impact on the partition of the island. At the time partition was widely seen as a temporary thing, soon to be abolished in favour of some measure of reunification. He argued, by way of intriguing long-term prophecy, that declaring a republic for the twenty-six counties would inevitably make partition permanent by eventually bringing in direct rule of Northern Ireland by London. Also,

Dublin would lose the firm support of Canada guaranteed under the Treaty of 1922, together with the automatic support of the other 'White Dominions' which Dublin enjoyed at that time. Furthermore, the country would be poorer because of the inevitable loss of imperial preference.[27] By abandoning the Treaty settlement, he was arguing, de Valera was throwing away any chance of reuniting Ireland. In the same year Frank MacDermot, a dissident politician from Coolavin, Co. Sligo, TD for Roscommon and war veteran, denounced the Italian invasion of Ethiopia ('Abyssinia'); Binchy wrote him a letter congratulating him on his anti-fascist stand.[28] At around the same time Binchy involved himself in a complicated legal wrangle concerning fisheries at Killorglin, Co. Kerry. The following year he again entered the ongoing controversy over the Senate with a short piece in *Studies*, in which he made a plea for the 1922 Senate, pointing to its pluralist composition, consisting of all classes and religions. He bemoaned the Seanad Electoral Act of 1928, which had turned it into a party assembly. 'Its intelligence, its temper and its manners alike deteriorated. It became in fact a slightly superior replica of the Dail.' He suggested 'vocationalism', a fashionable placebo at the time, candidates to be nominated by vocational 'nominating bodies'. De Valera seems to have taken up a rather convoluted version of this suggestion.[29] Binchy was to return briefly to the question of the Senate even after de Valera's new Constitution and general revamp of the Irish constitutional system had bedded down after 1937. As late as 1940 he did a long and sympathetic review in Sean O'Faolain's new literary magazine, *The Bell*, of Donal O'Sullivan's long, strangely arranged but highly informative general political history of independent Ireland, *The Irish Free State and its Senate*. The book is very hostile to de Valera and his constitutional reforms.[30] However, as early as 1937, Binchy's intellectual concerns were rapidly changing, and the growing international crisis increasingly preoccupied him. In 1936 Hitler invaded the Rhineland and encountered no resistance, although what was then his little horse-drawn army could easily have been thrown back by any real French show of force. The French were split pathologically, the left having elected a Jewish socialist as prime minister. Many in the army accepted the slogan, *Plutot Hitler que Blum*. Hitler was becoming unstoppable, due mainly to the pusillanimity of his enemies; he came to see the leaders of the western democracies as 'worms'.

The Cross and the Fasces

Early during the year 1937 Binchy was recruited by the British Foreign Office to undertake a study of fascism. He was deputed to study Italy, with particular emphasis on the relationships between the fascist state and the Catholic Church. According to O'Driscoll the British thought he was too biased against the Nazis to do a study of Germany.[31] This was almost certainly the case. There is also a simpler and more obvious reason for keeping him out of Germany; Binchy was self-evidently someone who would be unwelcome in Germany on the grounds of his published opinions of Hitler, and might possibly be in physical danger in the country. After all, his 1933 article would certainly have come to the attention of the Germans in Dublin, and would have been fed into the Gestapo machine, and this time he would not have had diplomatic immunity had he tried to visit the Reich. Many journalists who had lampooned the Nazi leader were murdered after the Nazi seizure of power. A British diplomat warned him against ever returning to Germany while the Nazi regime endured.[32]

While getting a start on his study of Italian politics, Binchy had an audience with Pius XI in May 1937, as part of an English-speaking group. The old man had had bouts of illness and was staying at his country residence at Castel Gandolfo. Daniel had expected a tough-looking healthy man, but instead he was shocked to see 'this frail figure with the ashen cheeks and sunken eyes with the wasted hand raised in benediction'.[33] However, he quickly became aware of an inner strength in this man, a certain driven quality in his personality and an 'indomitable will'. The Pope spoke of the persecution of the Church in Germany and Spain, and eventually thanked them for visiting 'the house of the old father who is the common father of all, who loves all his children, and loves them all the more because he knows he must leave them soon'. He was to die in February 1939. To Binchy and millions of people the Pope came to be seen as standing for good in a world of increasing horror and for the idea of peace in an international arena increasingly dominated by warlike ideologies and pathological hatreds. Binchy argued that the prestige of the Papacy was at the highest point it had ever attained since the days of the Reformation; in the United States, both Houses of Congress were to adjourn in 1939 out of respect for the pontiff on the occasion of his death, apparently for the first time ever.

1. Osborn Bergin

2. Daniel Binchy in mid-career

3. Daniel Binchy

4. Eamon de Valera

5. James Carney

6. Front row, right: Carl Marstrander. Back row, left: Richard Best

7. Osborn Bergin, Tomás O Criomhthain (an tOileánach), Daniel Binchy

8. Daniel Binchy in old age

Binchy saw the Papacy as being neither Right not Left in the parlance of the day, but seeking the common good according to ancient philosophical principles laid down many years earlier.

> A policy so firmly anchored to principles was perhaps bound to be misunderstood in a society where politics have become so divorced from morality that the needs and interests of the moment are the only factors taken into account. In a world of crooked lines the straight line looks strange and forbidding, if not abnormal; and so we have the curious spectacle of some politicians whose policy seemed for a time to run parallel to the Vatican's accusing it of 'inconsistency' for declining to follow them in a sharp swerve to one side or the other. Pius XI pursued his straight line, undeterred by accusations or threats. No Pope has more scrupulously rendered to Caesar the things that are Caesar's; even when he disliked Caesar's policy, provided that it did not menace the essential interests of religion, he declined to intervene.[34]

The same Pope who denounced the 'fetishes of Liberalism' was also quite willing to denounce 'the pagan brutality of Nazism.' When the Italian fascist government tried to shut down Catholic Action in the early thirties, he issued an Encyclical against the government, thereby possibly endangering the Lateran Treaty. When Italian fascism, in imitation of the Nazis, turned anti-semitic, his denunciation of this new racism was rapid. Pius XI prayed for the success of Franco in Spain, not because he sided with right-wing totalitarianism, but because the Catholic Church would not be persecuted unduly by the right wing, whereas a victory of a Stalinist left-wing totalitarianism would certainly result in religious persecution. Curiously, that well-known anti-clerical, George Orwell, came up with a similar pessimistic prognostication in *Homage to Catalonia*. There was no hope of a democratic Spain emerging from the civil war, no matter which side won, he thought.

This interest in current affairs was not a new departure for Binchy. Over a year previously, in late 1937, he had written a long review article for *Studies* which reflected some serious thinking on his part which was far removed from Ireland's dead medieval civilisation or even from contemporary Dunquin. It concerned three recent books on the Papacy, international affairs and its relationship to Italian fascism. The essay started with the comment that all three books were written by non-Catholics, but none of them displayed the usual lay or Protestant hostility to the Papacy or the Catholic Church which was a commonplace of much current affairs writing of that time in the English language. Even in Italy, the nineteenth-century Papacy had been despised and hated by the new intelligentsia and much of the middle class; in 1878, when Pius IX, the reactionary pontiff of Vatican I, had finally died, a mob of liberals and Freemasons ('the Giordano Bruno Lodge') had tried to throw the corpse in the Tiber. But by the thirties of the next century, the Papacy had survived everything, he argued. 'At no time since the Reformation has the Papacy stood higher in the opinion of the non-Catholic world than now.'[35] One writer (René Fulop-Miller) congratulated the Church's development of a social teaching which finally addressed the circumstances of the modern world in which the Catholic faithful found themselves, instead of trying to retreat to an imaginary medieval world. A second writer, F. A. Ridley, a convinced socialist, while hostile to the Papacy, rather admired, in Machiavellian mode, the way in which the Church had managed to survive in the circumstances of Italian fascism. He saw the Papacy as having constructed an anti-left alliance with Mussolini's Blackshirts. Conrad Eckhardt saw, accurately according to Binchy, that losing its temporal domains between 1860 and 1870 and eventually reaching a Concordat with the Italian state in 1929 were the best things that could have happened to the Church. Binchy wrote:

> Detached from the cares of temporal government himself, Leo XIII proceeded to state in modern idiom the Church's attitude to the temporal power in general. In a series of encyclicals which the intervening years have not robbed of their relevance to our time, all the new problems – political, social, cultural – were examined in the light of traditional teaching, and solutions advanced which have won the unstinted admiration of men like Herr Fulop-Miller. Those who call Leo XIII a 'Liberal' as opposed to his predecessors are merely concealing under a meaningless label their ignorance of his work; with the exception of Pius XI no Pontiff has formulated essential doctrine

so uncompromisingly. To call him a 'Modern' would be nearer to the truth: like the present Pope, he had an insatiable interest in the contemporary discoveries of the human spirit, and – again like Pius XI – he did not hesitate to hail the progress of science as furnishing new weapons for the Church's age-old mission.[36]

With regard to forms of government, the Church was agnostic, except for requiring that the ordinary rights of religious freedom and public morality were protected, he argued. Soviet totalitarianism and Nazi racism had been clearly denounced in the 1930s by the Papacy. The Concordat with the Mussolini government, claimed by Ridley to be the sealing of an alliance, was nothing of the sort, but a ratification of the transfer of temporal power from the Church to the Italian state which had happened long previously as a matter of historical fact. Binchy was, over the next few years, to expand this germ of an argument into a classic book-length study. He also found time to write a short technical piece, '*Aimser Chue*' for a *Festschrift* for Eoin MacNeill, to be published in 1940, concerning the temporary residence rights ('coshering') a noble had had in Gaelic medieval Ireland over a base tenant in winter.[37] The impression given to this amateur commentator is that the nobles of Gaelic Ireland were perfectly willing, and legally able, to eat the unfortunate tenants out of house and home in wintertime if they felt like it. However, Binchy's war work was to be Italy.

Church and State in Fascist Italy, a big book of 774 pages, was published in London in 1941.[38] It has been reprinted only once, in 1970, presumably because the regime it documented was shortly to disappear, as Binchy had intuited. Perhaps he did not anticipate such a sudden and complete collapse as occurred in 1943, due more to military defeat and the general stupidity of the régime than to any real popular rebellion, although real partisan resistance did indeed exist. In the introduction to the book Daniel rebuked himself for the slowness with which he habitually wrote, due to his own carefulness, which he referred to as his 'excessive scrupulosity'. Intriguingly, he was somewhat ahead of his time in using the term 'totalitarianism' to characterise not only fascism and Nazism, but also the Soviet Marxist regime. He abhorred all of these political systems. He was not completely uncritical of Pius XI:

... [He] was not, of course, blind to the religious dangers inherent in Fascism and its equivalents elsewhere, but he failed to recognise that these dangers nearly all sprang from the essential similarity between those systems and Communism, that all forms of authoritarianism – Fascist, Muscovite or Hitlerite – have far more in common with each other than any of them has with traditional Christian polity. Nor had he at the time of his election [as Pope in 1922] any real appreciation of the forces that give democracy in its hour of crisis a strength and toughness far greater than the most rigid authoritarian system can command; and like so many continental ecclesiastics, he identified democracy with that particular brand of secularist Liberalism which it had assumed in his own country.[39]

Binchy despised Benito Mussolini, because of what he saw as his low intellect and his poor character, but he gave him the rather weak accolade of being at least some improvement on Hitler. He saw him as a man of few convictions of any kind, who was thus able to assume a chameleon-like ability to change to fit a given political environment.

He possesses in rare degree the art of communicating totally inconsistent impressions to different people at the same time. Among those who have been in contact with him there exists a bewildering disparity of views on the most fundamental aspects of his character and beliefs ... in thought as in action he remains the supreme opportunist ... Principles to him are nothing more than useful pegs on which to hang a particular policy; if events necessitate a different policy other pegs can be easily found. As Mr. Voigt acutely remarks, he represents the irreligious type, using the term in its widest sense, as opposed to Hitler and Lenin, both of them men of passionate and permanent beliefs.[40]

On the other hand, Mussolini had a human side to him; when his brother Arnoldo died in 1932, the grief of the *Duce* was patently obvious. Arnoldo was apparently a man of decency who had pleaded publicly for a reconciliation between the Catholic Church and Benito. Possibly to mollify the Catholic Church, the fascists had suppressed the Freemasons in Italy in

1925. Daniel believed that Catholics had always exaggerated the political and commercial influence of Freemasons. But then, it could be said that Freemasonry in the English-speaking world was a much milder and more innocent social animal than the continental Grand Orient, or the semi-revolutionary lodges of France or Italy. He remarked, 'To a certain kind of Catholic mind, by no means confined to Italy, Masonry offers a useful scapegoat fulfilling the role which the same type of mind in other camps assigns to the Jesuits or the Jews.' His general analysis of the phenomenon of Freemasonry is brilliant: well-informed, moderate and entertaining.[41] However, he went on rather strangely to defend the Vatican's tolerance of the destruction of the democratic Catholic People's Party (the *Populari* or predecessor of the Christian Democrats, the Italian equivalent of the *Zentrum*, much admired by him in his German days). Somewhat feebly, he speculated and reported disappointedly:

> No doubt the Vatican's benevolent attitude towards the destruction of the *Partido Populare* had been largely based on the hope that its disappearance would eliminate the last excuse for friction between Fascism and the Catholic organisations of Italy. But this hope was doomed to swift disappointment; the efforts to secure a monopoly in the training of youth and the attacks on Catholic Action continued with unabated vigour. Already the totalitarian octopus was stretching forth its tentacles and there were ominous signs that Fascist theory was evolving on unchristian or even anti-Christian lines.[42]

It could be argued against Binchy that the consent to the abolition of the Catholic electoral organisations in Italy was the last of a long series of anti-democratic own goals by the Vatican, going back to its crazy pre-war prohibitions on Catholics voting in national elections in Italy, a tactic that handed the parliamentary assembly over to the Church's enemies: anti-clericals, Freemasons and socialists. It also had the effect of damaging seriously the emergence of a democratic and national political culture in Italy. Binchy pointed particularly to the existence of popular state-worship in Italy as early as 1924, and the Church's sensitivity to being identified with any secular regime. Therefore, the Concordat of 1929 had the great virtue of drawing a line between Church and State in Italy.[43] In fact, the

Concordat was initiated secretly by the fascists in 1926, in an attempt to buy the Church off. To some extent it succeeded, but it must have been something of a shock to the Blackshirts to realise how a genuine popular loyalty to the Church persisted in Italy despite their best efforts.

> Indeed, an impressive proof that the heart of Italy has remained unshakenly Catholic was provided by the peasantry, to whom the Fascist regime, like its predecessors a product of the towns, meant merely a change of masters; for the first time they abandoned their normal attitude of lethargic indifference towards public affairs when the great news came that the Government had made peace with the Holy Father. In the poorest hamlets of Sicily, in the loneliest outposts of the Alpine frontier, they flocked to their churches to join in the simple service of thanksgiving and to pray for the Pope who had 'given back God to Italy and Italy to God.'[44]

Interestingly, the Vatican encouraged the voters to turn in a 'yes' vote on the plebiscite the fascists organised on the issue of the Concordat, a rare instance of the Church of Pius XI appealing to popular opinion as expressed through the ballot box. The agreement resulted in the right of sanctuary being eliminated and there was to be no religious instruction in the universities from then on. The totalitarian regime was everywhere, Binchy observed, and its social penetration was at a formidable level, rivalled only by that of the Church itself. The state's party and police organs let the centre know what was going on in every parish in Italy. The fascists rejoiced in the destruction of bourgeois, Communist and democratic organisations and their being replaced by fascist fronts of various kinds. The newspapers were, of course, muzzled, including the avowedly Catholic ones. Even the Boy Scouts had, under apparently irresistible pressure, eventually to be ceded to the state by Pius XI in 1938.[45]

One of the keys to the Catholics' apparent quietism was the settled conviction that the fascist system was transient and would not, and could not, last for very long. This conviction was partly an echo of the long life of the Church as an institution, which had seen off nations, empires, kingdoms and entire civilisations over nearly two millennia. This could also work the other way; negotiating an agreement with the fascist state risked being stuck with such an agreement in a post-fascist future, a future which might even be democratic.

> To negotiate with a single-party State which made no attempt to consult the Italian people would expose the result of such negotiations to very special risks. The agreements might well be regarded as part and parcel of Fascism, destined to be thrown on the scrap-heap once the Fascist system had gone the way of all things human.[46]

This is more Binchy's thinking than Pius XII's, perhaps; his general theme was one of defence of the Concordat of 1929 despite its fascist origins, and the real test of the agreement would come with the disappearance of Mussolini and company. In February 1939, days before his own death, Pius XI sent £1,000, perhaps equating to US$1,500,000 in the currency of 2015, to an Irish Catholic committee dedicated to the aid of Jewish refugees from Nazism. Binchy's comment on the Pope's legacy was essentially a version of the Yankee proverb: 'good fences make good neighbours'.

> Pius XI, for all his attachment to the land of his birth, remained faithful to the universalist tradition of the Papacy. His attitude towards the reconciled Italy combined friendship with independence, and the precedent which he forged for his successors may well be summed up in the old proverb: love your neighbour – yet pull not down your hedge.[47]

A recurrent theme of Daniel's avowedly political work was the superiority of democracy to totalitarianisms of all types. In Italy he seems to have spoken to, and listened to, people of all walks of life, apparently having learned Italian very quickly, an achievement which for him would have been fairly easy. He seems to have been able to talk freely to the Italian man in the street. He clearly had an Irish instinct for public opinion and its potential importance in political life which many of his academic colleagues or clerical friends did not possess. Although the Church was silent and certainly very ambivalent on the question of the sovereignty of the people, democracy offered the Church a better deal than did any other form of government, he insisted. The Church had had its quarrels with democratic

115

governments and would of course have more in the coming times, but at least liberal democracy allowed it to protect itself and permitted it to keep the 'weapons of defence and counter-attack'. It could, under the democratic doctrine of free speech, appeal to the public through the newspapers and of course the pulpit. Under democratic conditions the Church:

> … can summon the faithful to its support and to oppose by all means those laws, institutions, or policies which it deems to be contrary to the interests of religion … The moral seems to be that nowadays, where popular liberty has been destroyed, religious liberty is bound to suffer also …[48]

It certainly had taken a while, but Pius XI eventually realised that totalitarian dictatorship, whether of left or of right, was actually a far greater danger to popular Christianity than were even the secularist liberals and democrats his predecessor, Pius IX, had done valiant and deluded battle against for so long ago. The last chapters of Binchy's book show many signs of being afterthoughts or simply restatements of ideas already set out in the main body of the work, composed as it was under wartime conditions in Ireland with no chance of any visits to an Italy which was about to be torn apart by warfare. Daniel was possibly under some kind of deadline from the British; they wanted the analysis before Italy collapsed, as was becoming increasingly likely as the tide of war turned gradually against the Axis. As a Parthian shot towards the end of the book, Binchy took to task, in an entertaining way, English Protestant zealots, some of them close to authority in wartime Britain, who seemed to regard Catholicism as a religion which kept the faithful in a dark ignorance worse than that of paganism, and the Italian version of Catholicism was seen by them as the worst version of this terrible international perversion of Christianity. Some of them saw the Church as an ally of Italian fascism, or even as being its creator. His defence of the Church was aimed in particular at this collection of English cultural survivors of the Reformation of three centuries before, a tradition still living as a component of an unselfconscious English imperial nationalism. 'The ordinary Italian is not disposed to compromise in matters of religious faith; he may be a Catholic, or he may become an atheist, but he will never be a Protestant.'[49] This sounds very much like an echo of Stephen Daedalus's famous reply to Cranly, two characters in the novel *A Portrait of the Artist as a Young Man* whose creator, James Joyce, had just died in Zurich. Stephen tells his friend that he has lost his Catholic faith, and Cranly asks him did this mean he was going to turn Protestant? Stephen answers that he had lost his faith, but not his self-respect; why should he reject an absurdity that is intellectually coherent for an absurdity that is intellectually incoherent?

Binchy's book got a rave review in Dublin from Father Edward J. Coyne SJ in *Studies* in late 1941. Binchy, said Coyne quite perceptively, 'has a keen sense of the dramatic and omits no opportunity of letting it be seen'. He used his wit, irony and humour to enliven his writing, but sometimes with a streak of malice. He saw a side to Binchy that was to display itself again later in his career.[50]

However, Binchy was trying to help Frank O'Connor, who was going through a difficult time; he was practically destitute, and his work at Radio Eireann had suddenly dried up. Apparently his making a broadcast through the BBC was seen by government people as a breach of neutrality, and it had been decided to cut off all employment for him, *while not actually telling him so*. Binchy, with his civil service experience, figured this out pretty quickly and remonstrated with P. J. Little, the Minister for Posts and Telegraphs. Not only was O'Connor not to broadcast in Dublin, he was not permitted to go to London to broadcast there; the Irish government refused him a visa to travel out of the twenty-six counties. Binchy pointed out that this amounted to depriving a man of his livelihood. Little suggested that O'Connor could use a pseudonym, like Proinsias O Conchobhair or Micheál O Donnabháin, as was a commonplace custom at the time. However, the writer flatly refused to do so.

Apparently the Church had him in its sights as well, for not being married in a manner accepted by it, and was able to block off his employment in a similar way, either separately or, more likely, in symbiosis with the state authorities. He was, in effect, living with a woman who was not regarded by the Archbishop as his wife, and this was giving public scandal. It also seems that the Archbishop was able to turn state work contracts on and off like a tap. It seems very probable that the Church's civilian arm, the Knights of Columbanus, was involved in this murky business, as it had penetrated the state apparatus and the semi-state bodies fairly thoroughly. It was also strong in the dimmer recesses of the universities. My own belief is that the Archbishop was the prime mover in this affair; O'Connor had, after all, perfect republican credentials from the Fianna Fáil point of view, being a veteran of the anti-Treaty IRA and a supporter of the Irish language. Irish democracy was real, but in its mean-mindedness it sometimes reflected a very nasty side to the Irish character.[51] Ironically, O'Connor did do some writing for the *Irish Independent* newspaper group during the war years under a pseudonym ('Ben Mayo'); apparently someone was looking out for him. It is said that the editor of the time, Hector Legge, was that honourable man.[52]

Binchy was fairly hostile to clerical power in Ireland, and often did not go to mass on Sundays. It was around this time that Binchy was travelling to Chatham House, the academic end of the Foreign Office, to work at the Italian Desk. There he met an Irish lady, Violet Conolly, who worked at the Russian desk; she was a formidable scholar of Soviet Russia, and had contributed articles on the subject to *Studies*. She was reportedly extremely fond of him, according to family folklore. The relationship apparently came to nothing.[53]

De Valera, Mathematics and Medievalism

Before, and eventually in tandem with, his Italian project, Binchy became involved in another intellectual task at home in Dublin: the creation of the Dublin Institute for Advanced Studies, another brainchild of the Taoiseach, and one which Binchy and his colleagues looked upon with far more favour than they did de Valera's Constitution. De Valera had already set up a folklore project, for which schoolchildren all over the country were organised to interview older people in their families with the idea of recording rapidly disappearing local customs, verse, stories and proverbs. The result was to be the magnificent folklore archive in University College Dublin which offers us a cultural photograph of rural Ireland in its last post-Famine generation, just before it vanished forever because of modernisation, mass education, radio and television. In a way it was an Irish version of Mass Observation in England.

Because of the Treaty split, one of the long-term side-effects was that the three colleges of the National University of Ireland in Dublin, Cork and Galway were controlled by pro-Treaty elements, usually of the Fine Gael political tradition. Trinity College Dublin remained predominantly unionist and, therefore, pro-British in tradition. Fianna Fáil was able to make some headway in Galway, the smallest of the three but little in the other two, and the party remained bereft of any real intellectual tradition. De Valera's quite genuine interest in a certain kind of higher education was snookered by this situation. His solution was to leapfrog the entire university system, such as it was, and set up a post-doctoral Institute of Advanced Studies. A note on the DIAS file in 1936 seems to reflect de Valera's thinking: '[An institute of advanced studies]…such as that of Princeton, where research work would be carried out under guidance of men of international reputation. Had in mind Conway, Whittaker and Schroedinger. Max Born and Einstein not available. Get in touch with Schroedinger and offer him asylum.'

For a start the Institute would have three Schools: a School of Celtic Studies and a School of Theoretical Physics to start up in October 1940, and then a School of Cosmic Physics to start on 26 March 1947.[54] The problem of how to organise the Meteorological Service and what to do with the Observatory at Dunsink was used as the occasion of de Valera's initiative. In April 1938 a Note dictated by the Taoiseach observed in a phrase worthy of the penny-pinchers of the Department of Finance, 'At the present time famous Jews could be got almost for what would enable them to live.'[55] Another Note of May 1938 again tacitly expressed the thought that Hitler's mad assault on German higher education could be a gift not only for higher education in Britain and America, but for Ireland also. This was written to the Taoiseach by E. T. Whittaker, an English scientist who had been the Astronomer Royal and who was acting as science adviser to de Valera, '[M. Von Lane] … is not a Jew, but the son of a high Prussian General, but he has always been opposed to Nazism and most courageously opposed the dismissal of his Jewish colleagues. I think he would be a splendid man to get if it is possible.'[56] Whittaker wrote again a few weeks later, 'If Schroedinger and Heitler could *both* be got, Dublin would be the most important centre for mathematical Physics in the world.'[57] Eventually, Erwin Schroedinger and Walter Heitler duly arrived in Dublin. Schroedinger seems to have been politically rather innocent. He had tried to flatter the Nazis, and was not Jewish, but he 'loathed the Nazis, their violence, their anti-intellectualism and their anti-semitism.' However, in the Reich, jobs like his were given to Nazi chancers, ideological fantasists, lunatics and apparatchiks; his career in Germany was destroyed. In the late thirties, he stopped off in Belgium first, where he was given several university appointments. He was given a transit visa through Britain to Ireland with the help of Frederick Lindemann (later Lord Cherwell), a famous Oxford physicist of the period, who engineered a transit visa for him. Eventually he showed up in Dublin in late September 1939 and was to stay there for eighteen years. Medawar and Pyke remark: 'The relative quietness of Dublin – Éire remained neutral during the war – suited him; he was very much a lone worker.'[58] Whittaker wrote a congratulatory and supportive letter to de Valera on 7 December 1942.

> This is an illustration of the principle I mentioned above, that the institution should be created for the men: for it is the fortunate circumstance that Erwin Schroedinger and Heitler were available, that has counted for the wonderful success of the institute. When the war ends, it will be possible to attract to Dublin every brilliant young theoretical physicist from an impoverished and starving Europe ...[59]

The projected School of Cosmic Physics was started in April 1943. Richard Best was one of the first people recruited to the School of Celtic Studies a few years earlier. A congratulatory letter was sent to him from E. H. Alton in Rome in October 1940. 'I am delighted that you are to be one of the great ones in the new institution. It has, in my eyes, already justified its existence. I knew that they should not overlook your claims but there is always a danger in this country where the inconceivable so frequently happens.'[60]

E. J. Gwynn of TCD wrote to Best, also in October, remarking entertainingly 'I am delighted – I always said there was some good in de Valera. You will need a bridle for O'Rahilly and a pair of spurs for Bergin.'[61]

Binchy was to serve as the first Director of the School of Celtic Studies, and had an important say on how it was to be set up and who should be recruited to it. Appointments included Best, Bergin and O'Rahilly.

By the time that Binchy wrote to his old friend William T. Cosgrave in 1943, it appears that he had finally found his berth. He noted that he much preferred to be working on Old Irish than to be writing on church and state in fascist Italy. The price of contentment, however, seems to have been a certain political bitterness; he strongly disagreed with the Fine Gael policy of going along with de Valera's policy of neutrality.[62] In 1943 he published a short pamphlet of 35 pages which was a sort of intellectual manifesto, *The Linguistic and Historical Value of the Irish Law Tracts.*[63]

Otherwise, his attitude towards the entire linguistic revival drive remained mildly sceptical. The Richard Best Papers for the thirties contain a fascinating series of letters and memoranda 'relating to the state of Irish studies since the foundation of Saorstát Eireann, the foundation of the Dublin Institute for Advanced Studies and the revision of the spelling of Irish.'[64] As early as 1931 the idea, first suggested by Thurneysen, of a dictionary of Old and Middle Irish, was floated, Blythe being an energetic supporter. The idea resurfaced in the mid-thirties under de Valera's government and, of course, the usual issue of the expense of endowing Irish-language scholarships for the assistants who were to compile the dictionary was aired. The Department of Education was sceptical in a very different way. In a minute of 15 October 1936 a senior civil servant observed rather acutely:

> After twenty-five years the burden and reputation of Irish scholarship is still almost entirely in the hands of those who had been recognised leaders in 1909.

> There are several reasons why this is so. Openings for those with a bent for scholarship in 1900–09 were rare then as now, but some found their way into positions of the Civil Service as then organised, where they were able to solve the problem of earning a living and pursuing the paths of scholarship. Such possibilities do not now exist.

In other words, Irish studies was beginning to display gerontocratic tendencies, partly because of the rationalisation of the civil service under the Irish Free State and partly because of the clientelist and occasionally corrupt nature of the universities. It was also observed rather coldly by the Department that the universities in the country were predominantly undergraduate, and that there were actually no exclusively postgraduate professorships. To tackle this ambitious task of studying medieval and Old Irish, students needed instruction not only in Old Irish, but also in Latin and German. Best's reaction in 1936 was melancholic; he felt that the tradition of pure scholarship 'as an end in itself, pursued throughout life, not merely as a source of livelihood, is largely wanting [in Ireland].'[65] In December 1936 Best commented again on the deplorable state of Irish-language studies. Obvious texts were unavailable, classic works were out of print and no adequate grammars existed. 'This state of things is not creditable to the nation. It makes more difficult the teaching of Irish in the secondary schools and universities and keeps the standard of that teaching low as compared with other modern languages or the classics.'[66]

During 1936 Binchy also wrote a thoughtful piece on the situation and how it might be remedied.

> Assuming that Irish research can be efficiently organised and successfully prosecuted, what will be its effect on the Government's policy of restoring Irish as the spoken language of the people? It cannot be too strongly emphasised that no amount of research will of itself achieve this purpose. No language can be restored by scholarship and by scholarship alone. On the other hand given the conditions which alone can make the revival possible – namely a real and active desire for it on the part of the majority of the people – the task will be greatly facilitated by the labours of trained scholars. Scholars cannot create a new literature. That is up to poets, novelists and authors generally.[67]

The universities were a 'disappointment', but in the absence of grammars and reference books it was impossible to impart a scholarly knowledge of the language in the few short years a student attended a university. Furthermore, many of the politicised language activists were too busy quarrelling with each other to get down to the task of converting the nation to their ideas and their cause.

> Nor has the revival movement itself – with some eminent exceptions – made any significant contribution to the scientific study of Irish.

It has concentrated mainly on propaganda, and many of its leaders have been too busily engaged in exalting or depreciating one or other of the modern dialects to spare any interest in the classical language, a knowledge of which would have done much to reconcile their differences.

We must therefore face the fact that the scholarly study of Irish is still in its infancy. We propose that the Government should revive the School of Irish Learning but on a much vaster scale.[68]

There were other voices over the years expressing unease about the merits of some of the members of the Irish Studies Committee set up by Government. In January 1938 Thomas O'Rahilly wrote to Best expressing a lack of confidence in a committee 'which includes among its members certain meddlesome individuals who, in my opinion, owing to their lack of scholarly qualifications ought to have been debarred from membership.'[69] As a veteran of the civil service, he was perhaps unusually privy to Irish politicians' fondness for patronage. He wrote again to the same effect some months later. He was also uneasy about the new DIAS itself the following year. 'There is a grave danger that the new Institute may turn out to be a mere racket – a way of providing free motorcars and fat salaries for a number of people.'[70] Many scholars felt that the entire cultural revival programme was being penetrated by party politics and that this might in time lead to the ruin of the whole effort and its collapse. That these latter fears were, to quite an extent, accurate was to become even clearer in the fifties. However, the scholarly wing of the movement continued to be successful. After the war, an attempt was made by O'Rahilly to recruit a younger first-class scholar, Kenneth Jackson, an Englishman working in the United States. Muiris Mac Conghail, a well-known Irish scholar, described him many years later in terms worthy of the god Lugh Lámh-Fhada as 'Ioldánach', or 'all-skilled'.[71] Jackson sounded out Best on the DIAS, evidently being uneasy about Irish office politics.

Is there any question that the Institute might be wound up, or fail or go bankrupt or be ended by a change of government or the eventual death of de Valera?

Do you think it would be possible for me, as an Englishman and a protestant, or should I be exposed to continual hostility for those reasons both within and without the institute? Is a possible change of government to an extreme Nationalist one likely to cause my ejection? Not knowing who my colleagues would be, I wonder whether I should be likely to be acceptable to them? One hears garbled rumours of feuds etc., and I should not like to have to enter into them.[72]

Unfortunately wartime feelings of mistrust possibly deriving from Ireland's neutrality and a residual political bitterness impelled Jackson eventually to go to Edinburgh instead. However, it is also probable that O'Rahilly, with his pessimism and outspokenness, was hoist with his own petard, having lost a fine scholar partly because of his own noisily expressed unease about the DIAS. Despite all this negativity, the DIAS prospered, ironically in part because of the wrecking of Europe and European higher education along with the general catastrophe. After the war, however, no more subjects were added to the Institute as originally envisaged. Professor Robert Dudley Edwards of UCD's History Department fought in vain during the 1960s for an 'Irish Institute of Historical Studies, either inside or outside the Institute of Advanced Studies' but got nowhere.[73]

During the war years Binchy was certainly productive as usual. In 1941 he produced *Críth Gablach* (Branched Purchase), a pioneering study of the laws governing social mobility, such as it was, in medieval Ireland.[74] In part this was a successor to the pioneering work of Eugene O'Curry back in the 1860s. It was, however, a pioneering work itself in that it attempted to transcribe a particularly difficult and much miscopied medieval text. Because it was not part of the *Senchas Már* it had been historically somewhat neglected. Internal evidence suggested an Ulster or Meath origin. It was a tract on the law of persons. As Binchy suggests, ancient Irish law never asserted the Roman principle of a general equality before the law and the differences in rank in Irish society had a legal as well as an economic and social significance. Binchy felt that it gave a schematic and almost caricatured picture of the ancient ranking system in Irish society but it was known from other sources that many of the prescriptions in *Críth Gablach* did not actually apply in everyday reality.

It is in fact quite clear that the compiler is sketching a highly conventionalised order of society, a kind of ideal state, and his work, *si parva licet componere magnis*, recalls some features of Plato's *Laws*. CG should therefore be regarded as a theoretical construction, which, although built of genuine legal materials, bears only a very limited relation to the realities of legal life in ancient Ireland.[75]

The text provides rules for legal blood-feuding in the wake of the murder of a high-ranking person, rules against satirising or defamation and the weight to be given in court to the testimony of people of different rank. It also provides for generational delays in the achievement of noble status after the material acquisition of the requisite wealth in land, servitors, cattle and slaves. It offers a general picture of a highly stratified society which did, indeed, allow for movement upward from a previously humble status; much as in Roman society it was possible even for the descendants of freed slaves to achieve high status. Ancient Irish society was quite capable of change and indeed witnessed considerable change in its thousand years of (more or less) recorded history. Binchy had dreamed of writing a history of Irish law from the sixth to the sixteenth century. He reminisced years later:

…it did not take me long to discover [in the thirties] that this was an utterly vain hope.

You see, I had failed to realise the fundamental convention on which all this written work was based: the fiction of immutability. In the official doctrine of the [Gaelic law] schools the old derived text was like the law of the Medes and the Persians, which 'changeth not' … it was the timeless wisdom of the ancients.[76]

Many years later, while dissenting from Binchy's argument that the status system in *Críth Gablach* and *Uraicecht Becc* was partly imaginary, Timothy Powell was to comment that in an inspection of medieval Irish law tracts '… the scholar is given a picture of society, albeit somewhat fragmentary in places, that suggests an astonishing degree of legal sophistication.'[77]

During the war years Binchy and Bergin between them produced a translation of Rudolf Thurneysen's gargantuan *A Grammar of Old Irish* from the original German.[78] The translation and revision had originally been embarked upon by the Department of Education, but after Thurneysen's death the civil servants offered it in uncompleted galley form to the new DIAS, which accepted the task quite readily. Binchy also found time to write a very complimentary review of James Meenan's *The Italian Corporate State* in 1944. Meenan covered much the same ground as Binchy's work of 1941, but with far more emphasis on the institutional structures of Italian fascism. The current fashion for vocationalism in Catholic Ireland prompted Meenan's study.

Notes

1   Sean O'Faolain, *Vive Moi!*, London: Rupert Hart-Davis, 1965, p.269.
2   Frank O'Connor, *My Father's Son*, London: Pan Books, 1971 (first published 1968), p.79.
3   Oliver St. John Gogarty, *Rolling Down the Lea*, London, Constable, 1950, p.116.
4   O'Connor, *My Father's Son*, p.80; John Garvin, conversations, 1970s.
5   Seán O Coileáin, 'Obituary of R. A. Breathnach' *Eigse*, Vol. 33, 2002, pp.229–232.
6   Ibid.
7   See O'Connor, *My Father's Son*, pp.88–89.
8   Warwick Gould, John Kelly and Deirdre Toomey (eds.), *The Collected letters of W. B. Yeats*, Vol. II, p.452, 25 September, 1899.
9   See O'Faolain, *Vive Moi*, pp.275–276.
10 George Plimpton (ed.), *Writers at Work*, London: Penguin, 1985, p.35.
11 Ibid., p.42.
12 NLI MS 11,000 (12), Richard Best Papers, 16 March 1934.
13 Daniel A. Binchy, *Sick-Maintenance in Irish Law*, Oxford: Oxford University Press, 1934; *Bretha Crólige*, Dublin: Offprint 1934; *Eriu*, Vol XII, Part 1, 1938, *Bretha Crólige*, pp.1–77; *Sick-Maintenance in Irish Law*, pp.78–134. See also Liam Breatnach, 'The Early Irish Law Text *Senchas Már* and the Question of its Date', Cambridge: the University, 2011.
14 See *Bretha Crólige, Eriu* version, pp.11–13.
15 Fergus Kelly, *A Guide to Early Irish Law*, Dublin: Institute for Advanced Studies, 1988, pp.214–224, 231.
16 Donnchadh O Corráin, Liam Breatnach and Aidan Breen, 'The Laws of the Irish,' *Peritia*, Vol. 3 (1984), pp.382–438.
17 See *Bretha Crólige*, p.35, sections 43, 44 of the MS.
18 See *Sick-Maintenance in Irish Law, Eriu* version, p.78.
19 Ibid., p.107.
20 Ibid., p.87.

21 Ibid., p.101.
22 Ibid., p.105.
23 Eoin MacNeill, Review of Bretha Crólige, *Studies*, Vol. XXIII, 1934, pp.709–711.
24 D. A. Binchy, 'President de Valera and the Senate,' in J. G. Douglas, *Speeches of Senator J. G. Douglas*, Dublin: Pamphlet, 1934, pp.1–22.
25 D. A, Binchy, Review of 'Two Blasket Autobiographies', *Studies*, Vol. XXIII, 1934, pp.545–58.
26 Donnchadh O Corráin, interview, 2 July 2014.
27 D. A. Binchy, 'Comment' on an article by Michael Tierney, *Studies*, Vol. XXIV (1935), pp.20–25.
28 NLI MS 1065/14/5, Frank MacDermot Papers.
29 'Proposals for a New Senate', *Studies*, Vol. XXV, 1936, pp.20–32, quote from p.21. On this controversy, see Tom Garvin, *The Irish Senate*, Dublin, Institute for Public Administration, 1969, pp.1–5.
30 Review of Donal O'Sullivan, *The Irish Free State and its Senate*, *The Bell*, Vol. 1, No.5, December 1940, pp.81–5.
31 M. O'Driscoll, *Ireland, Germany and the Nazis: Politics and Diplomacy 1919-1939*, Dublin: Four Courts Press, p.283.
32 Liam Breatnach, interview, 15 July 2014.
33 Daniel A. Binchy, 'Pope Pius XI', *Studies*, Vol. XXVIII, 1939, pp.1–12.
34 See Binchy, 'Pope Pius XI', p.6.
35 Daniel A. Binchy, 'The Papacy in a Changing World', Review Article, *Studies*, 1937, pp.641–647, quote from p.642.
36 Ibid., p.645
37 Daniel A. Binchy, '*Aimser Chue*', *Féil-Scríbhinn Eoin Mhic Néill, Ath Cliath*: 1940, pp.18–22.
38 D. A. Binchy, *Church and State in Fascist Italy*, Oxford: Oxford University Press, 1941.
39 Ibid., p.85.
40 Ibid., pp.102–103.
41 Ibid., quote at p.143; on Freemasonry, see pp.143–7.
42 Ibid., pp.162–3.
43 Ibid., pp.165–6.
44 Ibid., pp.194–5.
45 Ibid., pp.417–18.
46 Ibid., pp.239–40.
47 Ibid., p.302.
48 Ibid., p.329.
49 Ibid., pp.603–4.
50 Edward J. Coyne, 'Review' of *Church and State in Fascist Italy*, *Studies*, Vol XXX, 1941, pp.604–608.
51 James Matthews, *Voices: A Life of Frank O'Connor*, Dublin: Gill and Macmillan, 1983, pp.188–191.

52   Donnchadh Ó Corráin, interview, 28 June 2014.

53   Helen Burke née Binchy, interview, 11 July 2014.

54   AD UCD/P150/2609, de Valera Papers, 1936.

55   AD UCD /P150/2609, de Valera Papers, April 1 1938.

56   AD UCD/P150/2609, de Valera Papers, 4 May 1938.

57   AD UCD P150/2609, de Valera Papers, 25 May 1938.

58   Jean Medawar and David Pyke, *Hitler's Gift*, London: Piatkus, 2000, pp.72–3, 78.

59   AD UCD/P150/2609, de Valera Papers, 7 December 1942.

60   NLI MS 11,000 (3) Richard Best Papers, 8 October 1940.

61   NLI MS 11,001 (9) Richard Best Papers, 30 October 1940.

62   AD UCD P7b/106 (118) Richard Mulcahy Papers, 4 June 1943. I am indebted to Michael Laffan for this reference.

63   Daniel A. Binchy, *The Linguistic and Historical Value of the Irish Law Tracts*, London: Milford, 1943.

64   NLI MS 11,005 (1) Richard Best Papers, general description of file.

65   NLI MS 11,005 (1) Richard Best Papers, 15 October 1936; 28 October 1936.

66   NLI MS 11,005 (1) Richard Best Papers, 16 December 1936.

67   NLI MS 11,005 (3) Richard Best Papers, Daniel A. Binchy on Irish Studies: 'Review of Situation', 1936.

68   NLI MS 11,005 (3) Richard Best Papers, Daniel A. Binchy on Irish Studies: 'Review of Situation', 1936.

69   NLI MS (4) Richard Best Papers, 11 January 1938.

70   NLI MS 11,005 (4) Richard Best Papers, 2 April 1939.

71   Muiris Mac Congail, '*Máistir Léinn a Rinne*', *Irish Times*, 18 March 1991.

72   NLI MS 11,001 (16) Richard Best Papers, 17 November 1946.

73   David Quinn, Obituary of Robert Dudley Edwards, *Analecta Hibernica*, No. 35, Dublin: Irish Manuscripts Commission, 1992, pp.v-ix, quote at p.vii.

74   Daniel A. Binchy, *Críth Gablach*, Dublin: DIAS, 1970 (first published Dublin, Stationery Office, 1941).

75   *Críth Gablach*, p.xix.

76   Daniel A. Binchy, 'Lawyers and Chroniclers', in Brian O Cuiv (ed.), *Seven Centuries of Irish Learning, 1000–1700*, Dublin: Stationery Office, 1961, pp.58–71, quote on pp.61–62.

77   Timothy E. Powell, 'The Idea of the Lower Orders of Society and Social Stratification in Early Medieval Ireland', *Irish Historical Studies*, XXIX, November 1995, pp.475–89, quote at p.475.

78   R. Thurneysen, *A Grammar of Old Irish* Dublin: DIAS 2010 (first published in English, Dublin: DIAS 1946).

CHAPTER FOUR

SECLUSION AND
SCHOLARSHIP, 1942–1980

In 1946, while still at the Dublin Institute for Advanced Studies, Thomas O'Rahilly published his monumental account of Irish prehistory up to the coming of Christianity in the fifth century and the slow beginnings of a recorded Irish history. *Early Irish History and Mythology*, the fruit of years of work, was of an extraordinary length and contained many fascinating studies, particularly perhaps his analysis of classical geographers' descriptions of prehistoric Ireland.[1] Binchy was quietly doubtful about some of the argumentation. Amidst the volcanic energy of the study, its brilliance and its insights, there was also a fair amount of empirically ungrounded imagination. It contained a suspiciously detailed account of various tribal invasions of Ireland culminating in the 'Goidelic invasion' of the island some centuries before Christ. O'Rahilly also famously suggested that parts of Ireland had housed tribal groups that had, at one stage, spoken a British Celtic dialect, P-Celtic rather than Q-Celtic. Much of his sometimes over-imaginative argumentation of 1946, as if to validate Binchy's assessment, has been dismissed or refuted in detail since then.

It would be wrong to dismiss all of O'Rahilly's work in *Early Irish History and Mythology*, however. Luigi Luca Cavalli-Sforza argued in 2001 that there was a division among archaeologists and cultural prehistorians as to whether migrating farmers in prehistoric Europe brought agricultural and other skills with them by migration or 'invasion' or was it only the knowledge and technology of farming that spread: 'demic' diffusion versus cultural diffusion. Demic theories of migration of peoples were fashionable before the Second World War, and partly for political reasons of a modern kind, these were replaced largely by cultural theories of diffusion of ideas after the war. Warriors and tribes on the move, led by warrior kings, were replaced in the academic imagination by merchants like Pythias, storytellers and stonemasons visiting remote shores and leaving valuable objects such as tools, innovative ideas and skills behind them. The latter set of ideas tended to become dogma, particularly in the English-speaking world. The tide began to turn again with the work of Colin Renfrew, Cavalli-Sforza and his colleagues, the growth of DNA studies and the use of modern fast computers for principal components statistical analysis of both linguistic and biological data. Their mainly genetic evidence was cumulatively sympathetic to the demic hypothesis; cultural and technological change in Europe was to be associated with large movements of people in search of new land to farm as population growth pushed them out of settled land into more sparsely inhabited areas. The general direction over the last 10,000 years tended to be a slow movement, with some counter currents, from the south-east to the north-west.[2] Back in the 1940s, invasion, migration or 'demic' ideas were very much out of fashion, and O'Rahilly was sailing against the winds of opinion of the time.

Of the book in general, Bergin wrote a genial, complimentary and devastating review in 1949–50, which was not published until both O'Rahilly and Bergin had died. Bergin died in 1950, O'Rahilly in 1953, having retired from the DIAS in murky circumstances in 1950.[3] Binchy edited the review quietly for eventual publication in 1957 in *Irish Historical Studies*. Bergin had written:

> This is a great book. For more than thirty years the author has enjoyed the well-deserved reputation of being the leading authority on the language and literature of Ireland from the early modern period to the present day. Not content with this, however, it is clear that, without forsaking his old love, he has devoted more and more attention to the problems of pre-Christian Ireland, its people, languages and beliefs.[4]

According to Bergin, the volume was 'imposing'. O'Rahilly, Bergin wrote, had read an enormous amount in Irish, English, French and German. Parenthetically, it has been alleged that O'Rahilly could not read German. The book was an admirable compendium of information, but many of the author's conclusions were arguable. The probable fact that Ptolemy's famous map dated from information garnered in the fourth century BC and did not mention the Lagin or Goidels was taken by O'Rahilly to indicate that

130

the Gaels and/or Leinstermen had not yet moved in on the Green Isle. To myself, as an amateur, this appears thin evidence of anything; absence of evidence is not evidence of absence, but neither is it evidence of anything. However, Bergin continued:

> In the *Liber Hymnorum* the Irish are said to have worshipped demons, and elsewhere the pagan deities are identified as fallen angels. But the view that finally prevailed among the learned, and was firmly believed by Irish scholars down to the seventeenth century, was that these deities were really ancient kings and queens whose reigns could be dated after the lapse of thousands of years. Meanwhile in folk belief some of them have been reduced to the rank of 'fairies'.

> Since the year 1880 there has been progress in the study of comparative mythology and folklore, and in the editing of Early Irish texts. Disregarding Atkinson's pessimistic outlook, a number of scholars have endeavoured to solve what he held to be insoluble. Dr. O'Rahilly has investigated the theories of almost all writers who have discussed Celtic mythology and found all wanting. Like Homer's Teiresias in the world of the dead, 'he alone has stedfast wits; the rest are fleeting shades'.[5]

Bergin asked the reader to imagine if early Greek literature had perished leaving only fragments of Homer's *Iliad*, how would moderns be able to restore the 'charming figure' of Hector's wife Andromache. 'We can imagine a professor in Texas arguing that *Andromache* obviously means "slayer of men"'. She was therefore a goddess, and Hector, therefore, became a doublet of Zeus, our imaginary professor might have concluded. Bergin went on to object to O'Rahilly's aggressive style of argument and concluded:

> He would do well also to tone down the needless asperity of his comments on his fellow workers past and present. No doubt they were often inaccurate. And he had many models. The *odium philologium* displayed by great scholars of the past is notorious. But there is a more excellent way of indicating the heights to which he has climbed, often upon the shoulders of others. Even Dr. O'Rahilly has, as he

131

frankly admits, changed his views on some important points. In one case (p. 208) he oddly combines this with an attack on the readers who accepted the view he has now discarded – a form of palinode which seems unique in the history of scholarship. Continued railing is not the way to attract or convince. It awakens in the reader's mind the suspicion that (to those who meet him) it may be as dangerous to agree with him as to contradict him and the more cautious will be tempted to keep, as it were, on the other side of the road and simply ignore him. That would be a calamity, for his work marks an epoch in the study of Early Irish history and mythology. Like the Irish poets, I end as I began – this is a great book.[6]

Bergin's interestingly balanced review appeared too late to modify some people's hostile and dismissive reactions. Paul Grosjean SJ reported himself to be unimpressed by O'Rahilly's tome in 1951. Grosjean, a well-respected Celticist and Church historian in his own right, writing from a liberated Belgium and having spent a fair amount of time in a Nazi prison, had evidently lost none of his tart sense of humour when he wrote to Best in 1951 (in French as usual; my translation):

You have given me news also of the communication made by Aubrey Gwynn on Patrick, bishop of Dublin; a word on Bieler's brilliant career and an entire page, worthy of appearing in an anthology of your writings, on T. F. O'Rahilly … this man is assuredly capable of dropping an atomic bomb on the lot of us, but for the moment he would do well to dedicate his activity to running away on all fours; he has provoked three or four chain reactions which could easily blow up his entire laboratory and himself with it. The redoubtable Pokorny is busily correcting the proofs of a series of reflections on the etymologies contained in *Early Irish History and Mistology* [sic]. I'm not sure if this is to be explosive; it might just be laughing gas.[7]

The book received some genial and sympathetic reactions also, and actually became a semi-popular success among amateurs in Ireland because of its direct and easily read style. Strangely, O'Rahilly, despite his pretty conspicuous presence, always seems to have escaped the almost savage wit of Binchy's criticism; there must have been an underlying respect and liking there. Certainly Binchy had great respect for O'Rahilly's linguistic abilities.

Daniel had been awarded a Senior Fellowship in Corpus Christi College, Oxford, in 1946, presumably in part as a reward for his 'war work' on Italy, but of course mainly for his scholarly investigations. Paul Grosjean had predicted an Oxford award in a letter to Best in August 1945. 'The way you speak to me of Binchy convinces me that he is going to be nominated to Oxford and that the deed is already done. I'd like to be sure of it. Please do not neglect to transmit to him my congratulations and to wish him on my behalf a brilliant career in that very Welsh [*gallois*] milieu of Jesus College.'[8]

Daniel thus was out of the way in England for most of the O'Rahilly hullabaloo, seen by many at the time as a storm in a Celtic chalice. It is on this occasion that he announced his intention to write a fully edited transcript of all early Irish law manuscripts, a monumental task that he spent the next thirty years on, it finally seeing the light as the *Corpus Iuris Hibernici* in the late seventies in seven immense volumes. When asked how he would like the volumes bound, his tart humour asserted itself. 'I would like it bound in the hide of Robin Dudley Edwards, the thickest and most impenetrable hide in Ireland.'[9] Edwards, quite a warrior with words himself, would almost certainly have been delighted by the remark. The central idea of this thirty-year-long project was to complete the job commenced in a relatively amateur way by O'Donovan and O'Curry a century earlier. This almost Sysiphean task was to involve thousands of hours checking ambiguities in scripts, expanding abbreviations and being familiar with many different dialects of written Irish as the language changed over ten centuries. On top of this, medieval Latin was obligatory. He had also to be familiar with legal and philosophical concepts and social outlooks incomprehensible to modern-day Irish people. In effect he was reconstructing the sociology and institutions of a dead, half-forgotten and ridiculously romanticised civilisation, whose real and imagined features had long been caricatured and travestied for both nationalist and unionist political purposes. It was in connection with this project that, in 1943, he had published a short 'book' or rather a long article, *The Linguistic and Historical Value of the Irish Law Tracts*, a kind of declaration of intent of future work.[10] This was a version of a lecture he gave in England in the same year on which he commented, 'Few came to my lecture except a few old girl friends.'[11] Some years later, in 1955, he wrote a more elaborate declaration. It was, he wrote, a century since O'Donovan and O'Curry had transcribed and translated the principal Irish legal MSS as *The Ancient Laws of Ireland*. It had dated badly, in part owing to the great scientific work of Thurneysen, and Binchy was resolved to re-edit the lot, which he felt, prophetically, would take a quarter of a century. The law tracts, many of them dating back to the seventh century and many more having a provenance as late as the sixteenth century, presented a fairly intimidating task. He had evidently commenced this gargantuan task back in the thirties.[12]

Frank O'Connor visited him in Oxford in March 1948. De Valera's Fianna Fáil had been defeated in a general election in February after sixteen years in government and a government led by Fine Gael was now in power, radical republicans and liberals led by Sean MacBride shared power with old Free Staters, hatchets were being buried and change seemed to be in the air. The new Coalition government appeared to be relatively free of the geriatric tendencies which were increasingly evident within Fianna Fáil. Binchy and Myles Dillon were the two resident Irish Celticists in Oxford at the time. Binchy was residing fairly regally in quarters which once had been inhabited by Ruskin, which impressed O'Connor, but seemed to signify little to Binchy's austere soul. It seems to have been during this visit that O'Connor, a much-married man, asked Binchy during a late-night drinking session, why he never had married. 'Dan Binchy, why did you never get married?' The two old friends had had a few but Binchy apparently poured out a story that sobered O'Connor up a bit, a tragic account of the love of his life. Binchy was well aware of O'Connor's propensity to transform real-life experiences of other people into stories, and made the writer promise not to transform it into a story until both of them were over seventy.[13] O'Connor was never to achieve that age, but he had come to know a very private man as no one else did. Apparently the tale, whatever it was, impressed him mightily and haunted him for years. As far as I know, O'Connor never wrote the story. Years later, Michael O'Donovan/Frank O'Connor was seriously ill and dying in 1965 when, as James Matthews reports:

On Tuesday Michael was at Trinity again to attend a lecture by Dan Binchy. By now he could hardly walk, but he felt he could not let him down. Only the week before, in the course of conversation Michael jokingly asked Binchy how old he was. All the years he had kept his promise, not to write the story of Binchy's tragic love affair until Binchy was seventy, though it had haunted him as few others had ever done. Every poignant detail still resonated in O'Connor's imagination.[14]

Post-war *Accidie*

In 1945 Binchy published a highly enthusiastic review of Robin Flower's lyrical essay, *The Western Island*, in *Studies*. The review reflects a certain frustration or pessimism which seems to have come upon him during the war years, a dislike of the authoritarianism, intellectual isolationism and smugness that, in his view, had characterised neutral Ireland. He sensed that the entire cultural revival had run into deep trouble; many others were to come to agree with him over the next decades. In the review, he commented:

> I know of no work that gives so faithful a picture of the Gaeltacht and its people. Those who are without Irish will find in it the testament of an ancient culture from which the 'otherness' of Ireland ultimately springs. And even those who have been surfeited by a leaden diet of 'compulsory Irish' will, if they read this book, discover that the language, in its natural environment, is something vastly different from the dreary grind of their schooldays.[15]

Somewhat later, in the course of a review of a book on Scottish educational policy, he made a public sideswipe at the Irish linguistic revival programme. 'Our rulers – or should I say their catastrophic advisers? – have all along based their policy on the assumption that Gaelic is still the native language of the Irish people.'[16] This self-evident observation generated rage among Gaelic League nationalists, committed as they were to an opinion, apparently first expressed by Douglas Hyde in the 1890s, that Irish people were naturally Irish-speaking and their habitual speaking in

135

English was for them an unnatural act. In Scotland, where no such curious assumption prevailed, the language was far healthier in its native habitat than it was in Ireland where the language movement was being ruined by a doctrinal orthodoxy of surreal absurdity, he claimed with some asperity. This absurdity was enforced by government in the form of a bureaucratic Department of Education which refused to recruit its officials at graduate level. The Irish Department of Education disliked education; it made you independent-minded.

A similar half-concealed pessimism surfaced in a little article, '*Sé Cuisle na hEigse Cuisle na Tíre*' (The Pulse of Literary Heritage is the Pulse of the Country), which he wrote in lively Kerry Irish under his invented Irish name 'Domhnall O Bínnse' for his old school's annual magazine, *The Clongownian*, in 1947. In it he expressed some doubts about the future of the revival. He started by stating that literary heritage is the memory of the human race, and without it our language will die. He continued (in my translation):

> It is true that there is some Gaelic poetry [written nowadays], but the standard is not very high and as for [general] writing there is no book worth reading except for *The Islandman* and one or two others at best. By contrast, English writing is enormous, so much so that other countries want to read it … It will last hundreds of years. What a difference there is between them – one language almost dead while the other is under full sail and getting stronger all the time! And there is one cause for it – literature in English is strong and there is an absence of such strength in Irish.[17]

At about the same time he gave a friendly review to Myles Dillon's elegant book, *The Cycles of the Kings*, expressing similar pessimistic sentiments.

> I take leave to doubt whether the common reader will find the fare very stimulating. But for this Professor Dillon is in no way to blame; his translations and summaries are admirably done. The fault lies rather with the originals. And this prompts a final question: with respect to our neo-Gaelic enthusiasts, how much of Irish literature is worth reading for its own sake?[18]

His scepticism about the proposed revival of the Irish language as the usual spoken language of the people was not new. As early as 1938 he had commented rather philosophically in the *Studies* discussion about O'Faolain's *King of the Beggars* as reviewed by Michael Tierney:

> Ireland has remained in substance what O'Connell made her and continues to move along the lines which he laid down for her. He bade her speak the English tongue, and the victorious progress of that tongue is even to-day overwhelming the last feeble strongholds of the older language. He bade her think in terms of political and economic nationalism, and she has obeyed him but too well. No better instance could be found than in the career of the movement for the revival of Irish, which, in its origins a reaction against O'Connell's neglect of cultural nationalism, has eventually become political in the worst sense of the word, operating entirely with the weapons and the methods of political agitation. The very measure of the success which Professor Tierney ascribes to the Gaelic League in revolutionary politics is the measure of its abject failure to achieve the purpose for which it was called into being. It was far less trouble to create a revolution than to restore Irish, and so a stream that should have been kept aloof from and uncontaminated by political strife was mingled almost from its source by the turbid waters of Irish political nationalism.[19]

His more recent comments had, however, a more exasperated, impatient and even contemptuous tone. Myles Dillon noticed this *accidie* coming over Daniel in personal relationships. In late 1946, in Ireland between jobs in America and Scotland, he noticed an uncharacteristically anti-social mood in his old colleague. He wrote to Best:

> What you say of Binchy interests me. I saw more of him during those gloomy months in Ireland than of any other of my friends, and he was unfailing in hospitality and in help of various kinds; but he grows more angry with Ireland and the Irish. I agree with him in most things, but I have been as far removed [in America] that I feel less passionately about them. His devotion to Bergin is now almost his

only tie, and Bergin is a recluse too. From his letter I seemed to sense disappointment with Oxford, but I should be interested to hear what he has to say in conversation.[20]

A new waspishness occasionally manifested itself under his usually very controlled learned commentaries. In 1946 R. A. S. Macalister, a well-known Irish archaeologist, produced a large study of Celtic inscriptions on stone in the British Isles. Binchy reviewed it for *The Journal of the Royal Society for Antiquities in Ireland* in 1946.[21] In the course of a generally complimentary review he suggested, among other things, that Macalister did not know his Old Irish declensions. With regard to the derivation of the Ogham alphabet, he quoted disapprovingly Macalister's blunt and apparently unsubstantiated claim 'there is one alphabet, *and one only*,' which could have provided the background of the Ogham characters: 'the Chalcidic form of the Greek alphabet once current in Northern Italy'. This well-known, and apparently eccentric, view of Macalister's was not shared by two distinguished non-Irish experts, Carl Marstrander and Rudolf Thurneysen. Marstrander had made a strong case for the Runic script as the basis of Ogham, while Thurneysen had favoured the Latin alphabet. Macalister had ignored their arguments, and was possibly unaware of them. Binchy remarked, 'Dr. Macalister may not accept these theories, but this hardly dispenses him from at least attempting to refute them.' He then went on to give a rather funny example of the kind of highly colourful explanation Macalister was fond of and famous for.

> In attempting to solve the more obscure ciphers the author suffers from, if anything, an excess of ingenuity. The most famous example is the Colbinstown stone (No. 19), where by an elaborate process of translation, inversion, and re-transliteration he finally produces an Ogham inscription. But this solution, which had already appeared in print, has been described by Thurneysen (in general the most restrained of critics) as 'fantastic'.[22]

Apparently this ancient stone with Irish inscriptions on it had been defaced by something at a height coincident with the hubs of modern farmers' cartwheels. This broadside provoked an angry rejoinder from the older man, to which Binchy in turn retorted: 'Quarrelling with his reviewers is rapidly becoming a pastime with Dr. Macalister; the pages of Irish journals are strewn with his rejoinders and remonstrances.' When many disagree with him, Binchy observed, Macalister remains obdurate in his opinions. 'Here again, as in so many other matters connected with Irish studies, Dr. Macalister is *Athanasius contra mundum.*' He finished by directly questioning the older man's competence in the Irish language.[23] Macalister died in 1950. Binchy had another, posthumous and rather devastating, swipe at the old man's shade in 1952.[24] It may be no coincidence that Binchy's attacks on Macalister commenced in 1946, a year after MacNeill's death. Perhaps MacNeill had had a hand in restraining Binchy; Macalister was an old friend of MacNeill's and the latter had a long history of defending Macalister from the linguists in the academic movement. MacNeill was aware that language was Macalister's weak point; however, his point of view was that, as an archaeologist, Macalister was to be valued and encouraged.

Binchy moved back to Ireland from Oxford in 1950, and took up a Professorship at the DIAS. Perhaps his years in Oxford had sharpened his tongue, for he apparently now saw rampant amateurism all around him in Irish academia. In his eyes this amateurism was accompanied by a propensity to take advantage of the obscurity of the subject matter to retreat from scientific enquiry into oracular proclamation commonly unsupported by real evidence. His old intellectual enemy, non-scientific carelessness, had prospered in Ireland.

Even Thurneysen, his adored old mentor, who had died in 1940, did not escape his eagle eye completely. In 1952 he redated the old master's estimates of chronological position of a medieval manuscript on linguistic grounds back from the eleventh century to the eighth. This was *Eachtra Fergusa maic Léti*, a strange narrative involving an early king of Ulster, a drowning and rebirth among other rather odd things. He critiqued Thurneysen's ascription of authorship.

> I shall endeavour to show by linguistic evidence (1) that Thurneysen's date for the composition of the prose saga is at least three centuries too late; (2) that the ancient poem itself contains a summary of the main events of the saga, which accordingly was not the invention of

THE LIVES OF DANIEL BINCHY

'imaginative' commentators but an early and authentic member of the Ulidian cycle.[25]

However, he also relented a few years later. In a short article in 1958 he agreed with the old Swiss scholar about the probable date and provenance of what he had once thought of, following MacNeill, as a chunk, possibly a general introduction, to the *Senchas Már*. The *Uraicecht Becc*, 'Small Primer' he, like Thurneysen, allocated to the seventh century, rather than the previously consensual eleventh.[26] The latter date would have tied in with Brian Boroimhe, the eleventh-century king of the Dal Cais and victor at Clontarf in 1014. It would also have been supportive of a belief in the reality of a High-King Tara-based Irish state, and the ideas of Eoin MacNeill. Binchy was now sceptical about any such power centre; to an extent, this scepticism was itself actually a heretical political opinion in the hyper-nationalist Ireland of the time. Binchy admitted he was wrong to suggest that the text was part of the *Senchas*; he now concluded it was a fragment of an older legal corpus. In an appendix to the article he tacked on an almost casual remark:

> Incidentally, the four-fold classification, with the 'king of Ireland' at the apex, which some modern historians ascribe to the traditional law, is quite unknown to the [ancient] jurists; its origin is to be sought rather in the works of [P. W.] Joyce and [Eoin] MacNeill, as I hope to show in a future article.[27]

He went a little further. In 1958 he also published 'The Fair of Táiltiú and the Feast of Tara', in which he argued bluntly that The High-King's sovereignty over the other provincial kings was a fiction invented by the 'synthetic' historians of the O'Neills in the seventh and eighth centuries for political purposes.[28] This was a frontal attack on the intellectual legacy of Eoin MacNeill and the nationalist fantasy of a Gaelic polity peddled by patriots like Pearse in the pages of *An Claidheamh Soluis*, the Gaelic League organ, and other little patriotic magazines in the years before 1914. MacNeill, like so many of the others, had always believed in the antiquity and political authority of the Tara monarchy. Binchy stated in what some would see as an act of intellectual parricide:

In Oenach Tailten we have been dealing with a genuine historical institution whose extent and significance were grossly exaggerated in later legend. In the Feast of Tara, on the other hand, we are confronted with a primitive ritual which, some centuries after its disappearance, was resurrected by the pseudo-historians in a totally different guise. Indeed, the transformation of this archaic ceremony into a respectable institution of the 'central monarchy' is perhaps the most striking metamorphosis effected by the professional mythmakers.[29]

He had a particular go at Geoffrey Keating, the early-seventeenth-century 'pseudo-historian,' author of that highly entertaining book *Foras feasa ar Éirinn*, as the source used rather too eagerly by certain modern nationalist ideologues. He went further: 'But would it not be well first to examine the few contemporary records of the Feast in genuine historical documents and see how far (if at all) these can be reconciled with the later romantic tales in which Keating placed such childlike trust?'[30] The Feast of Tara, he claimed aggressively, was 'an archaic fertility rite of a type associated with primitive kingship the world over.'[31] Binchy concluded by reiterating:

To sum up then: the historical Feast of Tara was a primitive fertility rite culminating in the apotheosis of the sacred king. It was last held by Diarmait Mac Cerbaill in 560, after which it was discarded as a relic of paganism. More than three centuries later, however, the pseudo-historians resurrected it in the form of a 'constitutional organ' of the 'high-kingship', and we can trace the expansion of the legendary Feast of Tara until by Keating's day it has eclipsed the [authentic] Fair of Tailtiu in importance and become the equivalent of a 'national assembly' or 'Parliament.' In this strange guise it continues to haunt our textbooks and examination papers.[32]

This repetitive creation of an imaginary all-Ireland early medieval polity with representative institutions went on from the tenth to the seventeenth centuries. It became a satisfying story for those who disliked the Norman and English takeover of the island and who bristled at English and Scottish representations of the Irish as savages who had to be civilised by forces from the larger island; English law was needed for the lesser breeds. For similar political purposes this imagined polity was resurrected in the late nineteenth century by the Gaelic League and Sinn Féin. It certainly surfaced in the *Claidheamh Soluis* in the early years of the twentieth century, and even the inchoate scribblings of the Provisional IRA in the 1970s expressed vague notions about restoring something like the federal political organisation of a fantasised medieval polity. However, despite its doubtful history, the proposition that a developed Irish state was long in existence before the Anglo-Norman invasion lives on. In 1995, Bart Jaski argued '[In the late eighth century the] ... main political division in this period was between Leth Cuinn and Leth Moga, the spheres of influence of the kings of Tara and Cashel respectively.' However, he admitted that the title 'King of Ireland' reflected a person's achievements and often represented 'a claim rather than a measure of actual political domination'. In the ninth century, he points out, Máel Sechlann briefly dominated the entire island; thus an all-Ireland high-kingship was becoming gradually feasible in a way it had not been previously. Here he follows an argument of Binchy's, to the effect that the Vikings had had a modernising or 'developmental' impact on Gaelic society.[33]

During the 1950s Binchy spent a fair amount of time abroad. He was Visiting Professor at Harvard in 1954, he spent some time at the University of Wales, and was also a Lowell Scholar in Boston for a time.[34] His international reputation was now formidable. At Harvard he met Alfred North Whitehead and was inspired by him to write a little piece on the importance of education in topics of no practical utility. Uselessness concentrated the student's mind on the pure activity of learning and understanding without the distraction of utilitarian purpose.[35]

In 1958, Binchy gave a Thomas Davis lecture on Irish radio in which he summarised the results of his researches into ancient law at that date. He reminisced about his high hopes as a young man of discovering much about its historical development and the evolution of ancient Irish society from the legal commentaries. He realised, however, that the medieval commentators themselves commonly misunderstood the meaning of the texts.

> In medieval Ireland the lawyers owed much of their prestige to the fact that they were the custodians of ancient wisdom, and they

naturally made great play with their archaic texts, being well aware that the layman would never guess how limited was their knowledge of these texts.[36]

Thus, from the sociological point of view, the law texts had been something of a disappointment. On the other hand, Ireland was fortunate in that the chroniclers were far more successful than the lawyers in transmitting to posterity the narratives of their times and their own pasts. The Annals of the various provinces and districts were extraordinarily rich in incident and datings from the twelfth century on. The rise of the chroniclers was part of a general slow transformation of Irish society which was to culminate in the extinction of the Gaelic order in Ireland in the seventeenth century. The chroniclers were themselves a successful imported tradition, a pattern that has often been seen in Ireland: 'To put it very briefly, the lawyers represented an indigenous profession, the chroniclers an imported one.'[37] In this case, the conduit was mainly the Catholic Church and its religious orders, coming in from England and the continental mainland. The impact of outside forces on Irish society was a general theme of his thought, and in 1959 he published an elegant short article, 'The Passing of the Old Order', in which he argued succinctly that the Norse raids had forced a certain rather sluggish but detectable modernisation on Gaelic society. In particular, warfare, which had long been ritualised, began to become a serious and professionalised activity because of the military prowess of the Viking raiders. Of course, the towns of Ireland were essentially a Viking importation as well.[38] Tribal kingdoms began to take on a certain institutional solidity. However, the kingship of Brian in the early eleventh century had failed to produce an Irish state. Certainly Binchy was removing what he saw as the mythological features from traditional Irish historiography with a vengeance, presumably much to the irritation of many.

Many commentators both of the time and later on have noticed a mood of disappointment or disillusionment in the post-war Ireland of the late 1940s, not least of these W. J. Maloney, a correspondent of Eleanor Knott, who wrote to her from England in early 1947 offering an ironic explanation for a certain cultural decay in Ireland: mass education. 'When I was a boy in Ireland intent on the study of Gaelic I collected poems and long tales – never varied in the telling – from the illiterate peasants of Clare. Their literate children had no culture whatever.'[39] Ten years later he wrote off the entire linguistic revival in a similar vein:

> I agree with you about the sad state into which Irish has fallen among people who have no delight in idiom. I shudder at some of the official Irish I see from time to time and am sorry for the poor children who have to learn it at school. The movement for the revival of Irish got into the wrong hands at an early date. I think of those people I used to see in Dublin in my early days with a 'Fáinne' in their buttonholes and hardly a word of Irish in their heads. Patriotism is not enough as Edith Cavell said in another context.[40]

Binchy was sympathetic to this point of view, as was his old friend Frank O'Connor. As early as 1934, Binchy had sensed this desertion.

> The new generation has turned its back upon the rich storehouse from which the language of the old people drew its savour and its strength, the folk-tales handed down from generation to generation around the kitchen fire. Nowadays let one of the seniors begin a story, and in a flash the kitchen is emptied of the entire youthful population.[41]

This apathy, or even secret hostility, of the population made the minority who were sympathetic to revival more impassioned. During the winter of 1958–59 Binchy developed the habit of visiting O'Connor every Sunday at eleven o'clock in the morning at his apartment in Mespil Flats just off Upper Leeson Street and not too far from the house of Eoin MacNeill's descendants and Richard Best's old residence. This was reportedly in part to let his housekeeper think he had gone to Mass, but it suited both him and O'Connor. O'Connor was resolved to learn old Irish and, typically, threw himself into it as though it were the most important thing in the world. Binchy was delighted to teach him, much as Bergin had taught himself a generation earlier.[42] It is not clear how much Old or Middle Irish O'Connor actually learned, but it is clear that Binchy was almost intimidated by his enthusiasm and energy.

Patricks and Paddies

An old academic controversy blew up again in the 1950s and 1960s. St Patrick had been a cult figure in Ireland and elsewhere for centuries. He became a bone of contention between Catholics and Protestants, each side claiming him as the father figure. At a time when only Protestant churches were permitted to have steeples, the Dublin blind rhymester Zozimus sang in the early nineteenth century:

> Saint Patrick was a gentleman,
> He came of decent people:
> He built a church in Dublin town,
> And on it put a steeple.

Patrick is one of the few national patron saints to be an internationally celebrated figure, partly because his day, 17 March, became a national day for post-Yankee immigrants in the United States. It is also due to the extraordinarily wide Irish diaspora and, in particular, to the emergence of the Irish in the United States as the leader of, and organiser of, the Democratic Party, traditionally the party of the immigrant ethnicities produced by the American industrial revolution after the American Civil War. Schoolchildren in Ireland fifty years ago sang hymns ('Hail glorious Saint Patrick, dear Saint of our Isle' etc.) to his memory and treated him almost as a semi-divine figure. Academics trying to figure out who the saint was, where he came from, when he lived, if he had ever lived or whether he was one person or some kind of composite were likely to get into trouble by being innocently oblivious to the fact that they were undermining a beloved mythical personage in studying a probable historical figure. Back in 1942, T. F. O'Rahilly had published a short book arguing that Patrick was really a composite of at least two figures, Palladius and Patrick, and that the two had become confused in the annals and eventually also in the folk-mind.[43] Even the traditional date of the saint's arrival in Ireland itself (432 AD) had accreted to itself a semi-sacred status. Something of a fuss was generated, even in nervous little neutral Ireland; in fact it blew up in his face and he received a fair amount of abuse, some of it from the clergy. In the same year O'Rahilly wrote to Eleanor Knott in some irritation that the idea that Patrick was a composite figure was nothing new, and he appealed to various Victorian figures.[44] He expostulated that 'Shearman had had four [Patricks]!' He pointed out that George Petrie, the famous early-nineteenth-century Irish antiquarian, in his 'The History and Antiquities of Tara Hill', of 1839, had 'suggested that there were at least two Patricks: an early Patrick, who preceded Palladius was the author of the *Confessio*, and died *circa* 461, and a late Patrick, who died *circa* 492 and who may have been identical with Palladius. This is the nearest to my own views that I have met; but, as you will observe, the difference is as striking as the resemblance.'[45]

The DIAS was one of many targets of Brian O'Nolan or Myles na gCopaleen, author of the famous quip that after many years of intensive and very learned study, the great scholars of the Institute had concluded that there was no God but two Saint Patricks. Myles was also the author of a famous comic verse, more affectionate than derisive, 'Binchy and Bergin and Best', which got into Dublin oral folklore:

> They rose in their night-shift
> To write for the Zeitschrift,
> Binchy and Bergin and Best,
> They proved they were bosses
> At wrestling with glosses,
> Binchy and Bergin and Best,
> They made good recensions
> Of ancient declensions,
> And careful redactions
> To their three satisfactions,
> Binchy and Bergin and Best.[46]

O'Rahilly wrote to Knott in 1950 complaining indignantly about the satirist's 'offensive clowning'.[47] A decade later, in 1961, James Carney published *The Problem of Saint Patrick*.[48] This was an expansion of earlier work by O'Rahilly and himself on the saint which had also attracted some rather venomous clerical criticism and even personal abuse. In it, he argued from the regnal lists, which provided dates for the reigns of Irish kings, that Palladius had arrived in Ireland around 432 and that Patrick had arrived to succeed him on his death in 461, his mission lasting from 462 to his death in 492. All this multiplication of missionaries was effectively an assault on a semi-divinised account of the saint that had become a popular and much-loved *story* which legitimated the Irish Catholic Church and its marriage with the land and the people of Ireland. Patrick had been turned into a messianic figure in the popular imagination, and to question his existence appeared akin to blasphemy to many. As Father John Ryan put it quite oracularly, 'Patrick is the one Apostle of Ireland. There was none before him, there was none after him.'[49] Carney also argued in *The Problem of Saint Patrick* that many places traditionally associated with Patrick were designated thus for purposes akin to modern tourism. He was an entertaining writer, and his prose was conversational, clear and often witty. At one stage he documented entertainingly how a bald and sparse narrative can be blown up into a complete pseudo-history quite easily. One sentence in the *Confession* of Patrick could provoke an entire narrative.

> This whole theory began with a boat, some men, dogs, and a desert. By a process which I may call the absorption of the picturesque, a twentieth-century legend has been created: traders, cargo of wolfhounds, Gaul, Vandals, a usurping emperor, a peasant rising in Armorica, the arenas of Italy, high Italian officials playing for power and waiting for the Irish dogs, almost as for war material.[50]

For a while, in the 1950s, Binchy held his tongue, but the new waspishness, some of it well-aimed, did not fade. In the early sixties, certain Nazis tried to get wolf's nests in Ireland. One was a fellow called Hans Hartmann, a Nazi propagandist and quondam head of one of the Reich's radio services and, incidentally, a Celticist, who latched on to the Celticist industry in Ireland. He was welcomed quite politely by some of the Celtic Studies community in Ireland because he was an Irish speaker. Even that late on there was something left of that ancient respect for the enemy's enemy among the Celtic scholars in Irish academia. Someone tried to introduce Daniel to him by saying 'Have you met Dr. Hartmann?' Binchy said 'No, but I heard his voice', and turned on his heel.[51] He still hated and despised Nazis.

Binchy finally set off an intellectual atomic bomb of his own in 1962 in a famous long 'article' occupying 165 pages, or nearly an entire issue, of a new annual academic journal, *Studia Hibernica*.[52] He started by pointing to several different traditions in writings about Patrick. Even among more academic writers there was little agreement: some writers accepted the idea that there was only one Patrick, that he arrived around 432 AD, had a more-or-less triumphal progress around Ireland, found a pagan country and left it a Christianised one at his death, a demise fixed either in the 460s or, perhaps, in the 490s at the unlikely Mosaic age of about 120. Others, including Carney, argued rather tentatively that Palladius and Patrick had become entwined in the folk mind, Palladius having arrived in 432 whereas Patrick could be seen to have succeeded him on his death at some time in the 450s or 460s. Binchy's comment was radically agnostic:

> Personally, being uncommitted to either school, I think it very possible both dates are wrong – or at best approximations, for as I shall try to show, we have no evidence in favour of either which amounts to anything like proof in the eyes of a trained historian. Indeed, so uncertain is the chronology of St. Patrick that recently a distinguished medievalist has put forward a plausible argument that he died before the arrival of Palladius in 431, and we shall see that Dr. [Mario] Esposito's theory, whether or not one accepts it, deserves the most serious consideration.[53]

Something that clouded the scene further, he argued, was the emotional commitment of many writers, both modern and ancient, to the idea that there had to be one heroic Patrick, rather than a succession of missionaries or even a team of them. The traditional date of Patrick's death was put at 462, making 1962 the 1,500th anniversary. Binchy did not make the point, but it must be remembered that the Eucharistic Congress of 1932 was very much a living memory in 1962 and it had involved an extravagant display of Catholic triumphalism combined with a surge of popular nationalism, coinciding as it did with the coming to power of Eamon de Valera's Fianna Fáil party early in the same year. The ceremonies had culminated in a mass meeting of a million people in Dublin and the Phoenix Park. Binchy pointed to a popular 'religious nationalism' which could be just as strong an emotional force as political nationalism and, in Ireland, for obvious reasons, both of these forces existed and reinforced each other.

> This attitude is not really dictated by religious considerations: from the purely religious standpoint it would not matter a jot even if all the Patrician documents in the Book of Armagh were proved to be forgeries. But there is a nationalism in religious matters which can be as strong an emotional force as political nationalism and which reacts just as vehemently against any attempt by historians to query its foundations. [54]

Binchy took apart, at great length, the claimed evidence in favour of either the traditional narrative or the 'revisionist' one and, at length, concluded that the only real evidence that had survived from that epoch was the two written pieces traditionally ascribed to Patrick himself. All other evidence was guesswork, hearsay, forgery or fantasy. In particular, the dates on the regnal lists were extremely unreliable, having very probably been doctored in the seventh and eighth centuries to further the claims to the kingship of Tara of the Uí Néill dynasty.[55] Binchy commented, 'Personally I have a strong suspicion that the annals of the fifth and sixth century represented deliberate re-writing of history for the purpose of exalting the Uí Néill dynasties at the expense of their rivals.'[56] James Carney's 1961 book came in for severe criticism by Binchy, and academic folklore reports that the younger man was devastated by the occasional savagery of the criticism coming from his old colleague, and was apparently incapacitated for some days afterwards. Binchy was, however, also taking on several pious clerical scholars, including Francis Shaw, Aubrey Gwynn and John Ryan. At that time in Irish academia this was a pretty risky thing to have done, particularly if you had graduate students to defend and promote.[57]

Furthermore, the two authentic documents themselves reveal a Patrick who did not enjoy any triumphant progress through a pagan Ireland, but rather one who was humble, was ashamed of his poor education, had been persecuted, had been betrayed over a secret sin of his youth, had been in chains and had a career more akin to a slow martyrdom than to any great triumph. He struggles with his own guilt and spiritual inadequacy. Patrick never mentions any Irish High-King, but refers merely to 'Irish kings' (which proves nothing). As Binchy rightly remarked, '... the moral and spiritual greatness of the man shines through every stumbling sentence of his "rustic Latin".'[58] He concluded, 'Uncertainty is the occupational disease of all who work in the history of Ireland in the fifth and sixth centuries; it cripples the Patriciologist no less than the humbler political and social historian.' He finished with a wonderful remark about everyone's ignorance, '... why not learn to live with it?' He did admit to a certain leaning toward the Carney narrative himself, but insisted on his own permanent and incurable uncertainty. Some years later, a British scholar, R. P. C. Hanson, queered the pitch further by pointing out that the British Church was in a good position to send missionaries to Ireland during the first half of the fifth century but was in no such position during the second half owing to a huge Saxon invasion of Britain, accompanied by the removal to Armorica of a substantial proportion of the native British population. Hanson noted Binchy's tentative sympathy toward the Carney position, a sympathy which was unspoken.[59] Nicholas Williams has also pointed this out to me.

W. J. Maloney wrote to Knott in June 1962 congratulating her on her careful reading of what had apparently been Binchy's draft text.[60] A few weeks later he commented at greater length:

> ...'Patrick and His Biographers' is certainly a fine piece of work ... The irony, the wit and the erudition employed in controverting the biographers may not have an altogether salutary effect on them. It will enrage those who are the principle targets of Binchy's shafts. But the work I think will make them more careful for the future ... I shall be interested to hear how his victims react, in particular Fr. Shaw and Professor Carney. They had better be guarded in their replies or they may be chastised with scorpions.[61]

T. M. Charles-Edwards wrote of Binchy: 'He once said to me that he found it difficult to write without some target: several Irish scholars must have devoutly wished that the fluency of his prose had no such impediment ... Binchy's long article of 1962 on "Patrick and his Biographers: Ancient and Modern" is a notorious example of deflation – notorious because both brilliant and savage.'[62] In May 1962, Shán O Cuív wrote to Binchy congratulating him on his polemic. 'The Anti-Vivisection Society might be tempted to protest against some of your remarks, but it is a good thing to have pretentious humbug masquerading as scholarship shown up for what it is.'[63] Hanson ratified Binchy's argument in 1968.

> If anyone will take the trouble to read the very thorough refutation of Carney carried out by Binchy in his famous essay on St. Patrick and his biographers he will find it difficult to avoid the conclusion that … not only is the evidence of Muirchu and Tirechan for Laoghaire's (or anybody else's) celebrating a spring festival at Tara entirely worthless, but that in effect we have in their annals, in spite of their apparently careful attention to detail, no means whatever of dating Laoghaire's succession, career, or death.[64]

Many years later, Morfydd Owen was to describe this intellectually ruthless side of Binchy's character accurately in an obituary. He had a 'thorough and even relentless pursuit of learning.' He was difficult for younger scholars to approach, but once you had proven yourself intellectually, seemed serious about the subject, and were accepted, he would do almost anything for you. He could be grim and distant towards younger people, but was loyal to those whom he saw as capable, honest and determined.[65] This attitude towards young and unproven scholars was very common in his generation, and certainly not peculiar to Binchy; if you were young, you might be brilliant, but you really had to prove it on your own. In 1962, one astute American observer of the Irish intellectual scene, J. V. Kelleher, already known for his devastating comments about the linguistic revival policy and what he saw pretty accurately as the intellectual bankruptcy of the modern Irish political class, weighed in publicly on Binchy's side, remarking that:

> The Uí Néill emerge into history like a school of cuttlefish from a large ink-cloud of their own manufacture; and clouds and ink continued to be manufactured by them throughout their long career. Only one thing seems consistent, their claim of sole right to the Kingship of Tara … Nearly everything that one touches turns out to have been affected by the inventions of the historical revisionists. Even the

myths and sagas are not exempt, and certainly Irish hagiography is still full of decipherable political overtones. All this should remind us that in medieval Ireland there were no categorical divisions between history and literature or between sacred and profane electioneering.

...We no longer have a definite framework against which to arrange our ideas. Still, we have achieved a great liberation. We no longer know what isn't so and never was.[66]

Plus ça change, plus c'est la même chose. Modern Ireland is not all that different in its everyday democratic life. Robert Dudley Edwards, Professor of History at UCD, weighed in a little later on, in the pages of *Irish Historical Studies*. Edwards cited Michael Oakshott's well-known dictum to the effect that the historian should only reach those conclusions which the evidence obliges him to believe.

Infectious enthusiasm for maintaining a personal viewpoint can be described as the occupational hazard of the student of political and ecclesiastical controversy. Professor Carney has not escaped the censures of Professor D. A. Binchy ... [Binchy's censures] may appear merciless but, if not always charitable or accurate, at least they will do some good if they lead Professor Carney to accept, in evaluating evidence, the dictum of Oakshott. It now seems likely that future advances in the study of early Irish Christianity will depend on a more austere attitude to non-contemporary evidence, and a more determined attempt systematically to explore the early annals and genealogies without any preconceived ideas, much in the way that British historians are doing for the neighbouring island.[67]

W. L. Warren offered less strict rules of evidence in a piece published in 1969. Essentially he argued against induction from demonstrable facts, the principle he refers to as 'Ranke's Razor'.

... [The idea] that the historian's job is the pursuit of the knowable has admittedly done much to free historical polemic; but it has also promoted an academic attitude which dissuades the historian from venturing an opinion without clear evidence to bear him witness, and has inhibited the free play of that historical imagination which I hold to be essential to the solution of some of history's more fascinating problems ... The sin against Truth lies not in framing a theory for which one has no positive proof, but in clinging to a theory which has failed at the test.[68]

It could be argued that Michael Oakshott, a political philosopher, did no basic research into society ever in his entire life, and that it was a bit thick for him to lecture people who had to struggle with almost incomprehensible ancient societies, languages, political principles and religious systems. However, there is no stopping political philosophers, any more than lawyers, with their commonly impossible and often unreal criteria of truth.

J. F. Lydon, in a review of the first numbers of *Studia Hibernica*, complained specifically about Binchy. 'The "tribal" nature of Irish society (tuath = tribe = primary unit) is again trotted forth, though no real evidence is produced to support this important declaration of faith.'[69] However, he went along with Binchy on the Carney row.

Whatever about his medievalist colleagues, by 1962 Binchy was very evidently on cordial terms with his old Nemesis, Eamon de Valera, receiving an effusively friendly letter in Irish in 1962 from Dev as president of the country about his request to have a lectureship established in classical Latin at the DIAS.[70] On an even lighter note, Binchy sniped at the militant nationalists in a piece dealing with the renaming of his native town of Charleville as Rathluirc in the middle of the Anglo-Irish conflict in 1920 at the behest of the rebels. He pointed out that the town had never used that name before 1920 and it was often known casually to the locals as Rathgogan. Ráth Luirc had been a poetic phrase used in medieval times to refer to the island of Ireland. He noted that telephone operators consistently mispronounced the misnomer in various strange ways. He claimed that similar inaccurate 'renamings' existed all over the country.[71] He was certainly right; Charleville should have been renamed Rathgogan, or left as it was.

In 1966 he published a re-examination of the arguments concerning the laws of the physician which he had published a generation earlier, thereby fulfilling a promise made by him at that time. There was certainly nothing wrong with his memory.[72] In the same year appeared his first instalment of his massive study of Brehon law, the finished product to be published eventually in 1978.[73] Another study of the ancient Irish Fergus Mac Léti saga followed in which he argued rather intriguingly that Brehon lawyers were themselves the cultural descendants of the *filí* (poets) and that was the origin of their curious habit of basing many of their judgements on matter that was essentially fictional but was recorded in the sagas.[74]

Frank O'Connor had died in 1966, and his old friend Maurice Sheehy put together a collection of essays written by his old comrades, including Daniel. It must be remembered that O'Connor and Binchy had become friends in the 1920s partly because of their shared veneration for Russell and Bergin. In fact it was Bergin who had first called Binchy's attention to O'Connor's famous story, 'Guests of the Nation'. 'Read that story. It's one that deserves to live'[75] he had told him. Binchy wrote of O'Connor with an enormous and obvious affection:

> All his life he loved scholarship in Irish, and in later years it became almost an obsession with him according to his admirers in Britain and America, who, understandably, deplored the increasing amount of time he devoted to it. It seemed as though his intense love of Ireland, combined with his antipathy to all the works and pomps of contemporary Irish society, drew him more and more to the study of the Irish past. Every relic of that past was dear to him. For years he waged war almost single-handed on the disgraceful indifference of a native government to the national monuments supposedly in its care, and also denounced the officially sponsored vandalism which is rapidly destroying the character of our cities. But more than all else he cherished the *Eigenart* of the Irish mind, the 'otherness' that expressed itself for so long in Irish and more recently in English. *Nil hibernici alienum.*[76]

Despite his noisy anti-clericalism, O'Connor had had many priest friends as did most Irish Catholics whatever their private religious convictions might have been. Furthermore, he often wrote sympathetically about Irish priests and their emotional quandaries as he saw them. He used to preach to Binchy and other scholars that they were the last generation of educated Irish people who would ever have the privilege of hearing the Irish language as spoken by monoglots or near-monoglots, and they, as scholars, had the sacred duty of collecting all the traditional material, the poetry, sagas, laws, homilies and all the rest of it and transmitting it to posterity. Binchy was fascinated by O'Connor's natural virtuosity as a translator, and believed his translations of ancient and modern Irish poetry to be incomparable; Frank O'Connor/Michael O'Donovan was a natural prose and poetry writer, of a kind rare anywhere. In a self-revealing remark, Binchy reminisced, 'I myself am conscious of an even deeper debt. It was Michael's glowing interest in every branch of Irish scholarship that encouraged me to persevere with my own work. For despite the old poet's praise of a scholar's life – *aoibheann beatha an scoláire!* – I have often found myself querying both its purpose and its value.'[77]

O'Connor's encouragement helped Daniel continue and now he was without this 'unflagging sympathy'; evidently Michael was a kind of brother to him, in some ways more forceful than he was himself. However, he felt that his memories of Michael and his aggressive, even romantic, enthusiasm would sustain him during his 'few remaining years'. There seems to be a certain amount of self-sentimentalisation here, despite the extraordinary intellectual clarity that he usually exhibited. He evidently did not expect to live another twenty years; in fact he was to live even longer than that. A similarly affectionate memoir by him of Bergin appeared in 1970, as did an important collection of lectures on kingship in the British Isles.[78]

Around this time many of his old friends and colleagues began to die. Myles Dillon died in 1972, and David Greene wrote a rather philosophical obituary of him, commenting on the archaism of the entire intellectual tradition, or at least its fascination with the Gaelic past and relative dismissal of the present-day Irish language so beloved of de Valera, Delargy, the folklorists and the revivalists.

> His friend and contemporary Daniel Binchy has noted, in his memorial lecture on Osborn Bergin, the pull backwards which carried so many scholars from modern Irish to the older language; as he rightly says, it cannot be explained merely by the fascination of disciplines learned abroad, since both MacNeill and O'Rahilly took the same path while

remaining in Ireland. In Dillon's case, it is likely that the example of his teachers counted for a great deal in his decision.[79]

The fascination with the past can be explained in part as due to its vastness; after all, a small group of scholars had been presented with an entire civilisation to explore, one which had remained unexplored and misunderstood for centuries. In part, again it was obviously driven by nationalism.

In 1973, a much-delayed memorial volume was published in honour of Eoin MacNeill. In it Binchy gave a short assessment of his old teacher's contributions to the study of ancient Irish law.[80] He gave historical primacy to MacNeill in initiating the modern scientific study of Irish law, pioneering it even before two other famous scholars engaged in this difficult and highly technical task, Charles Plummer of Oxford and Rudolf Thurneysen of Bonn. It was MacNeill who figured out that regnal succession in Irish law was confined to a four-generation kin-group, an arrangement characteristic of many early Indo-European societies. Being locked up by the British in Mountjoy Jail during 1920–21, he was restricted in his access to sources, but like Henri Pirenne in a German prison camp a few years earlier, he resorted to memory when he had only a restricted access to books. He also used his intuitive flair for an ancient society; Binchy always admired this kind of thinking in others, having had a similar regard for Frank O'Connor's intuitive poetic sense; perhaps he sometimes felt his own logical, legalistic and somewhat cold intellectual style lacked something. Binchy pointed to MacNeill's clarity of mind as well. He had sorted out the modern almost pathological semantic confusion of the terms *fine*, *cenél* and *tuath*; the first referred to the four-generation kin group, the second was a general descent group from a common ancestor with no legal connotation and the last was a territorial designation for an area under a petty king and his subjects. MacNeill believed that there was no such thing as a clan system, and in the laws the term *clann* was used exclusively to mean 'children', as indeed it usually does in modern Irish. In Scotland the 'clan system' was the result of the collapse of a feudal political and social order that had itself replaced the old Gaelic system centuries earlier. Binchy admitted willingly that Irish kings began to amass power when under Norse military pressure, but stuck to his picture of the early high-kings as being weak politically, whatever about their ritualistic and symbolic importance. He continued to assert that MacNeill's picture of a developed Irish state was generated partly because of political nationalism. He also felt that it was almost certainly driven partly by an angry rejection of unionist claims that pre-British Ireland was incurably savage, fierce and wild to which Mother England came as a mother to her child, as the old parodic song has it.

Law in a Stateless Society

Thomas Hobbes famously stated, in the aftermath of the English Civil War, a war that was remembered with horror in England but also in Scotland and Ireland, that the life of man 'in a state of nature' or one without a state, was nasty, brutish and short. There was a contract between the individual and the state, essentially the understanding that the state should 'defend me and spend me'. That struggle was really a war of the three kingdoms, determining eventually whether Catholicism or Protestantism would prevail in the Isles, and whether the political structure of the Isles would be unitary or federal in some sense or other; the result was that it was to be unitary, with some slack given to Scotland. As a sort of comment on this widely-held idea of the horror of a stateless society without ever quite saying so, in 1973 Binchy published another of his blockbuster book-length long articles, this one being nearly fifty pages long, 'Distraint in Irish Law.'[81] This magnificent study was, in part, another return to an early topic, but was also a new departure. He was able now to put Irish ancient law into a comparative context, concluding that even in the context of other primitive legal systems, Brehon law as recorded in the *Senchas Már* and other texts was peculiarly archaic and also represented a pre-statist political order. The introduction of Christianity in the fifth century 'on top' of this political order had had the rather odd effect of giving the art of writing to a very archaic, even primitive, social order. It was sometimes argued that, as a result, an already powerful caste of lawyers had been allowed to freeze in written form and make permanent the hitherto orally transmitted rules and lore that had provided the framework of that society. Also, writing allowed them to record, rather solemnly, rules and institutions which had become dead letters even in their own day.

Irish law was, then, he claimed, a *museum*, containing features that had once been characteristic of most Indo-European peoples, something which Binchy had already argued with regard to kingship and 'primitive suretyship'. In the absence of the state as final enforcer of custom and law, the kin-group became the primary enforcer, and its rights of enforcement were themselves encoded in law. A primitive form of enforcement, for example, was for the creditor to seize goods belonging to the debtor forcibly and for him to hold them as surety until repayment occurred. Of course, these kinds of enforcement exist in modern legal systems, but usually only in some very restricted forms, and, in the English-speaking world, usually involving state local officials like the sheriff. In ancient law this right was routine, but was usually ring-fenced by rules governing the kind of goods that could be seized, their value and, naturally, the presence of trustworthy witnesses. In ancient German law, for example, 'male and female serfs, cows and dry stock' could be seized, but the seizure of horses and plough-oxen could be heavily penalised 'unless prior authorization by the king' had been gained.[82] Interestingly, here we see the primitive state making a tentative intervention, one that would eventually become sovereign.

In Irish Brehon law, in practice chattels, including livestock and human beings of inferior status, could be forfeit, but generally land was not. The distinction was obviously the classic one between moveable and immoveable goods. Furthermore, illegal distraint or confiscation of moveable goods (including human beings) could lead to heavy fines. These rules changed over the centuries, and later compilers and scribes often did not understand the earlier sets of rules. A basic condition was the legally recognised 'solidarity' of the *fine* or extended family. This entailed an obligation to ensure repayment falling on the shoulders of the head of the kinship group, and on his failure to meet the obligation, his next-of-kin. Intriguingly, certain exalted (*nemed* or 'sacred') personages, including kings, chief druids, Christian priests later on, and senior poets could enforce their own claims against their social inferiors without notice. The only redress the inferior had against a sacred personage was to fast against him; this seems to have been an unusual occurrence. It was almost proverbial for people to be advised to trade only with others of their own or inferior status; fat cats might not feel like repaying you, and you had little recourse against such a one. In some circumstances a right of trial by combat still existed. Personal honour was highly prized, and any threat to it had to be dealt with immediately by compensation. Binchy detected a certain slow improvement in the status of women in later strata of the *Senchas Már*.[83] Why this happened is obscure; Binchy himself was fond of appealing to external interventions from outside Ireland, either cultural or political, as causes. Probably economics and population growth had something to do with it.

Binchy concluded that the lawyers had gradually accrued to themselves some of the powers nowadays associated with the state.

> The unregulated reprisal of primitive society is first limited by according the man whose property has been seized for a debt owed by a member of his kindred the right to be informed of its whereabouts and the liability for which it has been impounded. Later the jurists succeed in establishing the practice of giving notice beforehand to the defendant or his surrogate, the periods of notice varying between one and ten days. If no move toward settlement of the claim is made before the period of notice expires, the requisite amount of livestock is seized, driven away and impounded, becoming forfeit after the lapse of twenty-four hours.

Later rules provided better terms for the defendant, and eventually a limited right of distraint was given to women.[84] Most of this system seems to have been set up before the seventh century, and there seem to have been local variations in the law from petty kingdom to petty kingdom, despite the universalist claims of the jurists. Furthermore, there was evidence of considerable evolution in the system, despite the usual claims made of historical immutability since the unrecorded era of the ancients. Binchy points out, 'Yet the fiction that the old order still endured was maintained right through the centuries.'[85] This quasi-religious and ahistorical belief in the static nature of both society and law seems itself to have been a principle of legitimation; this is how things have always been done, and who are you to question the wisdom of our great and revered ancestors? In his 1978 *summa* Binchy wrote, as a very old man, that trying to reconstruct the sociology of ancient Irish Celtic society through the records of a millennium of Brehon law was pretty problematic.

Finally there are a few engrossing problems still awaiting solution. How far do these records reflect existing conditions? How can the tribal society reflected in them be reconciled with the testimony of the Annals and more or less contemporary literary works in which powerful rulers and their kingdoms play such a leading role? Were the earlier jurists, too, like their successors, 'backward-looking' (to use Frank O'Connor's apt description of the Irish learned classes as a whole), their gaze still fixed on a dead past? Again, how and why was the text of the tracts, with its different linguistic strata, definitely empanelled about the end of the seventh century?[86]

A Gaelic Heritage?

Every now and then Binchy displayed his old penchant for commenting on the contemporary scene, almost as a refreshment after months or even years of absorption in the minutiae of a thousand years earlier. He was repeatedly struck over the years by how thoroughly the Irish had shed the entire cultural edifice of Gaelic Ireland, almost as though it never had been. Even the 'neo-Gaelic' terminology was an obvious fake.

> For the political and social structures of today, far from being the embodiment of the traditional Gaelic aspirations (as our politicians sometimes assert), are based primarily on representative democracy and central administration after the British model; and the only point at which they diverge from this model, the Republican form of government, has its source, not in native tradition (to which the very idea would have been abhorrent), but rather in the American and French Revolutions.[87]

There had been created by Irish political leaders a 'fictitious continuity' between modern Irish and Gaelic traditions. 'One might as well claim that the French Republic is the successor state to the Gaulish *civitates* described by Caesar' according to Binchy. This seems to be a sniping at de Valera's ideological posturing, in particular his 'Gaelic chieftain' rhetoric in hailing Douglas Hyde as First President of Ireland in 1938, and calling him heir to the Gaelic chiefs of olden days. Myles na gCopaleen used to guy the neo-Gaelic posturing of the patriots from a similar intellectual vantage-point to Binchy's. Actually, although all of this was obviously true, Binchy somewhat underestimated de Valera's originality, particularly in copying the American institution of Judicial Review ('the Marshallian device') and inserting it into the 1937 Constitution. The Irish use of judge-made law is clearly American in direct inspiration and is certainly not English. Neither, needless to say, is it Gaelic, but curiously enough, rather like modern Irish or American judges, the medieval Gaelic law-makers were lawyers and scribes rather than elected politicians.

Notes

1 Thomas F. O'Rahilly, *Early Irish History and Mythology*, Dublin: Dublin Institute for Advanced Studies, 1946.

2 Luigi Luca Cavalli-Sforza, *Genes, Peoples and Languages*, London: Penguin, 2001, pp.101–103 and *passim*.

3 Osborn Bergin, Review of Early Irish History and Mythology, *Irish Historical Studies*, Volume 40, 1957, pp.416–25.

4 Ibid., p.416.

5 Ibid., p.425.

6 Ibid.

7 NLI MS 11,000 (7), Richard Best Papers, 13 May 1951.

8 NLI MS 11,001 (6), Best Papers, Grosjean to Best 22 August 1945.

9 Donnchadh O Corráin, interview, 28 June 2014. *Corpus Iuris Hibernici*, Dublin Institute for Advanced Studies, Introductory Matter and Six Volumes, 1978.

10 Daniel A. Binchy, *The Linguistic and Historical Value of the Irish Law Tracts*, London: Milford, 1943.

11 Donnchadh Ó Corráin, interview, 28 June 2014.

12 Daniel A. Binchy, 'Irish Law Tracts Re-edited', *Eriu*, Volume 17, 1955, pp.52–85.

13 James Matthews, *Voices: A Life of Frank O'Connor*, Dublin: Gill and Macmillan, 1983, pp.238, 329.

14 Ibid., p.37.

15 Daniel A. Binchy, Review of Robin Flower, *The Western Island, Studies*, Volume XXXIV, 1945, pp.129–130.

16 Daniel A. Binchy, Review of John Lorne Campbell, *Gaelic in Scottish Education and Life* Edinburgh: 1945, in *The Bell*, Vol. 10, No. 3, 1945, pp.362–66, quote at p.365.

17 Domhnall O Bínnse, 'Sé Cuisle na hEigse Cuisle na Tíre', *The Clongownian*, 1947, pp.36–7.

18 Daniel A. Binchy, Review of Myles Dillon, *The Cycles of the Kings, The Bell*, Volume 13, No. 6, March 1947, pp.71–2.

19 D. A. Binchy, 'Comment', *Studies*, Volume XXVII (September 1938), pp.368–72, quote at p.369.
20 NLI MS 11,000 (17), Richard Best Papers, 29 November 1946.
21 Daniel A. Binchy, Review of R. A. S. Macalister, *Corpus inscriptionum insularum celticarum*, Dublin: Stationery Office, 1943, in *Journal of the Royal Society of Antiquaries of Ireland*, 1946, pp.56-7.
22 Ibid., p.57.
23 Daniel A. Binchy, Rejoinder to Macalister, *JRASI*, 1946, pp.143–145.
24 Daniel A. Binchy, Review of R. A. S. Macalister, *Lebor Gabála Erenn* Part 4, 1941, *Studia Celtica* Vol.2, part 1, 1952, pp.195–209.
25 Daniel A. Binchy, 'The Saga of Fercus maic Léiti', *Eriu*, 16, 1952, pp.33–48.
26 Daniel A. Binchy, 'The Date and Provenance of *Uraicecht Becc*,' *Eriu*, XVII, 1958, pp.44–54.
27 Ibid., p.54. The Joyce referred to is P. W. Joyce.
28 Daniel A. Binchy, 'The Fair of Tailtiu and the Feast of Tara', *Eriu*, Volume 18, 1958, pp.113–38.
29 Ibid., p.127.
30 Ibid., p.132.
31 Ibid., p.134.
32 Ibid., pp.137–38.
33 Bart Jaski, 'The Vikings and the Kingship of Tara,' *Peritia*, Volume 9, 1995, pp.310–53, quotes at pp.311, 313, 319.
34 Encomium by Michael Duignan on the occasion of Binchy being awarded an honorary doctorate by the National University of Ireland, 1973. DIAS, Binchy Papers, BIN/N/51.
35 D, A, Binchy, 'Latin as Means and as an End', TS article, n. d., DIAS BIN/N/ 51.
36 Daniel A. Binchy, 'Lawyers and Chroniclers', in Brian O Cuív, *Seven Centuries of Irish Learning, 1000–1700*, Dublin. Stationery Office, 1961, pp.58–71, quote at p.64.
37 Ibid., p.58.
38 Daniel A. Binchy, 'The Passing of the Old Order', in Brian O Cuív, *Proceedings of the [First] International Congress of Celtic Studies*, Dublin, Institute for Advanced Studies, 1959, pp.119–132.
39 RIA 12021, Eleanor Knott Papers, 24 March 1947.
40 RIA 12021, Eleanor Knott Papers, 6 January 1957.
41 Robert Kanigel, *On an Irish Island*, New York: Knopf, 2012, p.245.
42 James Mathews, *Voices: A Life of Frank O'Connor*, Dublin: Gill and Macmillan, 1983, p.329.
43 Thomas F. O'Rahilly, *The Two Patricks*, Dublin: Institute for Advanced Studies, 1942.
44 RIA 12021/78, Eleanor Knott papers, 25 August 1942, O'Rahilly to Knott.
45 Ibid.
46 Myles na Gopaleen, *The Best of Myles*, London: Picador, 1968, pp.266–67.
47 RIA 12021/78, Eleanor Knott Papers, 16 October 1950. O'Rahilly to Knott.
48 James Carney, *The Problem of Saint Patrick*, Dublin: Dublin Institute for Advanced Studies, 1961.

49 Ibid., p.158.

50 Ibid., p.169.

51 *Irish Independent*, 8 March 2014.

52 Daniel A. Binchy, 'Patrick and His Biographers, Ancient and Modern' *Studia Hibernica*, Vol. II , 1962, pp.7–173.

53 Ibid., p.7.

54 Ibid., p.17.

55 Ibid., pp.67–69.

56 Ibid.

57 Donnchadh O Corráin, interview, 28 June 2014.

58 See Binchy, 'Patrick and His Biographers,' p.165.

59 R. P. C. Hanson, *Saint Patrick: His Origins and Career*, Oxford: Oxford University Press, 1968, pp.27–28. The bibliography of writings on Patrick is apparently limitless. See Cormac Bourke, 'Patrick', *Dictionary of Irish Biography*, Volume 7, pp.117–25.

60 RIA 12021, Eleanor Knott Papers, 15 June 1962.

61 Ibid.

62 Máire Herbert and Kevin Murray (eds.), *Retrospect and Prospect in Celtic Studies*, Cork: Congress of Celtic Studies, University College Cork, 1999, p.19.

63 DIAS, Binchy Papers, BIN/P/45.

64 See Hanson, *St. Patrick*, pp.26–27.

65 Obituary of Daniel Binchy, *Studia Celtica*, Vols. 24–25, pp.153–155.

66 J. V. Kelleher, 'Early Irish History and Pseudo-History', *Studia Hibernica*, Volume III, 1963, pp.113–127, quote at pp.125–127.

67 *Irish Historical Studies*, Vol. XIII, No. 52, September 1963, pp.367–369 quote at p.369.

68 *Historical Studies*, Vol. VII, 1969, London: Routledge and Kegan Paul, pp.1–20, quote at pp.1–2.

69 J. F. Lydon, 'Review' of *Studia Hibernica*, Nos. 1–3, *Irish Historical Studies*, Volume XIV, No. 56, September 1965, pp.386–389, quote at p.387.

70 UCD P150/2609, Eamon de Valera Papers, 27 November 1962.

71 Daniel A, Binchy, 'The Old Name of Charleville, Co. Cork', *Eigse*, Volume 10, 1961–1963, pp.211–235.

72 Daniel A. Binchy, 'Bretha Déin Chécht', *Eriu*, Volume 20, 1966, pp.1–65.

73 Daniel A. Binchy, 'Ancient Irish Law', *Irish Jurist*, New Series, Volume 1, Part 1, Summer 1966, pp.84–92.

74 Daniel A. Binchy, 'Eachtra Fergusa Maic Léti' in Myles Dillon (ed.), *Irish Sagas*, Cork: Mercier, 1968, pp.40–52.

75 Daniel A. Binchy, 'The Scholar-Gypsy', in Maurice Sheehy, *Michael/Frank: Studies on Frank O'Connor*, Dublin: Gill and Macmillan, 1969, pp.16–22.

76 Ibid., p.17.

77 Ibid., p.21 (Irish: The life of the scholar is beautiful).

78 Daniel A. Binchy, *Osborn Bergin*, Dublin: pamphlet, 1970; *Celtic and Anglo-Saxon Kingship*, Oxford: Oxford University Press, 1970.

79 David Greene, Obituary of Myles Dillon, *Lochlann*, Volume 6, 1974, pp.189–91.

80 Daniel A. Binchy, 'MacNeill's Study of the Ancient Irish Laws', in F. X. Martin and J. F. Byrne, *The Scholar Revolutionary*, Shannon, Irish University Press, 1973, pp.39–48.

81 Daniel A. Binchy, 'Distraint in Irish Law', *Celtica*, Volume 10, 1973, pp.22–71.

82 Ibid., p.23.

83 Ibid., pp.58–9.

84 Ibid., p.65.

85 Ibid., p.67.

86 Daniel A. Binchy, *Corpus Iuris Hibernici*, Introduction, Dublin Institute for Advanced Studies, 1978, p.xxi.

87 Daniel A. Binchy, 'Irish History and Irish Law: II', *Studia Hibernica*, Volume 16, pp.7–45, quotes at pp.8–9.

CHAPTER FIVE

ROMANTICISM AND THE IRISH PAST, 1945–1989

In 1947 Sean O'Faolain remarked famously in *The Irish*, 'Little though they know it, the dominating problem for all Irish politicians, ever since the founding of the Free State, has been what to do with their lovely Past. (O lost, and by the wind grieved, ghost come back again!)'[1] This was a remark that might have amused Binchy mightily, but there was an important truth in it. Irish governments were saddled with a popular ideology of national spiritual and linguistic renewal and restoration which was both impossible to achieve and internally contradictory. Even the lost Ireland that was to be restored and with which the new state claimed continuity was itself little understood. Eventually many people realised this, often slowly and reluctantly, and quietly abandoned parts or all of the programme. Very appositely, a scholar of a later generation, Seán O Coileáin, remarked in 1999 'Many scholars of all periods, but particularly of modern Irish, will have entered the field fired by a cultural ideal that has been silently abandoned.'[2]

The late nineteenth century and the early twentieth century in Europe was a territory of strange beliefs, ideologies and pseudo-religions. It was a time of spiritualism, associated with Madame Blavatsky generally, and, in Ireland, with W. B. Yeats. There even was, and still is, a thing called 'Celtic Spirituality', associated historically with Yeats and latterly with half-educated pop singers. Theosophy was fashionable, and even got into O'Casey's plays. At the same time it was the age of Einstein and Darwin, where the Biblical account of the formation of the Earth, and even the scientific system of Newton, were both being demolished by the cosmic physics of the modern world, and by archaeology and biology. It was a time when people were still coming to terms with the biological history of the planet as rewritten by Wallace and Darwin. The relationships between the languages of Europe were being gradually worked out. The universities of Germany were the main drivers of these new sets of ideas until Hitler wrecked them, possibly irreversibly. After Hitler, the leadership of the world's universities passed for a long time to the English-speaking world, much enriched by the fleeing intelligentsia of the Reich. These émigré scholars included Einstein, Schroedinger and many of the people who gave the United States the atomic bomb. Not for nothing, they became referred to collectively as 'Hitler's Gift'.

Imaginary and Real Pasts

Chris Wickham, writing about history and pseudo-history among the barbarian successor states to the western Roman Empire, has commented:

> By 650 every 'barbarian' kingdom had its own traditions, some of them claiming to go back centuries, and those doubtless were by then core elements in the founding myths of many of their inhabitants; all the same, founding myths not only do not have to be true, but also do not have to be old. Each of the Romano-Germanic kingdoms had a bricolage of beliefs and identities with very varying roots, and these, to repeat, could change, and be reconfigured in each generation to fit new needs. Historians tend to give more attention to the account that Clovis's grandfather was the son of a sea-monster, than to the account that the Franks were descended from the Trojans, which seems more 'literary', less 'authentic'; but the first record of each of these traditions appears in the same seventh-century source, and it is hard to say that one was more widely believed than the other.[3]

Daniel Binchy and many other Irish academics and publicists spent their intellectual lives, whether or not they admitted it, dealing with a culturally and politically powerful nationalist romanticism that glorified semi-imaginary versions of the Irish past, reinforced by a religiously powerful celebration of an imagined pious version of that same past ('The Isle of Saints and Scholars', etc.). Both sets of ideas, or rather attitudes, one political and the other religious, were very Victorian. Romantics and clericalists clashed, but deep down they were on the same side: Ireland and the Irish past were special, and deserved special treatment. John-Paul McCarthy has commented penetratingly about this mentality, commenting that Pearse himself represented it in 'his morbidly introspective personality'.[4] Pearse and his acolytes looked to the reconstruction of an imagined or even daydreamed past and many of them covertly wished for a deeply illiberal Ireland in which the general body of the people was to be infantilised, denied the riches of an Anglophone civilisation and forced to speak a language most of their ancestors had decided to abandon long previously. This political tradition, much ignored and evaded in their daily lives by the real peoples of Ireland, became an orthodoxy which legitimated the banning of the best of modern Irish literature in the English language, the promotion of a patriotic pseudo-history, the neglect of the sciences and the denial about the awareness of the new art of film. Occasionally it seemed as though the movement, come to power, had turned into one which wished to wipe out the actual intellectual culture of the country. Modern dance, particularly ballet, was distrusted and discouraged. In a curious way, the better academic Celticists were attacking this political tradition, and in their quiet way were undermining it gradually. Their real alliance was, even if they did not always quite realise it, with the satirists some of them disapproved of: James Joyce, Eimar O'Duffy, Denis Johnston and Brian Nolan (Myles na gCopaleen) were on their side even when they laughed at the academics. These writers were also laughing at their intellectual enemies, the professional neo-Gaelic revivalists, and were laughing more loudly and more hurtfully at them.

From the point of view of the political scientist, these rather solemn or even ridiculous official doctrines or ideological attitudes were very convenient for power seekers in an emergent populist democracy such as the independent Ireland of the time. If you were rhetorically loyal to Faith and Fatherland, no one could gainsay you, and a public discourse that derived itself from these popular assumptions or axioms reigned supreme from about 1890 to about 1960. To some extent it still prevails among nationalists in Northern Ireland, but even there it is fading fast. In the late nineteenth century, anti-clerical Fenians and pious clericals found themselves allied, the former often subordinated to the latter. What is interesting about Binchy, other than his powerful intellect and enormous contribution to our understanding of the Irish past, is his consistent abjuration of Irish romanticism in favour of an aspiration towards a scientific understanding of medieval Ireland. The picture he, in particular, gives us of medieval Ireland goes flatly against the romantic visions of writers as different from each other as Thomas Moore, Alice Stopford Green, Aodh de Blácam or, to some extent, even Eoin MacNeill himself. The Ireland uncovered by Binchy, his colleagues and their predecessors has certain features which orthodox nationalists and certain kinds of Irish Catholic of the time certainly disliked. Some of these unpopular propositions ran something like the following.

Gaelic society was stateless:

The High-Kingship of Tara had no state apparatus, taxing powers or military force of a size sufficient to control the territory of the entire island; in modern parlance, Ireland was politically underdeveloped. It is actually unclear whether the 'High-Kingship' really existed at any time earlier than the seventh century. Perhaps it did; absence of evidence is not necessarily evidence of absence. Binchy tended to think that the seventh-century scribes describing fifth-century events simply transferred their own political circumstances back to earlier times. At any rate, real power, in so far as it was held by anyone in particular, was in the hands of the great provincial kings, and Tara was more a ritualistic than a governmental centre. Binchy pointed out with approval in 1976 that Donnchadh O Corráin, then one of a small group of rising young scholars in Celtic Studies, had demolished the nineteenth-century idea that Gaelic Ireland had a law-bound system of regnal succession. These would-be kings were violent and powerful men, accustomed to getting their way, and succession tended to be a pretty rough-and-ready process, blood being often spilt. Royal blood was notionally sacred, but the individuals who possessed it were certainly not particularly sacred. Within the extended families of royalty, brother killed brother in a perpetual power struggle. The system of recognised relationships was one that actually had an incentive to murder built into it. Binchy quotes cheerfully, with direct reference to O Corráin's work:

The good old rule!
… the simple plan
That they should take, who have the power
And they should keep who can.[5]

Christianisation led to an alternative power structure derived from episcopal and monastic institutions which, like everything else, tended to be captured by local tribal forces. However, there was competition to appropriate the High-Kingship by one or other of the great provincial kingdoms; in particular the two sets of Uí Néill tribal kingships. Munster held itself aloof for centuries under the long-lived Eóghanacht dynasty of Cashel. The well-known Victorian English medievalist, H. M. Chadwick described this condition elsewhere in early medieval Europe succinctly: '…in the heroic age the state appears to have been regarded as little more than the property of an individual – or rather perhaps of a family, which itself was intimately connected with a number of other families in similar positions.'[6]

There was no state-backed legislative process at island-wide level by which laws could be promulgated or abolished. Doris Edel writes a century later:

For the brithem, as for his Hindu colleague, the idea of a lawgiver was inconceivable, at least in theory: the law was in existence since time immemorial and only needed to be preserved and interpreted. This was the task of the legal schools in various parts of the island … As the redactors of the legal records adhered to the fiction of immutability, the image of the society that emerges from those texts has a timeless quality, at least at first sight. Evidently, early Ireland also underwent social changes which called for an adaptation of the law, but when a new rule was introduced, the old one was not dropped, but maintained beside the one that replaced it. A practical guideline for the beginner in the field is that the form of an institution which is treated at great length in a given text was, almost certainly, the later to emerge and that it superseded the forms which are treated more succinctly.[7]

This is very probably exaggerated, but the basic point still stands: in effect, there was no overarching Gaelic polity in medieval Ireland. Law was customary and theoretically immutable, although quietly changed all the time. Fergus Kelly puts it neatly:

> Not surprisingly, there are often inconsistencies between different sources. Thus, according to one law-text, *Bretha Crólige*, a person who injures another illegally must arrange for him to be brought away on sick-maintenance (*othrus*), and cared for until he has recovered. However, another text, *Crith Gablach*, states that the institution of sick-maintenance is obsolete, and has been replaced by the payment of appropriate fines.[8]

Significantly, the hierarchical and deeply unequal character of Gaelic society was tempered by various processes and institutions, chief among them the Church. As we have seen, honour-prices were equal and independent of social status in canon law, but in native law (*fénachas*) honour-price varied violently between people of different status and the sexes. The senior priests and nobles were *nemed* (sacred) and when they had a debt, the only recourse of the poor person was to fast against them, thereby assaulting the dignity of the powerful debtor.

This statelessness and traditionalism of the law contrasted not only with the extraordinarily early emergence of what was to become a powerful and aggressive imperial polity centred on south-east England, but also the emergence, under Gaelic aegis but with Norman administrative machinery, of a weak, but real, Scottish polity in the ninth century commencing with the reign of Kenneth MacAlpine. Gaelic kingdoms in Scotland were usually geographically much larger than their ancestral kingdoms in Ireland. In Ireland Máel Sechlann in the ninth century got close to taking over the high-kingship and building it up, but could not overcome the essential provincialism of Irish political power centres. Again, Brian Borumha failed to create an all-Ireland polity in the eleventh century and after his death in 1014 Gaelic society continued as a jigsaw of contending tribal kingships. The absence of coinage and the near equation of land with riches provoked fragmentation because one had to conquer the land and hold it; coinage permitted one to simply cut the other guy's pay, or just pay him off. Coinage therefore made a centralised state of some sort possible.[9] However, in Ireland, some coinage did exist, and silver was used by weight as a store of value from relatively early times.

Ironically, as Binchy argued several times, this very political incoherence and 'vegetable' character (to use his own term) of kingship was itself to act as a bulwark against a rapid and total conquest of the island. Such resistance as occurred tended toward passivity and evasion rather than military defence. When the Anglo-Normans finally moved into Ireland in the late twelfth century there was little resistance to them for a long time, and even then such resistance as there was turned out to be more likely to be cultural and behavioural rather than military until such time as the English, finally united under the Tudors, chose to actually exercise their Lordship of Ireland four centuries later. In the twelfth century the towns fell to the Anglo-Normans immediately, but the conquerors themselves tended, particularly in rural areas, to go native; an enormous proportion of Irish surnames are derived from Gaelicised versions of the Norse and Norman invaders' names. Furthermore, urban Ireland, such as it was, declined in the fourteenth century due to a natural calamity, the Black Death, leading to a Gaelic resurgence over the next century and a half. Essentially the Irish kept speaking Irish and kept to the mountains and the far west for centuries, until the final collapses of 1603 and 1691 following the battles of Kinsale and Aughrim.

A lot of this went against the preferences and opinions of some of Binchy's fellow scholars. Certainly it seems that his loyalty to MacNeill preserved the older man from any direct attack on his work by his old student during his own lifetime. It is not clear, however, how much is left of MacNeill's *Phases of Irish History* or the master's other writings by the time Binchy was finished with his arguments. However, much of the time he was, rather obediently, simply echoing MacNeill, and always deferred rhetorically to the knowledge and wisdom of his old teacher.

Binchy's picture of the provincial kings as almost powerless has been criticised academically. His old student and colleague Thomas Charles-Edwards argued quite reasonably that provincial kings did develop military capabilities after the coming of the Vikings, did extract dues and services and acted as judges whose verdicts could be made stick. After all, Irish kings did manage eventually to see off the Vikings militarily. Following him, Janet Nelson suggested that provincial kings could 'intermittently' command local kings. 'A shift from dietary metaphor to the language of power allows the conclusion that throughout the early medieval period, say down to the eleventh century, royal power was wielded at different levels which prescribed different styles of governance.'[10] Again, Proinsias mac Cana, writing in 1987, argued that these 'modern' developments were accompanied by mythological legitimation. In this pseudo-historical tradition Fionn mac Cumhail and his Fianna outlaws are gradually expanded into a loyal national militia of a long-existent Irish Tara-based state.

> Ireland was spared serious foreign intervention until the Norse incursions began at the end of the eighth century, but when it came it produced a ... reflex assimilation of myth to history (and history to myth). The Norsemen were equated to the Fomoire, and this provided an occasion for assigning a quasi-historical role as protector of the national territory to Fionn and his *Fian* ... D. A. Binchy has said of the Norse invasions that, while it would be anachronistic to claim that they created a common sentiment of national identity, they did evoke that sense of 'otherness that lies at the basis of nationalism', and even though I cannot accept his formulation of the problem without some qualification, there can be little doubt that the events of the ninth century brought about a certain politicisation of the cultural concept of nationality which coincided neatly with the (partial) historicization of the role of the *Fiana* as the protectors of Ireland. Moreover this development more or less coincided with the propagation of the doctrine of the 'high kingship' by which the learned historians of the establishment sought to impose on behalf of the Uí Néill dynasty the notion that the king of Tara was of right the over-king of all Ireland; from the tenth century what has been described as a political fiction – the 'high-kingship' – had become virtually a historical fact. This was all part of a sequence of profound socio-political, cultural and religious change which extended from about the end of the tenth century to the end of the twelfth, and one small element in this sequence of change was the nationalization of the *Fiana*.[11]

Mac Cana went on to observe that the anachronistic linking of Fionn and the *Fiana* with the high-kingship and Cormac mac Airt, notionally a third-century high-king, happened in the tenth century as part of this great cultural shift – a new piece of pseudo-history to bolster a germ of national identity.

However, Binchy himself acknowledged the occurrence of such shifts in the wake of the Viking raids in his 1962 piece, 'The Passing of the Old Order', very nearly a classic exercise in comparative political science. There he upholds the picture of an unorganised and almost incoherent congeries of small 'Balkan' statelets, this very incoherence making the country difficult to conquer, but does remark on the growing military capability of the Irish kings after the eighth century; they were ceasing to be quite the 'vegetables' he liked to call them. He was quite the political developmentalist, and consistently argued that Gaelic society in Ireland had the capacity to change. He also understood that it did change under internal pressures as well as under external influences such as the Viking raids and, of course, the coming of the Normans. However, despite these cavils, no one has retrieved, in any convincing way, the MacNeill vision of an all-Ireland political order centred on Tara. However, the *idea* of an all-Ireland kingship certainly did exist in early medieval Ireland; the O'Neills aspired to it and Brian very nearly got there in the early eleventh century. O Corráin has analysed some of the mythical legitimations that were manufactured to bolster the Uí Néill claims to sovereignty over the entire island. Commonly it involved the ancestral hero, Niall, embracing a hideous hag sexually. The hag is transformed into a beauty; the moral is, sovereignty is ugly until you possess it, and then it becomes attractive. 'On internal evidence, the tale is Uí Néill dynastic propaganda of the eleventh century, though some elements which make it up are as old, perhaps, as the eighth century.' [12] Again, Terence O'Connor made a last-minute shot at the high-kingship in the twelfth century. Perhaps another century of isolation might have given Gaelic Ireland the opportunity to create a native state. However, it didn't happen, and the Normans eventually did that job for them.

The weakness of secular institutions was balanced by the power of the monastic church, itself increasingly coming under pressure from outside to reform itself and to conform to western European organisational standards.

By 1152 the transmutation of the Irish church, though not yet complete, was inevitable. A Roman hierarchy, continental religious orders, and legatine commissions were removing the chief anomalies of the traditional system, while new styles in building and sculpture marked the transformation. And at the same time men of learning were transcribing, compiling, glossing and composing, in the pride of their unique heritage.[13]

It should be emphasised that this stateless condition combined with a powerful ecclesiastical apparatus, was not unique to Ireland, nor was Ireland extraordinarily remiss in not succeeding in building a state in the first millennium; Scandinavian countries were late state-formers, and Sweden was particularly delayed. In Scandinavia, Denmark was the most politically developed, and played a leadership role for the other countries much like that which England played in the British Isles. Norway, which became linguistically danified in the south in the eighteenth century, resembles Ireland and England strangely in its cultural relationship with the old imperial power, Denmark. However, unlike England, Denmark turned out to be too small to dominate the other countries, although it did try to do so in the form of the short-lived fourteenth-century Union of Kalmar. The first Russian state, centred on Kiev in the Ukraine, seems to have been as much a Scandinavian creation as a Russian.

Gaelic Ireland was deeply inegalitarian:

It was intensely aristocratic, and political power was concentrated in the hands of certain privileged and landed extended families. An elaborate set of laws of entitlement and inheritance meant that property was kept strictly within the minutely mapped kinship system (*deirbhfhine*) of the extended family. This element of common ownership by a family, such ownership being subject to laws of succession, was the origin of Connolly's famous mistake, the proposition that Gaelic society was, in some way, a form of 'primitive communism', as suggested by various historical anthropologists of the nineteenth century; it was nothing of the kind, but did have a generic similarity to other north European tribal systems. As O'Faolain famously argued in his anti-romantic polemical defence of O'Connell, *King of the Beggars*, almost certainly after conversations in the early thirties with people like Binchy, Gaelic society was highly exploitative and its lower orders were thoroughly despised by the upper crust. Furthermore, after its fall, the writers who had benefited from it sentimentalised it and scorned the common folk who had not prospered particularly under it. O'Faolain comments angrily that, in the early nineteenth century during the time of O'Connell, the old Gaelic world offered them nothing, and modern Irish democracy had to be founded on English, American and French ideas and traditions.

> All through the century it is the same. We can see these seven million helots finding no practical aid from the traditions of the old world that is ended. It was not possible that they should, for that old world was not a democratic world, and they had never shared much in its good things, and they had, as a class, never got much out of it. It had been chiefly an aristocratic order, and its figureheads had been those people whom [Aogán] O'Rahilly listed as the losers by its fall – the clerics, the learned, the chieftains, the bards, the nobles. How much the plebs lost is impossible to say. They do not make many appearances in the annals of the old Irish world; indeed I do not know a single indigenous Irish piece in prose or verse, composed before 1600, which deals with the life and interests of what we may call the lower orders; whereas elsewhere one thinks readily of scores of things that record, or were written to please, humanity in its humblest station – all those *fabliaux* that were a revolt against the rigidity and conventionality of the knightly life, the heartily vulgar tales of Chaucer, the saga of *Havelok the Dane*, where the hero is a common fisherman, and where the life of a fisherman is recorded with evident delight, the whole satire of Langland, all those popular German tales like *Tyl Eulenspiegel* or *Reynard the Fox* ... Of that direct reflection of a popular form of life, nothing was ever preserved in Ireland. We do not even know how the people dressed; or where they lived before the thatched, white-washed cabins were built.[14]

Back in the first millennium, there were free tribes and unfree tribes in a system vaguely reminiscent of the Indian caste system. Upward mobility existed in Gaelic society, but the law put restraints on it of an intergenerational kind. These restraints tended to weaken as the centuries wore on. The law provided for different levels of civil rights, depending on your rank in society. Even different levels of veracity were accepted from people of high rank than from people of low rank. Slaves and women could generally not testify in court. Warfare sometimes tended to be ritualised and was commonly regarded as a somewhat aristocratic activity. State-building was slow and incomplete even at the end of the pre-Norman period. H. M. Chadwick put it well, if rather datedly, in a comparative perspective a century ago:

> On the whole warfare is the state of affairs most commonly involved in heroic stories. It is a fact worth noting however that this warfare invariably takes the form of hand-to-hand fighting and very frequently that of a series of single combats ... in regard to social organisations the outstanding feature of the Teutonic and Greek heroic eras was the weakening of the ties of kindred and the growth of the bond of allegiance. In political organisation ... the chief feature of both periods was the development of an irresponsible type of kingship resting upon military prestige, the foundation of kingdoms with no national basis and the growth of relations between one kingdom and another. In religion ... the predominant character in both cases was the subordination of chtonic and tribal cults to the worship of a number of universally recognised and highly anthropomorphic deities, together with the belief in a common distant land of souls. Lastly we observe that the Gaulish heroic age appears to have possessed almost all the same characteristics while in regard to social and political organisation analogies are to be found in the heroic ages of the Cumbrian Welsh and the Christian Servians though hardly – or only to a very slight extent – in that of the Mohammedan Servians.[15]

Chadwick cites the famous 'democratic' incident in *The Iliad* in which the commoner Thersites is the only warrior in the Greek army who proposes that they all should go home, that ordinary Greek people have no quarrel with the Trojans. He is shouted down and sneered at by Achilles and his aristocratic comrades. This Chadwick claims as the exception which proves the rule that heroic eras in stateless barbarian societies were essentially aristocratic and honour-driven.[16]

Gaelic society was non-feminist:

Binchy and his colleagues made it perfectly clear that women in Irish society had few privileges, and, until quite late on, could not bear witness; their evidence was not accepted, any more than was that of slaves. Some limited concessions were eventually made to them. Early Celtic society admittedly gives us some historical examples of female military leaders, the British Queen Boadicca being the best-known historically. The legendary Maeve of the *Táin Bó Cúailnge* is presented as being reckless and of doubtful wisdom, in consistent contrast to her wise and reluctant husband Aillil, always wary of warfare. During the invasion of Ulster, Aillil wisely fears the threat of Cú Chulainn, a superhero and of course possessed of such supernatural powers as befit a supernatural hero. At one stage Maeve, in what seems to be an echo of the Melian declaration of the Athenians in the Pelopennesian War, is asked by Ailill when the Galióin of Leinster declare their neutrality and refuse to march with the Men of Eire on Ulster, 'Well what are we going to do with them, if they can neither stay nor come?' Maeve answers, 'Kill them.' Ailill answers, 'This is a woman's counsel, and no mistake, a bad thing to say.' Her speech was regarded as unlucky.[17]

Even Maeve (Medb) owes her status to her father's status.

> Once when their royal bed had been made ready for Ailil and Medb, they conversed as they lay on the pillows.
> 'It is a true saying, girl,' said Ailill, 'that the wife of a good man is well off.'
> 'It is true,' said the girl. 'Why do you say so?'
> 'Because,' said Ailill, 'you are better off today than the day I married you.'
> 'I was well off without you,' said Medb.
> 'I did not hear or know it, except that you were an heiress and that your nearest neighbours were robbing and plundering you.'

'That is not so,' said Medb, 'for my father, Eochu Feidlech son of Finn, was high king of Ireland.'[18]

None of this really proves anything, but there seem to be echoes here of Penelope's predicament in *The Odyssey*, endlessly fending off the suitors pending her man coming home from the wars. There was apparently some tradition of female warriors in pre-Christian Ireland as in other pagan Celtic societies; in the sixth century the Church reportedly tried to forbid women from being soldiers, thus demonstrating a pre-existing 'Amazon' tradition. The Church was very much in favour of the subordination of women. Multiple wives, up to a maximum of three with different statuses, were permitted. On the other hand, Maeve was credited in another saga (*Táin Bó Flidais*) with pretty impressive powers over Fergus Mac Roích, as retold by his ghost:

> Another version [of the *Táin*] says that, while he was king of Ulster for seven years, the sun did not rise over the edge of Emain Macha, and that his kingship was called 'the black reign of Fergus'; but the text also praises his generosity. His huge size is emphasised; he ate and drank for seven men and it took seven women to fulfil his needs until he met Medb.[19]

Gaelic society was slave-holding:

A myth much cherished by people of left-republican political views exists to the effect that Gaelic Ireland knew not the slave, despite the rather well-known autobiographical testimony of St Patrick. Slaves were commonly taken in battle, or in piratical raids on western Britain, but they could also be bought and sold and they were legally priced; interestingly, women slaves often seem to have been more valuable than male slaves. Slavery also existed in Viking Ireland and it seems that the Viking settlements internationalised the slave trade in the far west of Europe. There was, famously, a trade route dealing with furs and slaves running south from Scandinavia through the British Isles and down to western Iberia and North Africa. Wine was among the goods going the other way up to the Isles and on to Scandinavia. Portuguese wine, which was sent north almost as ballast, seems to be the remote origin of the curious modern Norwegian habit of drinking red wine with fish. In Viking times Dublin had one of the biggest slave markets in Europe and was a centre for the creation of eunuch slaves for the North African market. A woman slave or *cumal* was the unit of value, along with cattle, before coinage made its very delayed entry into Irish society. As Chris Wickham puts it with a certain amount of geographical uncertainty, ninth-century Dublin

> ... was the most powerful and dangerous of these new [city-state] polities and in the 850s it became the focus of substantial reinforcements, but the Vikings never engaged in large-scale territorial conquest in Ireland. It was too difficult, with all those tiny kingdoms, and also not hugely remunerative, as there were too few stores of moveable wealth (as in eastern Europe, slaves were Ireland's most valuable exportable commodity). Dublin's main political ambitions looked westwards [*sic*], to the Irish Sea and York.[20]

Dublin is sometimes described as the most English city in Ireland, but no one has ever, to my knowledge, suggested that it actually *is* in England or perhaps Holland.

Saint Patrick probably existed, but was no triumphalist:
Irish schoolchildren a generation or two ago were taught of a St Patrick who was close to being some kind of national godlet, in a hymn written by a Sister Agnes:

> Hail glorious Saint Patrick, dear saint of our isle,
> On us thy poor children bestow a sweet smile;
> And now thou art high in the mansions above,
> On Erin's green valleys look down in thy love.
> ...
> Ever bless and defend the sweet land of our birth,
> Where the shamrock still blooms as when thou wert on earth,
> And our hearts shall yet burn, wherever we roam,
> For God and Saint Patrick, and our native home.

While it is apparently clear that he existed, it is equally clear that his life was one of poverty and persecution as one of many Christian missionaries in an often hostile mission environment, commonly involving imprisonment and possible martyrdom. His personal modesty and humility are obvious as is his devotion to his religion and to his mission. It is also possible that the *story* of Patrick that has come down to us is, in part, due to confusion of several different historical figures, one of whom might indeed have performed great conversions. We do not know. Francis John Byrne remarks that Carney's late date for Patrick's arrival has much to support it. However, he goes on to say eirenically:

> It is clearly impossible to hope that we shall ever be able to give exact dates for his mission, but a difference of thirty years cannot be dismissed as the mere hesitation over a year or two normal in the early annals. Unfortunately, Patrick's own writings are ambiguous; he mentions no Irish personal names and only one place-name, and his references to Britain and Gaul are almost equally tantalising. We know so little about the state of Britain in the fifth century that to try to correct Irish chronology with the help of British is to explain *obscurum per obscurius* The internal evidence of Patrick's writings does perhaps favour the earlier dating, especially in view of the confidence the saint expresses in his *Romanitas*, and the lack of explicit references to the chaos which we presume to have prevailed in the late fifth century. But this is far from conclusive: our ignorance of the state of Britain (or of that region of it with which Patrick was familiar) forbids us to rule the later chronology out of court.[21]

Gaelic society was capable of change, and underwent great changes in the half-millennium 432–1169:

Gaelic society was not static in some unreal Platonic way as imagined by some of the Victorian patriots, including Pearse. Movement toward state-formation occurred, eventually to be interrupted by the Norse raids and settlements after 800 and, of course, the Anglo-Norman take-over after 1169. From the seventh century on, a very gradual and often unadmitted loosening up of the ties between social status and property levels occurred. Although the laws were held to be changeless, it is clear that they did change, and forgetfulness took care of obsolete legal provisions. Furthermore, linguistic change made those provisions increasingly illegible and incomprehensible to later copyists and lawyers. Dead-letter laws are not a modern invention and are an inevitable feature of any legal system set up to regulate a changing society. Binchy makes the point that Irish law was not unique in having no case law; Roman law and most legal systems in medieval Europe also lacked it. The role of case law and *stare decisis* is characteristic of Common Law, developed in England and used almost everywhere in the English-speaking world.[22] The Irish and Welsh, however, preferred mythological decisions derived from legendary material to real decisions upon which new decisions might be made afterwards. Robin Chapman Stacey has written: 'As anyone familiar with the sources will know, tales in the Irish law books very often act as origin legends for offences or the judgements pertaining to them ... [the principle that] a person's status and behaviour could and indeed *should* have an impact on the legal rights that person would enjoy made a system based on precedent not only impossible but undesirable.'[23] Donnchadh O Corráin puts it more cynically: '... the bulk of the early historical sources are literary and highly conventionalised products of specialist learned classes' retainers of the contemporary holders of power, who were at pains to legitimise all change by giving it the sanction of immemorial custom and who ruthlessly reshaped the past to justify the present.'[24] Pseudo-history had its uses: the now peaceful Vikings of the new Irish towns were used as whipping boys by the emergent Gaelic provincial kings who were taxing them and borrowing their technology.[25]

By the eleventh century Ireland was moving toward a more-or-less feudal society long before the Norman invasion, partly due to the growth of population, as several scholars have suggested. Also, intervention from outside Ireland was a significant source of change, the two obvious external agents of such change before Norman times being the Catholic Church, particularly in the form of the various orders sent into the country from the ninth century on, and the Viking incursions after 800. Strangely, one great western European development apparently passed the Irish by: the twelfth-century religious and intellectual renaissance.

The Church in Gaelic society gradually mutated toward a European norm:

As Kathleen Hughes has put it, paralleling Binchy, the intervention of the Vikings either galvanised or broke something in Gaelic society, strengthening the kingship and ecclesiastical systems. 'Respect and veneration had been accorded to the Church for so long that the Viking treatment left men bewildered.'[26]

> Ireland was submerged by confusion and anarchy. It was as if a shoal of sharks had got into a paddling pool. Inevitably the changed political situation caused partial disintegration of the old legal stability. The security of the pre-Viking system depended on its balance, for though there was no strong executive authority each grade of authority had been kept in control by those above it. Without warning, and through no fault of his own, a man could be bereft of all the material adjuncts which marked his position, without hope of compensation. Small wonder that the Irish law tracts now 'atrophy, and the theory of Irish law becomes ever more widely divorced from its practice'.[27]

This was apparently true of late-ninth- and tenth-century secular and ecclesiastical law in Ireland. Some sense, if not of nationality but of Binchy's 'otherness', seems to have emerged. Building in stone started in the ninth and tenth centuries, the high crosses and round towers generally dating from that era.

> By the tenth century the Church had adapted itself to the conditions brought by the Viking swords, and had achieved a material recovery. Her men of learning were in touch with England and the Continent, while Scandinavian civilization was influencing her men of art. The illuminators and smiths had lost some of their finesse, but the sculptors and masons had extended their activity. And while the stone crosses displayed the old and new testament iconography, the monastic story-tellers recounted their dialogues, visions and voyages in prose and verse, for the delight of the crowds.[28]

All of this speaks of foreign influence. Brian Borumha sees the High-Kingship as the legitimation of the rule of an Emperor of the Irish, although this 'institution' dies with him. The echo of Charlemagne and Rome is obvious. However, the provincial kings became more organised and powerful: more *modern*.

Medieval Ireland had a common literary Latin culture with Britain:
One modern authority remarks fairly typically:

> ...our survey of insular writing and manuscript illumination provides eloquent evidence for the existence of one single Latin literate culture. The view that there were two such cultures, with either the Irish or the Anglo-Saxon one being superior, is in need of revision. There was but one insular Latin culture, in which linguistic, artistic, and, at least from the seventh century onwards, religious barriers could be overcome. Ireland and her neighbour had their place in the tapestry of early medieval Latin culture; both played their part, to the best of their abilities, in the European network of exchange of scholars, books and ideas. Those scholars were not bothered by anything like nineteenth-century Romanticism and nationalism.[29]

Medieval Ireland was commonly imagined as being highly nationalistic, and fantasies of Fionn and his Fianna warriors defending the sacred isle against foreign invaders proliferated during the nineteenth century. These dreams bore little relationship to the reality.

Much Traditional Irish History is Mythical:
Bergin was fond of saying that euhemerism was extraordinarily strong in the Irish pseudo-historical tradition. This refers to the propensity of early scribes, perhaps particularly the monks, to take pagan gods and demi-gods and convert them into allegedly historical ancient kings and queens, warriors, seers and magicians. A second source of this process is the habit of the saga writers themselves of permitting divine or semi-divine figures to behave in ways that resemble the ordinary behaviour of

183

everyday human beings. It was as though, in 2,000 years time, historians were to write that the Second World War in Europe was won by the Americans, British and Russians because their armies had the great warriors Superman, Captain America, Dan Dare and Stakhanov, whereas the Germans only had Siegfried.

Fionn mac Cumhaill is a prime example of this process. Originally a personification of a god of knowledge, he is eventually 'nationalised' by the province of Leinster and gradually turned into a wise warrior.[30] Eventually he is made a chief-of-staff to Cormac mac Airt, the legendary fourth-century high-king of Ireland, and the Fianna, originally masterless men in armed bands, is transmogrified by the storytellers into a mighty Irish army. Medieval versions of Fionn are evidently tainted with Arthurian literature, a tradition that is similarly mythical and ultimately Celtic in origin. Fionn is represented as defending Ireland against foreign invaders, both real ones (Norsemen) and, in earlier versions of the tales, imaginary supernatural ones (Fomorians). 'The gradual development of tradition meant a gradual change in the portrayal of Fionn's background. In the earliest phase he was a solitary seer-figure, then he became the wise leader of a Fianna band and finally the leader of a great army.'[31] The greatest force behind euhemerism seems to have been the monks who were charged with the task of writing down these legends while eliminating the more obvious traces of a Celtic pantheon or other religious systems of ideas.

On the other hand, Irish society in pre-Norman times seems to have a relatively high level of literacy and an almost religious veneration for the few, hand-written books that there were. Books were bought for fantastic prices because of their rarity and for their possible sacred or magic character.

The Breakers of Myth

These findings, unwelcome to some ideologues and modern successors to the ancient Irish craft of pseudo-history, were, of course, not just Binchy's or even his generation's, but the fruit of the joint efforts of many Irish and foreign scholars over 100 years, starting with George Petrie, Eugene O'Curry and John O'Donovan in the middle years of the nineteenth century. They were succeeded by a formidable group of late Victorian and early-twentieth-century scholars under the aegis of Kuno Meyer, Rudolf Thurneysen, Osborn Bergin and Richard Best. Germany was the obvious intellectual centre of the international Celtic Studies movement and it was in Germany's universities that the grammar and vocabulary of Old Irish were first studied by modern methods and made available to later Irish scholars. The Irish scholars had an impressive international network of scholars in Britain, western Europe and, to some extent, in North America as well. This group can claim to be one of the most important intellectual movements in modern Ireland, as important in its way as the much better-known literary movement associated with William Butler Yeats, John Millington Synge and James Joyce or the movement towards a new scientific history associated with Moody, Quinn and Edwards from the thirties on. It is quite evident that the latter movement was heavily influenced by the earlier medievalists. Outside academia, the Celticists' efforts were resisted by many, particularly nationalist ideologues of a kind Ireland seems always to have with her, and, in the past, clerical historians addicted to a heroised version of Irish religious history. Of course, professional Celticists were themselves not immune to the virus of romantic thinking, but the scientific style of argument tended to win out in the long run among their ranks.

There was another reason for this outcome. As O'Faolain said in the mid-sixties, the learning of Irish lost its 'magical power to bind hearts together'. It had lost its mystique, because the political fight in which it had been a weapon to use was over. Instead of looking to the past and its possible restoration, the Irish were going full tilt into modernity, and the Irish language was being left to die, the bridge with the past being gradually demolished. Even as early as 1958, a Swiss scholar at the Institute for Advanced Studies felt able to say 'We are dealing with the ruins of a language.' O'Faolain wrote sadly, 'So the old life dies, the old symbols wither away, and I and my like who warmed our hands at the fires of the past are torn in two as we stand on this side of the bridge and look back in anguish at the doomed Ireland beyond it.'[32]

In fact, it seems to me that the move toward a scientific history in this country owes more to the Celtic Studies people than is ever acknowledged, although Robert Dudley Edwards did publicly acknowledge Binchy's intellectually austere stand. However, Binchy did note an unwillingness among Irish historians to engage with the Irish language, particularly in its earlier forms; interdisciplinary scholars who did develop such an interest tended to be linguists.[33] Many modern Irish historians have been trained in England, and this seems to have had the curious effect of inoculating some of them against the Gaelic past of the island, a past that has had profound and often unrecognised echoes in modern English-speaking Ireland in both Irish jurisdictions; one gets the feeling with some of them that they feel they have been dealing with an island which has always been English-speaking. However, the disease of nationalist and romantic fantasy has receded quite noticeably over the last thirty years or so, partly due to the very unromantic exploits of the Provisional IRA, but also because of the efforts of Irish historians, medievalists and other scholars to create a reasonably objective and non-fantasist account of the collective experience of human beings on the island. Certainly, the present generation of Irish people has, even at a popular level, a much more reasoned, unromantic and almost everyday understanding of ancient Ireland; our historical perspective is now much more far-reaching and far more accurate than that of people a century ago.

A dissident view has been offered by Alfred Smith:

> The impetus given to geographical studies by early nineteenth-century scholars was not to last. Already by the closing years of the [nineteenth] century the emphasis on Germanic scholarship on the importance of philology in the study of a nation's past combined with the rise of nationalism within Ireland itself to push the broader and more liberal Anglo-Irish tradition to one side. Whatever liberalism had remained within the Gaelic League in the appreciation of literature was replaced by a rigorous professionalism in Irish scholarship, combined with a heavy and stultifying emphasis on philology.[34]

Smith goes on to argue that 'pedantry' has taken over the field; 'Unfortunately, writers who have held up the progress of research into the origins of Irish Christianity by squabbling over the details of Patrick's mission, have largely ignored evidence for the independent evangelisation of the Leinstermen from fifth-century Britain.'[35]

Whatever about the pedantry of genuine scholars, another, far less benign, force has been the rise of an aggressive and commercialised philistinism in Irish universities, a modernist philistinism of a startling level of ignorance which is being reflected, quite justly, in the weakening of the country's third-level colleges in the international ratings. A contempt for non-applied and inexpensive humanist research and argument has done immeasurable damage to the intellectual life of the country. It is not realised by these people that the humanities and the social sciences are culturally specific in a way that the natural sciences are not, and that Ireland has a natural academic advantage in being a small but important cultural province of the English-speaking world; they have been throwing away a free cultural resource. This attempt to commercialise the universities was cheered on by the journalists, particularly the 'educationalists' in the *Irish Times*. Professor Morgan Kelly of UCD commented in 2014:

> ... the flames have engulfed the other engine that powered our take-off in the 1990s: the universities. Irish universities were never any great shakes but they did do one thing well, which was to produce a lot of well-trained graduates at extraordinarily low cost to the taxpayer. ... With a bigger slice of a shrinking pie going to administration, the numbers of academics in Irish universities have fallen sharply – by more than 20 per cent in UCD – with more able young academics making up a disproportionate share of the exodus. Irish universities have plummeted in international rankings, with UCD falling from 100th to 200th in the world in the reputable Times Higher Education Rankings, the second steepest fall ever recorded.[36]

It is quite possible that a young Daniel Binchy would never have been hired by a twenty-first-century Irish university.

The End

Binchy lived in Castleknock during his later years, partly to be near his beloved horses in the Phoenix Park. Towards the end of his life most of his old friends were already dead, but he retained his old wittiness and sharpness despite illness in his last years. Sean O'Faoláin, in his own last years, failed to recognise him and muddled him up with his son. 'He did the shopping, wrote to friends, talked on the phone with Dan Binchy. "A truly terrific thing has happened to me with Dan Binchy. I quite literally have ceased to remember him – he is become the Irish mirror of my son (in is it New Zealand or America?)".'[37] However, he outlived Binchy by two years. Daniel died in May 1989. A Welsh colleague, Morfydd Owen, described him in an extraordinary obituary as being:

> ...extremely entertaining company, witty, urbane and possessing of a great wealth of anecdote ... Lawyer, historian and linguist, few scholars have shown such many-faceted versatility and distinction and fewer still have experienced such a varied and rich education and career. Even fewer have shown such thorough and even relentless pursuit of learning ... As in the case of most great men, tales about Binchy's life and character are multitudinous. 'I am a truculent fellow' he once said of himself and indeed his writings as well as his behaviour show that he did not suffer fools gladly. He belonged to a generation of Celticists who did not believe in encouraging the young. Any young scholar was expected to perform a series of *anoethau* before they were accepted by him. Those whom he accepted, he accepted wholeheartedly and was loyal in his support of them, a loyalty they reciprocated. For despite his truculence, he could be a person of great warmth of feeling and he could be very human. His fondness for horses and riding was legendary.[38]

Unlike some of the other (mainly Irish) obituarists, the Welsh scholar made sure, interestingly enough, to refer at length to Binchy's alternative career in the thirties as a diplomat and public intellectual in an independent country. 'He had also been a man very much aware of the problems of his own times' as was demonstrated by his many reviews of books on current affairs and contemporary political science. His Italian study owed much to the work of British political scientist Herman Finer. 'His analysis of the problems of contemporary society reveal the same acute social and historical sensitivity' that had made him so successful an analyst of the social structure of Celtic societies.[39] He was a brilliant conversationalist.

This description of him was paralleled many years earlier by W. J. Maloney in a letter to Eleanor Knott in 1960. Kate O'Brien was the well-known Irish novelist, much persecuted by the Irish government's prehistoric censorship system.

> [Daniel Binchy and Kate O'Brien] lunched with me in London yesterday and we had a grand talk, in the Irish manner, on subjects of great variety and no mundane importance. My wife said when I was leaving home that she was sure I would come back hoarse. I told her that with two such conversationalists as Daniel Binchy and Kate O'Brien I would never reach that stage.[40]

In a fond homily at his funeral, Donal Cregan made some penetrating if affectionate observations. It was difficult to describe Binchy's profession, Cregan observed, as he was a 'Renaissance man'. He was a lawyer, a diplomat, a linguist of very high quality, a political scientist *avant la lettre*, a Celtic scholar, a historian of some note, a linguistic expert, but had always described himself as an early medieval historian.

> He was a man of formidable intelligence and a highly critical and sceptical cast of mind. Hence he set high standards for himself, and his students were also expected, if not to reach these standards, at least to aspire to them. 'When students want encouragement or consolation', he once said to me, 'they go to Myles [Dillon] … but', he added darkly 'they come to me when they want to learn the truth.' This was not quite the whole truth, as many younger scholars could testify who benefited from his encouragement and advice, but mostly his kindnesses were done by stealth.[41]

Binchy was a secret giver to charity, in particular to people whom he knew were on their uppers one way or another, and he never spoke about it. Again, his kindnesses were stealthy while his intellectual strictness and occasional cruelty were public. Despite his anti-clericalism, he was, apparently, a strongly believing Catholic, regretted (quite correctly) the disappearance of Latin in the Irish school system and liked Newman's ideas on university education. However, he seems to have habitually dodged going to Mass on holydays of obligation; he shared O'Connor's views on clerical power in Ireland. He loved painting, and sometimes presented paintings he liked to friends and relatives. As we have seen, he had highly developed political views, despising right-wing authoritarianism and anathematising atheistic communism. He was a firm believer, as early as the 1930s, in a natural alliance between the Catholic Church and democracy and did believe in the spiritual and civilising role of the Church in a secularising and post-religious western world. He seems to have harboured a certain bitterness in old age, and had a sense that his subject, ancient Irish law, would evaporate once he had gone; a certain self-obsession mixed with an historical pessimism seems to have existed.[42] Charles-Edwards, his old student and colleague, recalled his strange composite personality in a rather entertaining way:

> In remembering D. A. Binchy, I recall a man of quite exceptional brilliance of mind allied with a sharpness, even a fierceness, of temperament. Perhaps I can suggest what manner of man he was by saying that if he was French in the clarity of his intellect and German in his sense of the high claims of scholarship, and if his manner was at least somewhat English, the acerbity of the language he could deploy was wholly Irish.[43]

Pádraig Breatnach also described him accurately as a formidable scholar: interestingly, he used a Chadwickian phrase to describe Binchy and his comrades. 'In many ways he was our last link with the "heroic age" of Celtic Studies, and that consideration apart altogether from his own pre-eminence made it a privilege for us – *nani in umeris gigantum* – to know him.'[44] Fergus Kelly, in an obituary published by the School of Celtic Studies, remarked:

> As one who first came in contact with him as a postgraduate scholar at the Dublin Institute for Advanced Studies, I was immediately struck by his extraordinarily formidable personality. To attend a seminar under his direction was both an inspiring and intimidating experience: grammatical errors or inadequate preparation of the text elicited reactions ranging from chilly to quite ferocious. This

belligerent streak in his make-up also lent a sharp cutting edge to some of his writings. Indeed, it must be admitted that he often went too far in his denunciations of other scholars and their ideas.[45]

An anonymous obituary in *The Clongownian* observed affectionately 'His innate courtesy and cant-stripping wryness – a combination of Charleville sharpness and Kilmallock insouciance – brought a breath of fresh air to turgid liturgies in Berlin. He was a brilliant diplomat because he was a brilliant endearing man. He touched nothing he did not adorn.'[46]

De mortuis nihil nisi bonum, indeed.

Notes

1 Sean O'Faolain, *The Irish*, Harmondsworth, Pelican, 1969, p.145. First edition published 1947.
2 Seán Ó Coileáin, 'Society and Scholarship: Play in the Modern World', in Herbert and Murphy, *Retrospect and Prospect in Celtic Studies*, pp.45–56, quote from p. 55.
3 Chris Wickham, *The Inheritance of Rome*, London: Penguin, 2010, p.99.
4 *Sunday Independent*, 6 April 2014.
5 'Irish History and Irish Law II', *Studia Hibernica*, 1976, pp.7–46, 41–2, 44.
6 H. M. Chadwick, *The Heroic Age*, Cambridge: Cambridge University Press, 1912, pp.333–334.
7 Doris Edel, *The Celtic West and Europe*, Dublin: Four Courts Press, 2001, p.52.
8 Fergus Kelly, *A Guide to Early Irish Law*, Dublin: Institute for Advanced Studies, 1988, pp.1–2.
9 Chris Wickham, *The Inheritance of Rome*, London: Penguin, 2010, pp.103–4.
10 Janet Nelson, 'The Limits of Power in Medieval Europe', in *Power in History: Historical Studies XXVII*, Dublin, Irish Academic Press, 2011, pp.3–24, citation at p.5. T. Charles-Edwards, 'Celtic Kings: "Priestly Vegetables?"' in S. Baxter et al., *Early Medieval Studies in Memory of Patrick Wormald*, Farnham, 2001, pp.65–80; P. Wormald, 'Celtic and Anglo-Saxon Kingship: Some Further Thoughts', in P. Szarmach (ed.), *Sources for Anglo-Saxon Culture*, Kalamazoo, Michigan, 1988, pp.151–183.
11 Mac Cana, Proinsias, '*Fianaighecht* in the pre-Norman Period' in Bo Almqvist, Séamas O Catháin et al., *The Heroic Process*, Dublin: Glendale 1987, pp.75–99, quote at pp.98–99.
12 Donnchadh O Corráin, 'Legend as Critic', *Historical Studies*, Volume XVI, Cork: University Press, 1987, pp.23–38, quote at p.33.
13 Kathleen Hughes, *The Church in Early Irish Society*, London: Methuen, 1966, p.274.
14 Sean O'Faolain, *King of the Beggars*, London: Nelson, 1938, pp.32–3.

15 H. M. Chadwick, *The Heroic Age*, Cambridge: Cambridge University Press, 1967 (first published 1912), pp.440–443.

16 See Chadwick, *Heroic Age*, p.228

17 See Edel, *The Celtic West*, pp.164–5.

18 J. E. Caerwyn Milliams and Patrick K. Ford, *The Irish Literary Tradition*, Cardiff: University of Wales, 1992, pp.16–17. See Donnchadh O Corráin, 'Women and the Law in Early Ireland', *Historical Studies*, Vol. XIX, Belfast: 1995, Queen's University, pp.45–57.

19 Muireann Ní Bhrolcháin, *An Introduction to Early Irish Literature*, Dublin: Four Courts Press, 2009, p.47.

20 Chris Wickham, *The Inheritance of Rome*, London: Penguin, 2009, p.496.

21 Francis John Byrne, *Irish Kings and High-Kings* London, Batsford, 1973, p.79.

22 See Binchy, 'Irish History and Irish Law I', pp.27–8.

23 Robin Chapman Stacey, 'Law and Literature in Medieval Ireland and Wales', in Helen Fulton, *Medieval Celtic Literature and Society*, pp.65–82, quote at p.73.

24 Donnchadh O Corráin, 'Nationalism and Kingship in pre-Norman Ireland', *Historical Studies*, Volume XI, Belfast: Appletree, 1978, pp.1–36, quote at p.12.

25 Ibid., pp.31–32.

26 Kathleen Hughes, *The Church in Early Irish Society*, London: Methuen, 1966, pp.199–200.

27 Ibid., pp. 205–6.

28 See Hughes, *The Church*, p.237.

29 Marco Mostert, 'Celtic, Anglo-Saxon or Insular? Some Considerations on "Irish" Manuscript Production and their Implications for insular Latin Culture, c. A. D. 500–800', in Doris Edel (ed.), *Cultural Identity and Cultural Integration: Ireland and Europe in the Early Middle Ages*, Dublin: Four Courts Press, 1995, pp.92–115, quote at p.109.

30 Dáithí O hOgáin, *Fionn mac Cumhaill: Images of the Gaelic Hero*, Dublin: Gill and Macmillan, 1987, p.25.

31 Ibid., p.151,

32 Sean O'Faolain, *Vive Moi!* London: Rupert-Davis, 1967, p.114.

33 See Binchy, 'Irish History and Irish Law II', p.7.

34 Alfred Smith, *Celtic Leinster*, Dublin: Irish Academic Press, 1982, p.2.

35 Ibid., pp.3, 9.

36 *Irish Times*, 14 March 2014.

37 Maurice Harmon, *Seán O'Faoláin*, London: Constable, 1994, p.275.

38 Obituary of Binchy by Morfydd E. Owen, *Studia Celtica*, Volume XXIV-XXV, 19891990, pp.153–157.

39 Ibid., p.154.

40 RIA 12021/51–57, W. J. Maloney, Eleanor Knott Papers, 31 October 1960.

41 Donal Cregan, Obituary of Binchy, *Irish University Review*, Volume 19, No. 2, Autumn 1989, pp.310–13, quote at p.312. Liam Breatnach put me on to this quote long ago.
42 Fergus Kelly, interview, 19 August 2014.
43 T. M. Charles-Edwards, Obituary of Daniel Binchy, *The Pelican*, 1968–69, p.72.
44 Pádraig Breatnach, Obituary of Binchy, *Eigse*, Volume XXIV, 1990, pp.153–4. Latin: 'dwarves on the shoulders of giants'.
45 Fergus Kelly, Obituary of Daniel Binchy, *Newsletter of the School of Celtic Studies*, No. 3, 1989, pp.10–14, quote at p.13.
46 'J. P. D', Obituary of Binchy, *The Clongownian*, 1989, p.97.

LIST OF PLATES

1. Osborn Bergin

2. Daniel Binchy in mid-career

3. Daniel Binchy

4. Eamon de Valera

5. James Carney

6. Front row, right: Carl Marstrander. Back row, left: Richard Best

7. Osborn Bergin, Tomás O Criomhthain (an tOileánach), Daniel Binchy

8. Daniel Binchy in old age

(All images courtesy of the Dublin Institute for Advanced Studies)

SELECT BIBLIOGRAPHY

Almqvist, Bo, et al., *The Heroic Process*, Dublin: Glendale, 1987.

Bewley, Charles, *Memoirs of a Wild Goose*, Dublin: Lilliput, 1989.

Binchy, Daniel A. and Myles Dillon (eds), *Studies in Irish Law*, Dublin, 1936.

Binchy, Daniel A., *Church and State in Fascist Italy*, Oxford: Oxford University Press, 1941.

Binchy, Daniel A., *Corpus Iuris Hibernici*, Dublin: Institute for Advanced Studies, 1978.

Binchy, Daniel A., *Críth Gablach*, Dublin: Institute for Advanced Studies, 1970.

Binchy, Daniel A., *Osborn Bergin*, Dublin: University College Dublin, 1970.

Binchy, Daniel A., *Sick-Maintenance in Irish Law*, Oxford: Oxford University Press, 1934.

Binchy, Daniel A., *The Linguistic and Historical Value of the Irish Law Tracts*, London: Milford, 1943.

Byrne, Francis John, *Irish Kings and High-Kings*, London: Batsford, 1973.

Carney, James, *The Problem of Saint Patrick*, Dublin: Institute for Advanced Studies, 1961.

Cavalli-Sforza, *Genes, Peoples and Languages*, London: Penguin, 2001.

Chadwick, H. M., *The Heroic Age*, Cambridge: Cambridge University Press, 1912.

Edel, Doris, *The Celtic West and Europe*, Dublin: Four Courts, 2001.

Fanning, Ronan et al. (eds), *Documents on Irish Foreign Policy*, Dublin: Royal Irish Academy, in progress since 1998.

Garvin, Tom, *Nationalist Revolutionaries in Ireland*, Dublin: Gill and Macmillan, 2005.

Hanson, R. P. C. *Saint Patrick: His Origins and Career*, London: Oxford University Press, 1968.

Harmon, Maurice, *Sean O'Faolain*, London: Constable, 1994.

Herbert, Máire and Kevin Murray (eds), *Retrospect and Prospect in Celtic Studies*, Cork: Congress of Celtic Studies, University College Cork, 1999.

Hughes, Kathleen, *The Church in Early Irish Society*, London: Methuen, 1966.

Hutchinson, John, *The Dynamics of Cultural Nationalism*, London: Allen & Unwin, 1987.

Kelly, Fergus, *A Guide to Early Irish Law*, Dublin Institute for Advanced Studies, 1988.

Matthews, James, *Voices: A Life of Frank O'Connor*, Dublin: Gill and Macmillan, 1983.

McCormack, W. J., *Fool of the Family: A Life of J. M. Synge*, London: Weidenfeld and Nicholson, 2000.

Medawar, Jean and David Pyke, *Hitler's Gift*, London, Piatkus, 2001.

Ní Bhrolcháin, Muireann, *An Introduction to Early Irish Literature*, Dublin: Four Courts, 2009.

O Dochartaigh, Pól, *Julius Pokorny, 1887-1970*, Dublin: Four Courts, 2004.

O hOgáin, Dáithí, *Fionn mac Cumhaill: Images of the Gaelic Hero*, Dublin: Gill and Macmillan, 1987.

O'Brien, Máire Cruise, *The Same Age as the State*, Dublin: O'Brien Press, 2003.

O'Connor, Frank, *My Father's Son*, London: Pan Books, 1971.

O'Crohan, Tomás, *The Islander*, Dublin: Gill and Macmillan, 2012.

O'Curry, Eugene, *Manners and Customs of the Ancient Irish*, London: Williams and Norgate, three vols., 1873.

O'Driscoll, Mervyn, *Ireland, Germany and the Nazis: Politics and Diplomacy, 1919-1939*. Dublin: Four Courts, 2004.

O'Faolain, Sean, *King of the Beggars*, London: Nelson, 1938.

O'Faolain, Sean, *The Irish*, Harmondsworth: Pelican, 1969.

O'Faolain, Sean, *Vive Moi!*, London: Rupert Hart-Davis, 1967.

O'Rahilly, Thomas F., *Early Irish History and Mythology*, Dublin: Institute for Advanced Studies, 1946.

O'Rahilly, Thomas F., *The Two Patricks*, Dublin: Institute for Advanced Studies, 1942.

Roth, Andreas, *Mr. Bewley in Berlin*, Dublin: Four Courts, 2000.

Sheehy, Maurice (ed.), *Michael / Frank, Studies on Frank O'Connor*, Dublin: Gill and Macmillan, 1969.

Smith, Alfred, *Celtic Leinster*, Dublin: Irish Academic Press, 1982.

Thurneysen, R., *A Grammar of Old Irish*, Dublin: Institute for Advanced Studies, 2010.

Wickham, Chris, *The Inheritance of Rome*, London: Penguin, 2010.

Williams, J. E. Caerwyn and Patrick K. Ford, *The Irish Literary Tradition*, Cardiff: University of Wales, 1992.

INDEX

personal life 87, 118, 134–5, 189
personality, reclusiveness and 57
politics and 39, 91–2
pseudonym, Domhnall Ó Binnse 136
religion and 118, 144, 189–90
return from Berlin (1932) 86–7, 97
return from Oxford (1950) 139
'scientific' temperament 61, 139,
    167–8
Thomas Davis lecture (1958) 142–3
Thurneysen's obituary 12–13
writings 50, 57
'Aimser Chue' 111
article in *Berliner Tagesblatt* 78
article on Hitler in *Studies* 42, 47,
    92, 102
Bretha Crólige translation 102
Church and State in Fascist Italy 111,
    117
Corpus Iuris Hibernici 133
Críth Gablach (Branched
    Purchase) 124–5, 170
'Distraint in Irish Law' 157
essay on German constitutional
    order 85
'Fair of Táiltiú and the Feast of Tara,
    The' 140
Fergus Mac Léti saga, study of 154
'Irish Ambassador at the Spanish
    Court, 1569–1574, An' 50
laws of the physician, re-examination
    of (1966) 153–4
*Linguistic and Historical Value of the
    Irish Law Tracts, The* 121, 134
Mein Kampf (Hitler), critique of 44
'Passing of the Old Order, The' 143,
    173
'Patrick and his Biographers: Ancient
    and Modern' 150–1
regnal succession, essay on 63–4
'Sé Cuisle na hEigse Cuisle na
    Tíre' 136
Sick-Maintenance in Irish Law 104
translation of *Grammar of Old Irish,
    A* 125
Binchy family 38–9

Binchy, Maeve 9–10
Blasket Islands 25, 26, 55, 56, 106
Boadicca, Queen 177
Boland, Frederick H. 40, 84
Brady, Ciaran 59
Breatnach, Liam 103
Breatnach, Pádraig 41, 190
Breatnach, R.A. 100
Breen, Aidan 103
Breen, Dan 93–4
Brehon law 157–60
    Binchy and 57, 102, 154, 157–60
    enforcement and 158
    illegal distraint/confiscation 158
    personal honour and 159
    sacred personages and 158
    status of women and 159
Brennan, Robert 40
Bretha Crólige
    Binchy's translation of 102
    judgements of blood-lying 103
    late Latin medical texts 102
    laws concerning injuries inflicted 103
    penalty system 103
    sick-maintenance (*othrus*) and 170
    specific and itemised
        entitlements 103–4
    Thurneysen's rediscovery of 102
Brian Boroimhe/Borumha, High
    King 140, 143, 170, 173, 183
Briscoe, Ben 93
Britain 5, 79, 180, 186
British Commonwealth 63, 67, 97
British Foreign Office 79, 108
Browne, Margaret 23
Brüning, Heinrich 46, 72, 73, 74, 79
    alliance of 'red and black' 79–80, 85
    Binchy's memoir of 102
    Binchy's perception of 73–4, 75,
        79–80
    land reform plans and 72, 74
    Zentrum party and 74, 79
Byrne, Francis John 30, 180

Carney, James 31–2, 180
    Binchy's critique of 32, 149, 150, 152